P9-CRO-992

TIME LIFE

BOOK OF REPAIR AND RESTORATION

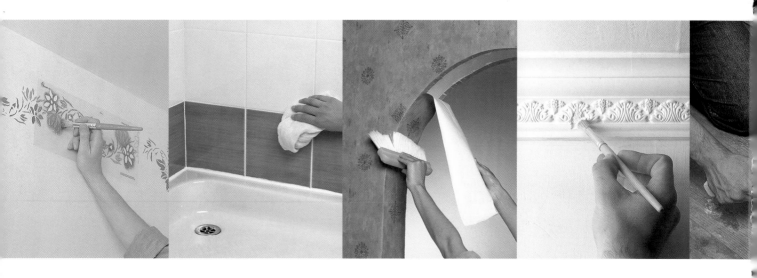

TIME LIFE

BOOK OF REPAIR AND RESTORATION

*Making the house
you own the
home of your dreams*

DAVID HOLLOWAY   MIKE LAWRENCE   JOHN MCGOWAN

CONSULTING EDITOR
TONY WILKINS

TIME LIFE BOOKS

ALEXANDRIA, VIRGINIA

TIME
LIFE
BOOKS

Time-Life Books is a division of Time Life Inc.

TIME LIFE INC.
PRESIDENT AND CEO: George Artandi

TIME-LIFE CUSTOM PUBLISHING
Vice President and Publisher   Terry Newell
Vice President of Sales and Marketing   Neil Levin
Director of Acquisitions and Editorial Resources   Jennifer Pearce
Director of Creative Services   Laura Ciccone McNeill
Director of Special Markets   Liz Ziehl
Project Manager   Jennie Halfant

First printing. Printed in Germany
TIME-LIFE is a trademark of Time Warner Inc. U.S.A.

Library of Congress Cataloging-in-Publication Data
Holloway, David, 1944-
Time life book of repair and restoration : making the house you own the
home of your dreams / David Holloway, Mike Lawrence, John
McGowan : forward by Stewart Walton.
p. cm.
Includes index.
ISBN 0-7370-0307-3 (hardcover)
1. Dwellings--Maintenance and repair Amateurs' manuals.
2. Dwellings--Remodeling Amateurs' manuals. 3. Interior decoration
Amateurs' manuals. I. Lawrence, Mike 1947- . II. McGowan, John.
III. Time-Life Books. IV.. Title.
TH4817.3.H637 1999
643'.7--dc21   99-23717
                                                  CIP

Books produced by Time-Life Custom Publishing are available at a
special bulk discount for promotional and premium use. Custom
adaptations can also be created to meet your specific marketing goals.
Call 1-800-323-5255.

Note: Every effort has been taken to ensure that all information in this
book is correct and compatible with national standards generally
accepted at the time of publication. This book is not intended to replace
manufacturers' instructions in the use of their tools or materials—always
follow their safety guidelines. The authors and publisher disclaim any
liability for loss, injury, or damage incurred as a consequence, directly or
indirectly, of the use and application of the contents of this book.

A Marshall Edition
Conceived, edited, and designed by Marshall Editions Ltd
The Orangery, 161 New Bond Street
London W1Y 9PA

Project Editor   Theresa Lane
U.S. Consultant   John Warde
Editorial Assistance   John Plowman
Art Editor   Amzie Viladot Lorente
Managing Editor   Clare Currie
Managing Art Editor   Helen Spencer
Editorial Coordinator   Rebecca Clunes

FOREWORD

At some time, and in one way or another, every room in the house will require some attention. This could be only a new coat of paint to freshen up the walls, or it could mean a complete overhaul from ceiling to floor. Whatever the scope of your project, *The Time-Life Book of Repair and Restoration* shows all the relevant techniques to get the best results, as well as provides all the necessary details on choosing the materials to decorate your home. By taking the time to follow the instructions carefully—and without skipping the preparation work—you can redecorate your home with professional results. In fact, you may find the most difficult part of the job is deciding on the colors, patterns, and textures for each room.

ABOUT THIS BOOK

At the start of each chapter, a "directory" section gives a brief summary of the information you'll find in the subsequent pages, a guide to how long it may take to complete the job, and a recommended level of skill. Within each chapter you'll find pages filled with "options" to help you choose the materials for the job and to give you design ideas. Having decided on the decoration for your room, follow the step-by-step pages to master the techniques. Clear photographs illustrate each of the steps, and lists are supplied of all the materials and tools you'll need for the job. You'll also find helpful hints from the professionals and ideas for alternative treatments. Cross-references to other pages will guide you to pertinent preparation instructions or to additional techniques to help finish a job. Whether you want to complete a single task or combine techniques to come up with your own ideas, all the help and advice you need is at hand.

CONTENTS

Chapter 4
FLOORS 172

Chapter 5
SHELVING AND
STORAGE 218

ASSESSING YOUR SITUATION

There is no straightforward answer to how much time and effort will be required to redecorate a room from ceiling to floor. There are a number of factors to consider, including the present condition of the room, your experience and ability to use tools, and the amount of free days you have in which to tackle the work.

A room in good condition in a new house may simply need painting to suit your personal tastes—potentially, a simple job of two or three days' work if the walls only require a washing down and a sanding of any old gloss paint before applying the new paint. Even the novice do-it-yourselfer would not find the job daunting. However, in an old house where the room may have been poorly decorated many times over, or where there is dampness, rotting wood, or numerous cracks in the ceiling and walls (see pp.12–13), you are looking at the worst case scenario; it may take months before the room can be completely redecorated.

DOING THE JOB RIGHT

Preparation—in which the surfaces are made clean, smooth, and even and any repair work is undertaken—is the key to successful decorating. Unfortunately, preparation must be done thoroughly, which can take considerable time. How much time is difficult to gauge because, although you can estimate how long the obvious problems will take to fix, you have no idea what might be lurking behind old wallpaper, flaking ceiling paint, or a damp patch. Wood paneling might have been fixed to disguise uneven walls, and a thick wallcovering might have been hung as a quick, less expensive solution to repairing badly cracked plaster walls.

Lifting up an old floor covering may expose one or more cracked or damaged floorboards. You may have to repair or replace several boards before you lay down the new floor covering.

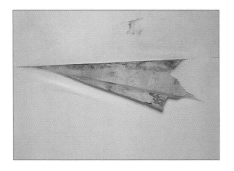

Moisture has stained this wallpaper and caused it to peel—the cause of the moisture must be resolved before attempting any redecoration.

This wall was stripped of peeling wallpaper with the plan of painting the room. However, the wall needs extra preparation before it will be ready for painting. The mantlepiece also requires work before it will be ready for decoration.

Often there is no way of knowing the condition of the walls, ceilings, and floors until whatever material that is covering the surface has been removed—but there are some clues. For example, a wet patch on wallpaper above the opening of a fireplace is a sign of dampness in the flue caused by a lack of ventilation or by a rainwater leak. Inspect the areas around windows and exterior doors, which are subjected to wet conditions. They could be affected by wet rot—clues include cracked paint and dark wood (see pp.60–61). You should also look for decay if you take up a floor covering (see pp.40–41). In each of these cases, any problems will require some remedial work before you redecorate.

Deeply indented, chipped paint on wood trim indicates that many coats of paint have been applied over the years. It is probably time to strip the trim back to bare wood; however, if there is just the odd chip and the rest of the surfaces are sound, then you can leave the paint alone because it will provide a sound, flat surface to paint on. You don't want to make unnecessary work and expense for yourself. The same goes for lining paper on the ceiling; if it's sound and adheres well, it may be better to leave it there because it could be covering a lot of cosmetic repair work.

Because there are so many corners in this kitchen, additional time was allocated to allow for the cutting of all the wall tiles. The countertop also required more time to custom fit it.

Dark, pulpy, soft wood is a sign of wet rot, which is found in damp areas. You can test for it by inserting a screwdriver, awl, or sharp knife into the wood.

OTHER CONSIDERATIONS

Apart from the basic aspect of straightforward decorating, you may want to make changes to the room such as removing an old fireplace mantelpiece or putting one in. Cabinets or shelves may need removing, replacing, or installing, or you may want to replace a door. Don't forget that old plumbing and electrical wiring might be factors.

The size and shape of the room also come into the equation. The bigger the room, the longer it will take to hang wallpaper. If the room has more than its fair share of alcoves, arches, windows, and doors, then hanging wallpaper is going to take far longer than in a simple rectangular room.

The vital thing is to calculate for the worst, then you won't be frustrated by unexpected delays. It is very upsetting to think you can decorate a room in a weekend, only to find that on Sunday evening you're still doing the preparation work. Don't be tempted to cut corners—it may only create more work in the future.

PLANNING THE CAMPAIGN

When decorating just a single room, other rooms in the house can be affected by becoming temporary storage space for furniture and ornaments. Few people like living in clutter, so it's best to tackle the work in a continuous session. If you only have a weekend to spare, consider waiting until you can take time off from work.

The summer is the best season for decorating: days are warmer and longer and open windows won't create cold working conditions. Painting in a cold temperature can adversely affect the finish. It's also not a good idea to paint in poor or artificial light, because it can be difficult—especially when using white paint—to see which areas have been painted or whether the paint has dripped. If you must decorate in winter, plan to do all your painting while there is natural light. You can always do the other jobs with artificial light.

BEFORE THE DECORATION

If you're doing major renovations that involve changing the use of a room, you may need to obtain a building permit from the office of your local building inspector. For example, a bedroom must have a window and a bathroom must have a source of ventilation.

If you want to install new electrical outlets, switches, or wall or ceiling light fixtures, then make sure the work is done before you start decorating. Plan the positions of these items carefully—repositioning them can mean having to redecorate a complete wall. The same applies to plumbing, gas, and water fixtures. If you employ professionals to do the work, make sure it is completed before you take time off to decorate. It can be frustrating to start your vacation while tradesmen are still finishing a job. You should

Preparation for this room included stripping wallpaper from below the picture rails and removing the floor covering. Wallboard was mounted on one wall to create a smooth surface, and a new baseboard was attached to it. Molding was added to the other baseboards to match the style.

Damaged floorboards were replaced in this room. The ceiling and walls will be redecorated before the new floor covering is installed.

The kitchen above was transformed with careful planning (see right). An electrician changed the track lighting to down lights and a plumber installed a new sink before any decoration began, including installing new countertops and painting the ceiling and walls.

remember they can get it wrong when it comes to time estimates—sometimes through no fault of their own, but because of an unexpected problem.

Make a list of all the materials and equipment you'll need and make sure you have everything before you get started. This may mean waiting for a delivery of a custom-ordered kitchen countertop or visiting a home center to pick up sandpaper or screws. When you're ready to start the work, have everything at hand, including stepladders and plastic bags for disposing of garbage.

ORDER OF WORK

If you are decorating a whole house, work from the top downward. By doing so, the inevitable dust will make its way downstairs to the unfinished rooms below. However, if you do choose to decorate the downstairs first, make sure that any upstairs room to be decorated is kept as dust-free as possible. This may mean taking occasional breaks when sanding a floor, for example, to clean up the debris.

Once you decide where to start, clear away as much furniture from the room as possible. Whatever has to remain should be piled in the center of the room, then completely covered up— paint splashes have a way of ending up in the unlikeliest places.

The first job is to tackle any structural work or major repairs. Dealing with rot (see pp.12–13) may mean replacing a number of floorboards. Putting in shelves or cabinets can be left until last, provided there is no risk of damaging any new decorations.

Generally speaking, a room should be prepared and decorated from the ceiling downward. Clearly you wouldn't paper a wall before painting the ceiling, because you would almost certainly get paint splashes on the new wallpaper below. So the order is ceiling, walls, woodwork (such as doors, casings, and baseboards) and metalwork (such as radiators). The exception is when hanging wallpaper—you should paint the woodwork and metalwork beforehand.

THE BIG ISSUES

Some problems in a house are best treated by an expert, including termites and dry rot. In fact, some mortgage and insurance companies may insist on a guarantee from a professional.

WATER INFILTRATION

Because water can seep from saturated ground soil to the inside of a basement by capillary action, buildings are constructed to be waterproof. However, wet patches can occur in a basement if there are cracks or holes in the walls or floor. These should be repaired using hydraulic cement. A high water table, improper soil grading, or poor drainage can allow water to enter the basement. You may need the soil regraded, the foundation waterproofed, drainage pipes installed around the perimeter of the house, or a sump pump.

Another place where water can enter a house is through a damaged roof, even if only one shingle is missing. Because the water can travel along the interior structure of the house, it may be difficult to trace the source of the leak to repair it.

Other locations where water can penetrate include around windows, doors, and dryer vents, and where outdoor structures, such as steps or decks, contact concrete walls. Make sure these are sealed with a silicone or polyurethane sealant.

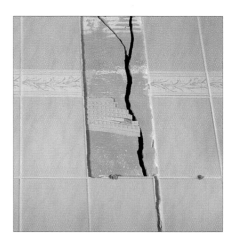

Ceramic tiles removed from this bathroom wall exposed the wide cracks created by the settling of the house. This is a situation that should be rectified only by a professional.

CONDENSATION

Although a different problem, condensation is sometimes incorrectly diagnosed as water infiltration. It occurs when warm, moist air contacts a cold surface—such as an outside wall or glass window pane—and is cooled. Cold air holds less water vapor than warm air, and the difference is deposited on the cold surface as water droplets—the mist or frost that appears on windows on a cold morning is one example. The typical symptoms of condensation are mildew and random damp patches on walls, which usually become worse in cold weather.

To distinguish between water infiltration and condensation, dry the damp area with a hair dryer, then place a piece of plastic kitchen wrap or aluminum foil about 2 feet square (600 mm sq) over it, and seal all four edges with duct tape. Moisture should form on one surface of the plastic or foil after a few days. If it is on the room side, the problem is condensation; on the underside, water infiltration.

Treatment for condensation will depend on the cause. It may simply be a matter of heating a cold room, adding ventilation in a bathroom or kitchen (or a blocked chimney), or insulating an attic or cold water pipes.

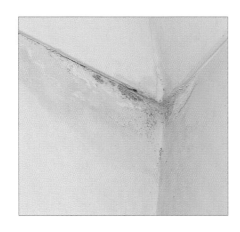

The mildew in this corner may be caused by either water infiltration or condensation. Before redecorating, the cause of the damp must be isolated and treated, and the mold must be removed.

The underside of the floorboards in a poorly ventilated crawlspace is host to the fruiting body of dry rot. The spores spread rapidly.

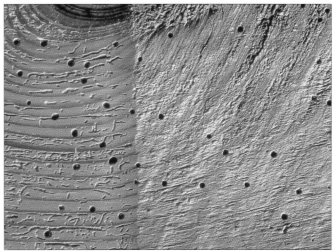

The main sign of woodboring beetles is the exit holes. The dark section has been planed to show the tunnels inside the wood.

INFESTATIONS

Termites feed on the cellulose in wood, and they can cause serious structural damage to wood buildings. Although they nest underground, termites can build shelter tubes to reach the wood. Modern buildings are constructed with wood members away from the ground, and some local codes require metal termite shields to be installed above the top of the foundation walls. However, termites can still manage to enter the home. When the soil temperate is between 50–55°F (10–12°C), or year-round in the South, inspect for shelter tubes in the basement, crawl space, near the foundation, and near openings where pipes enter the house. Seal any cracks in the foundation and holes in the shields. Termites are difficult to eradicate and require professional extermination.

Carpenter ants can pose a problem to wood sills and joists in houses in northern states. They prefer moist wood; look for course sawdust. Woodboring beetles will attack all structural wood in a house, including roof rafters, floor joists, and floorboards. Their exit holes are easy to spot—look for piles of powdery sawdust to indicate a new infestation. Carpenter ants and woodboring beetles are easy to eradicate if caught early.

Wood can also be attacked by wet rot (see pp.8–9) and dry rot, which are types of fungi. Wet rot only occurs in damp wood and can be found in window frames and exterior wood. After treating the cause of the damp wood, dig out and replace the damaged wood (see pp.60–61).

Dry rot is more serious. Once established, it can transfer from wet wood to dry wood. It can cause severe structural damage and should be treated only by a professional. Signs of its presence are cracks across the wood grain, a musty smell, and growths like cotton wool and mushroom on the wood. It is often discovered in poorly ventilated areas such as basements or under floorboards.

SETTLING

When otherwise firm, undisturbed soil on which a foundation is built is either undermined or softened by moisture, it can cause movement in the house. In colder climates, repeated freezing and thawing of the soil, known as frost-heaving, also causes house movement. If there is too much movement, wide cracks will appear in the walls, especially near windows and doors, and bricks may split. You must call in professional help to have the foundation of the house underpinned.

PREPARATION DIRECTORY

STRIPPING A ROOM

SKILL LEVEL Low
TIME FRAME ½ day
SPECIAL TOOLS Voltage tester
SEE PAGES 18–19

Remove items from a wall or ceiling, including shelves and curtain rail brackets. Wall outlets, switches, and light fixtures can be pulled forward after turning off the electricity.

DEALING WITH PLASTER CRACKS AND STAINS

SKILL LEVEL Low
TIME FRAME Under 2 hours
SPECIAL TOOLS Flexible putty knife, caulking gun
SEE PAGES 20–21

Repair small cracks and dents with filler; use caulking compound for cracks at baseboards or a door or window frame. Cover stains with a sealer before painting.

PATCHING HOLES IN WALLS

SKILL LEVEL Medium
TIME FRAME Under 2 hours
SPECIAL TOOLS Wallboard saw, hawk, trowel
SEE PAGES 22–23

Repair small holes in wallboard with joint compound and wallboard tape; patch a larger hole with a piece of wallboard supported with backing strips. Fill holes in a plaster wall with plaster.

REPAIRING DAMAGE TO A CEILING

SKILL LEVEL Medium
TIME FRAME Under 2 hours
SPECIAL TOOLS Flexible putty knife
SEE PAGES 24–25

Repairs include fixing a nail that has "popped" in a wallboard ceiling, as well as filling holes in plaster and wallboard ceilings. Larger holes in plaster ceilings have to be reinforced with expanded metal mesh.

STRIPPING OLD WALLPAPER

SKILL LEVEL Low
TIME FRAME 2 hours to ½ day
SPECIAL TOOLS Wire brush, steam stripper
SEE PAGES 26–27

You should remove an old wallcovering before hanging a new one. Some wallcoverings peel away from the wall; others must be scored, soaked, and scraped off or removed with steam.

REMOVING OTHER WALL DECORATIONS

SKILL LEVEL Low to medium
TIME FRAME ½ to 1 day
SPECIAL TOOLS Wide cold chisel, ballpeen or small sledgehammer, heat gun, crowbar
SEE PAGES 28–29

You may have to pry off ceramic tiles or paneling.

WASHING DOWN AND PREPARING SURFACES

SKILL LEVEL Low
TIME FRAME Under 2 hours
SPECIAL TOOLS None
SEE PAGES 30–31

Paintwork may need attention such as scraping off flaking paint, filling, and sanding. Wash walls with detergent or TSP. If wallpapering, scrape off any remaining paper after stripping the walls. How to eradicate any mold. See lead paint warning.

STRIPPING PAINT FROM WOOD TRIM

SKILL LEVEL Low
TIME FRAME 2 hours to 1 day
SPECIAL TOOLS Shavehook, narrow scraper, heat gun
SEE PAGES 32–33

Remove faking, badly chipped, or cracked paint with a heat gun or chemical stripper. (See lead paint warning.) Chemical strippers are preferred on moldings, where heat can cause scorching, and near windows, where heat can crack glass.

STRIPPING AND PREPARING METAL

SKILL LEVEL Low
TIME FRAME Under 2 hours
SPECIAL TOOLS Wire brush, electric drill plus wire brush attachment, safety glasses, dust mask
SEE PAGES 34–35

Clean a rusty cast iron fireplace or baluster with emery paper or by wire brushing. Fill pitting with an epoxy-base filler. To remove paint in intricate areas, use a chemical stripper.

POINTED PUTTY KNIFE   SHAVEHOOK   NARROW PUTTY KNIFE   WIDE-BLADE PUTTY KNIFE

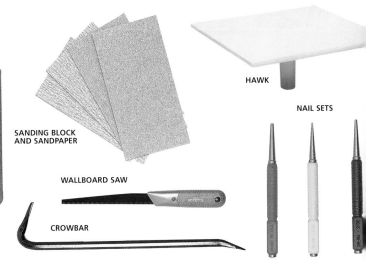

SANDING BLOCK AND SANDPAPER

HAWK

NAIL SETS

WALLBOARD SAW

CROWBAR

REMOVING BASEBOARDS AND OTHER MOLDINGS

SKILL LEVEL Medium
TIME FRAME ½ day
SPECIAL TOOLS Cold chisel, sledge hammer, crowbar
SEE PAGES 36–37

Repair old baseboards. To remove a board, pry it away from the wall. You may need to remove other moldings such as picture rails.

REPLACING BASEBOARDS

SKILL LEVEL Medium
TIME FRAME ½ to 1 day
SPECIAL TOOLS Coping saw, miter frame and saw (or tenon saw and miter box), block plane
SEE PAGES 38–39

Attach new baseboards by using panel adhesive or screws. If on a plaster wall, buy a new board of the same depth or greater.

REMOVING FLOOR COVERINGS

SKILL LEVEL Low to medium
TIME FRAME 2 hours to 1 day
SPECIAL TOOLS Tack lifter, crowbar, heat gun, cold chisel, ballpeen or sledgehammer
SEE PAGES 40–41

Pry away a fitted carpet from tackless strips that have been fitted around the room; these can be reused. Pull foam-backed carpet away from double-sided tape. If sheet vinyl or vinyl tiles are stuck down, use a heat gun and scraper to remove the adhesive. Pry up ceramic tiles and wooden floors.

MAKING MINOR REPAIRS TO A WOOD FLOOR

SKILL LEVEL Low to high
TIME FRAME 2 hours to 2 days
SPECIAL TOOLS Hammer, nail set, block plane
SEE PAGES 42–43

Drive protruding nail heads below the surface. If any floorboards are loose, secure them with screws (this usually cures a squeaking board). Repair any floorboards that have split and fill in any large gaps with a piece of wood shaped to fit.

REPLACING A DAMAGED FLOORBOARD

SKILL LEVEL Medium
TIME FRAME 2 hours to 1 day
SPECIAL TOOLS Wide cold chisel, circular saw (or floorboard saw), jigsaw
SEE PAGES 44–45

Replace a damaged floorboard before laying down a new flooring material; the technique for removing the board will depend on whether it has square edges or is tongued and grooved. Fit a new floorboard of the same thickness.

LAYING A HARDBOARD UNDERLAYMENT

SKILL LEVEL Medium
TIME FRAME ½ day
SPECIAL TOOLS None
SEE PAGES 46–47

Hardboard is a suitable underlay for many types of flooring such as carpet and sheet vinyl. Condition the boards to the room's atmosphere, then start laying them in one corner of the room; stagger the boards to avoid joints aligning.

MINOR CONCRETE FLOOR DEFECTS

SKILL LEVEL Low to medium
TIME FRAME 2 hours to ½ day
SPECIAL TOOLS Wide cold chisel, small sledgehammer, trowel
SEE PAGES 48–49

Deep cracks should be inspected and repaired by a professional. Prime minor cracks with a bonding agent before filling with mortar. If a concrete floor is dusty, apply a coat of concrete floor sealer. Dampness can be cured in a modern house by brushing on a coat of waterproofing emulsion.

LEVELING A CONCRETE FLOOR

SKILL LEVEL Medium
TIME FRAME ½ to 1 day
SPECIAL TOOLS Trowel, steel float
SEE PAGES 50–51

First clean the floor and fill any cracks with the compound. Level out hollows with a floor-leveling compound, which is spread out with a trowel—it should find its own level as it is left to dry. For a large area or a complete room, apply the compound in small batches (it dries quickly). If you are not successful the first time, sprinkle water on the compound and try again.

RUBBER GLOVES

FLOAT

PINCERS

SLEDGEHAMMER

TACK LIFTER

ELECTRICIAN'S SCREWDRIVER

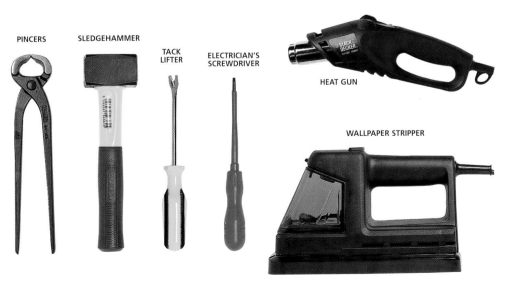

HEAT GUN

WALLPAPER STRIPPER

STRIPPING A ROOM

YOU WILL NEED

Pulling out a switch or socket
Voltage tester
Screwdriver
Masking tape

Removing a ceiling light
Polythene plastic bag
Masking tape

Removing a standard ceiling light fixture
Voltage tester
Masking tape
Pen
Screwdriver
Electrician's tape

Stripping other wall fixtures
Screwdriver
Plastic bag
Masking tape
Matchsticks **or** toothpicks

SEE ALSO

Assessing your situation
pp.8–9
Planning the campaign
pp.10–11

You should never be tempted to try decorating around items that are fitted to a wall or ceiling. These include shelves, light switches, and light fixtures. The end result will be poor, the fitting may become smeared with paint, and the whole process will take much longer than it would if the object were simply removed and replaced afterward. The exception is with some electrical fittings—outlets, switches, and ceiling fixtures. With these, it is usually possible to pull forward the cover plate, decorate, then put the plate back.

When stripping a room, the best way to work is to go around the room and systematically remove anything that can interfere with the decoration. Keep each fitting and its screws in a separate polythene bag so they are easily found when the time comes to replace them. Always turn off the electricity to a fixture before working on it (see *Helpful hints*, facing page).

LIGHT FIXTURES

After you have turned off the power at the service panel, remove any wall light fixtures, standard ceiling light fixtures, spotlights, or fluorescent striplights. You will usually have to remove the glass diffuser cover, either by releasing setscrews on the side of the fixture or a cap nut at the center of the cover, before you can remove the body of the fixture to reach the wiring. White wires are neutral, and black wires, or white wires with a black section, are hot. You can put tape on the wires and label them if you're concerned about rejoining them properly, or hire an electrician.

Any bare wires from the ceiling or walls must be protected by covering them with electrician's tape. You may have to restore power to the circuit while decorating takes place, or all the lights and outlets on that circuit will be out of action. Use additional lighting from lamps for the decoration.

PULLING OUT A SWITCH OR SOCKET

With the electricity turned off, release the mounting screws and pull the plate away from the wall. You can leave the switch or outlet in this position until the decoration has been completed. As further protection from paint, you should always apply masking tape to the edges of the switch.

REMOVING A DOWNLIGHT

This light fixture simply drops down from its hole in the ceiling. If it isn't heavy and you're painting the ceiling, tape a polythene bag around the body. If you're covering the ceiling with lining paper or wallpaper, detach the body from the wires (see *Removing a standard ceiling light fixture*).

CEILING FIXTURES

The methods for disconnecting ceiling fixtures are slightly different but the principles are the same: after turning the power off, remove the diffuser, disconnect the fixture from the mounting hardware, then—after using a voltage tester to ensure that the electricity is off—disconnect the wires. Make sure you use the wire connectors when you rejoin the wires.

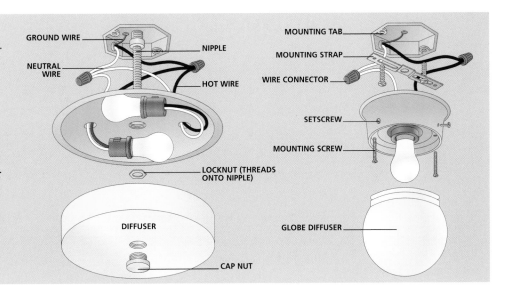

GROUND WIRE
NIPPLE
NEUTRAL WIRE
HOT WIRE
LOCKNUT (THREADS ONTO NIPPLE)
DIFFUSER
CAP NUT

MOUNTING TAB
MOUNTING STRAP
WIRE CONNECTOR
SETSCREW
MOUNTING SCREW
GLOBE DIFFUSER

STRIPPING OTHER WALL FIXTURES

1 You may have shelves, towel racks, mirrors, curtain rods, and so on to remove. This will simply be a question of unscrewing their supports such as one or more brackets. You may want someone to help you handle large, cumbersome items such as curtain rods.

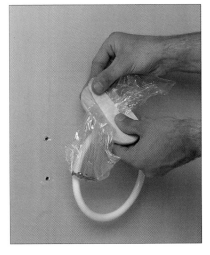

2 The best way to avoid losing the screws and other hardware that normally hold the items in place is to seal them in a plastic bag, then tape the bag to the item.

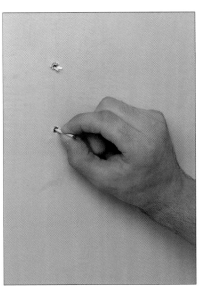

3 To avoid wiring and pipes buried in the walls, try using the original mounting holes to rehang the items once you finish the decoration. Because wallpaper will cover the holes, insert into them toothpicks or matchsticks trimmed to protrude slightly from the wall—they will poke through the wallpaper.

Helpful hints

The most important rule when working with electricity in the home is safety. It might be tempting to think that you can wallpaper around a switch by simply pulling the cover plate forward because you're unlikely to touch any wiring—but you could touch an exposed wire, with disastrous consequences.

It takes just a few seconds to go to the service panel and isolate the switch, outlet, or light fixture by turning the power off at the fuse or circuit breaker for that circuit. Then use a voltage tester to check that the switch, outlet, or light is "dead." This ensures you have disconnected the correct circuit.

DEALING WITH PLASTER CRACKS AND STAINS

Superficial cracks and small dents in plaster can be repaired quickly with joint compound or spackling used for wallboard. If there are a lot of fine hairline cracks, cover a plaster surface with lining paper or spun fiberglass wall covering.

Joint compound comes ready-to-use in tubs of various sizes. For large jobs, 5-gallon buckets are economical. Spackling has the same qualities as joint compound but is smoother and better-suited to walls that will be painted. It comes in small containers and squeeze tubes.

DIFFICULT CRACKS

Not all cracks should be filled with joint compound or spackling. Normal seasonal movement of the house structure can cause cracks at joints. Filling them usually fails because the movement creates additional cracks. If they are where the walls meet the ceiling, the real answer is to hide them by attaching crown molding (see p.148). Cracks above a baseboard or around window and door frames need a different treatment. You can use joint compound if you first squeeze strips of plastic filler rod into the gap as a base, but the best solution is to use a caulking compound. It remains flexible, so it keeps the gap closed despite any movement.

Minor damage in a decorative plaster cornice or ceiling rose can be repaired. However, most ornate repairs are best left to the professional.

TREATING STAINS

Most stains are due to water damage or tobacco smoke. Stains seep through paint, but you can prime a water stain. For a room stained by tobacco smoke, try a strong detergent or trisodium phosphate (TSP) on painted surfaces. If it doesn't work, you'll have to remove the paint. Wallpaper must be stripped (see pp.26–27).

REPAIRING A CRACK

1 Using the edge of a pointed filling knife or the corner of a flexible putty, "undercut" the crack—the idea is to widen the crack below the surface, forming an inverted V cavity, with the point of the V exposed to the surface. This will help the filler stay in place.

2 Remove any loose debris from the work area with an old paint brush. Using a flexible putty knife, firmly press either joint compound or spackling into the crack, forcing it into the cavity.

3 Hold the putty knife at an angle perpendicular to the work and scrape away the excess filler, but leave it slightly protruding from the surface. A more experienced person can smooth the filler level with the surface. Let the filler dry.

4 A wood or cork sanding block will help you achieve a smooth finish. Wrap a piece of fine wet-or-dry sandpaper around the sanding block and, holding it flat against the work, sand the filler until it is flush with the surface.

USING A CAULKING COMPOUND

TREATING A WATER STAIN

For a crack above a baseboard or around a window or door, squeeze a bead of caulking compound along it, making sure it contacts both surfaces. A slow, continuous movement will avoid creating ripples in the bead; you can use a wet fingertip to smooth the compound.

You can apply a coat of shellac-base stain-killing primer over a water stain—white ones are more often available—but first deal with the cause of the problem, such as a plumbing leak, and allow the ceiling to dry before applying it. The primer will seal the surface and form a good base for paint.

FILLING CHIPPED MOLDING

1 If the damage to a plaster molding is small, you can make the repair yourself. Carefully remove any loose sections or debris with a small paint brush.

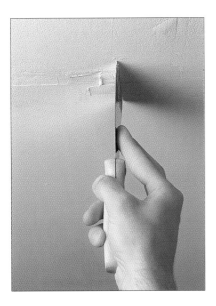

2 Fill in the damage with a two-part acrylic or polyester filler, using a small artist's clay modelling tool or a similar device to mold it. Try to match the profile of the surrounding pattern.

PATCHING HOLES IN WALLS

YOU WILL NEED

Patching a wallboard hole
Wallboard saw
Carpenter's level
Pencil
Hammer
Utility knife
Nail punch
Flexible putty knife
Sanding block
Fine sandpaper

Filling a hole in plaster
Hawk
Trowel
Wood straightedge
Fine sandpaper

MATERIALS

Patching a wallboard hole
1 inch x 3 inch (25 mm x 50 mm) furring strip
Box nails
Wallboard nails
Wallboard
Wallboard tape
Joint compound

Filling a hole in plaster
Patching plaster

SEE ALSO

Dealing with plaster cracks and stains pp.20–21
Repairing damage to a ceiling pp.24–25

Holes in wallboard often occur as a result of physical damage or by the removal of a fixture. If the hole is more than 3½ inches (87 mm) wide, it requires patching with wallboard. Before making the repair, locate the vertical studs on either side of the damage. You can do this by either tapping the wallboard until you hear a dull thud (instead of a hollow sound) or by using a stud detector.

DAMAGED PLASTER WALLS

Holes in plaster develop for the same reasons as for wallboard, as well as because of dampness. In the latter case, deal with the dampness before making a repair. There are different types of plaster available, but the best one for the do-it-yourselfer is one-coat patching plaster.

A condition known as blown plaster occurs when the plaster loses contact with the wall and bulges out. You should tap the bulge with a cold chisel and ballpeen hammer to remove all loose plaster, working back to a sound edge around the damage. Brush away all dust, dampen the repair with clean water, and fill the hole with plaster.

LATH-AND-PLASTER WALLS

Repair a hole in a lath-and-plaster wall in the same way as for wallboard. If you cannot find wallboard of the same thickness as the plaster, nail new, thicker laths to the studs so that a thin piece of plasterboard lies flush with the surface or just below it.

Helpful hints

Plaster walls are often damaged at external corners. Use a putty knife to fill and smooth the plaster on one wall, then on the flanking wall. After the compound stiffens, run a wet sponge down the corner to blunt the edge—a pointed edge is more susceptible to damage.

To patch a hole in wallboard less than 3½ inches (87 mm) wide, use a flexible putty knife to press in joint compound; when dry, sand it flush with the surface. (Joint compound will fill dents, too.)

PATCHING A WALLBOARD HOLE

1 Using a wallboard saw, cut back the damaged area flush with the edge of the stud; then extend it 1 inch (25 mm) to the center of the stud—use a carpenter's level to draw a vertical guide line on the stud. Repeat the procedure on the other side of the damaged area.

2 The top and bottom edges of the repair also need to be cut to create a rectangular opening. Use the level to draw horizontal guide lines, making sure you extend them beyond the damage before you make the cuts.

3 To provide support for the top and bottom edges of the wallboard, use box nails to secure 1 inch x 3 inch (25 mm x 50 mm) furring strips between the studs. Position the nails at a 45° angle (this is called toe-nailing), driving them through the battens and into the studs.

4 Using a utility knife and straight-edge, score and break a piece of wallboard to an exact fit. Use wallboard nails ½ inch (12 mm) from the edge (so they will go into the studs behind), at 6 inch (150 mm) intervals. Drive the nails flush to the surface; then without breaking the paper, dimple the surface with a hammer blow.

5 Seal the seams with wallboard tape. Coat the tape with joint compound, smoothing and blending it onto the surrounding surface. Let it dry for 24 hours, then apply a second coat of compound. Sand the work smooth before finishing with paint.

FILLING A HOLE IN PLASTER

1 Hold a hawk loaded with plaster close to the wall at a 45° angle. Scoop up some of the plaster with a trowel and sweep it into the bottom of the repair area. Don't press the trowel flat against the wall or the plaster will fall away. Continue, working up the repair area, until it is filled.

2 To level the plaster with the wall, use a wood straightedge (one with planed straight edges) or screed that is wider than the repair. Working from the bottom, rest the wood on the wall and zig-zag it from side to side as you move it up.

3 To create a fine surface for painting, let dry, then sand it smooth with fine abrasive paper wrapped around a wood strip.

REPAIRING DAMAGE TO A CEILING

A ceiling can suffer the same wear and tear as a wall, but it may also be damaged by a leak. Make sure you repair the cause of the leak and let the ceiling dry before making a repair to the ceiling.

WALLBOARD CEILINGS

A fairly common, minor defect in a wallboard ceiling is a protruding nail head—this is often referred to as a "popped" nail. Wallboard panels are nailed to the ceiling joists above them, and sometimes a nail can work its way loose. It is easy to repair, and you can follow the same procedure if a nail has popped from a stud on a wall.

A small hole can be covered with fiberglass or paper wallboard tape and covered with a joint compound, but a hole larger than 3½ inches (87 mm) requires a backing piece to serve as a base for the compound. You'll need a scrap of wallboard slightly longer and wider than the hole.

LATH-AND-PLASTER CEILINGS

Most older houses were constructed with lath-and-plaster ceilings. This type of ceiling was formed by nailing thin battens (laths) to the joists above and then adding plaster. This was forced through the small gaps between the laths so that, when set, the plaster was anchored in place.

How a hole is filled depends on its size and the condition of the laths. If the laths are not broken, coat them with latex bonding agent to make them less absorbent before filling the repair. If the laths are broken and the hole measures less than 3 inches (75 mm) across, simply push scrunched up newspaper into it to serve as a backing before plastering the hole. Where a hole is more than 3 inches (75 mm) across, you'll need to use fine expanded metal mesh as a backing piece for the plaster. Expanded metal mesh can be bought at building supply stores.

FIXING A POPPED NAIL

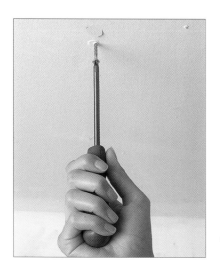

Insert a wallboard screw 2 inches (50 mm) away from the nail, ensuring that it goes into the joist above. Remove any debris covering the protruding nail, and use a nail set and hammer to knock it below the surface. Cover the hole with joint compound (see pp.20–21).

PATCHING WALLBOARD

1 Cut a wallboard patch 1 inch (25 mm) larger than the damaged area, and drill a hole through the middle. Slip a length of string 6 inches (150 mm) long through it, and tie a nail to the string on the back side of the board. The nail will prevent the string exiting the hole.

2 Apply joint compound around the edges of the front of the wallboard, then slip the piece through the hole—the front side of the board should face outward. Use the string to pull the board against the back of the wallboard surrounding the hole, then pull the string taut and let compound set.

3 Apply a layer of joint compound and cover it with a fiberglass mesh tape. Build up layers to bring the patch almost flush with the surface; allow the compound to harden between layers. Cut off the string before adding a final layer flush with the surface. After the compound is dry, sand it smooth (see pp.20–21).

REPAIRING LATH AND PLASTER

1 Use an old paint brush to remove any dust and debris from the areas to be repaired, wearing safety goggles and a dust mask.

2 If the laths are damaged, use tinsnips to trim the expanded mesh to size. Then fit the mesh in place by curling its edges around the back of the laths. The mesh is flexible, so this should be easy to do.

3 Use a cold chisel and ball peen hammer to undercut the edges of the hole so that the plaster will have a better grip (see pp.20–21). Make sure you do this gently to avoid creating any further damage. Once again, use the old paint brush to remove any debris. Coat the edges with latex bonding agent.

4 Place an excess of patching plaster onto a float and push it up into the repair until it is flat against the ceiling, forcing the paster through the holes in the mesh; slide the float over the repair. Scrape off as much excess plaster as you can and sand it smooth when the patch is dry (see pp.20–21).

STRIPPING OLD WALLPAPER

YOU WILL NEED

Using a liquid stripper
Stiff wire brush **or** scoring tool
Bucket
Water
Sponge
Wallcovering scraper
Detergent
Liquid wallpaper stripper

Using a steam stripper
Steam stripper
Water
Wallcovering scraper
Detergent

Peeling away vinyls
Utility knife (if required)
see *Using water to strip* above

SEE ALSO

Dealing with plaster cracks and stains pp.20–21

There are various forms of wallpaper or, more correctly, wallcoverings. Apart from straight-forward paper, there are washables, vinyls, and natural fibers, among others. One thing they all have in common is that they must be stripped off before hanging a new wallcovering. Hanging new wallcovering on top of an old one can cause both coverings to bubble.

STRIPPING THE WALL

How difficult it is to strip a wall depends on the wallcovering material and on the paste used—an over-diluted paste may hold a wallcovering in place but is not strong enough to withstand a soaking with water. The wall may be damp, which is fine for helping you get the wallcovering off; however, it is not a surface on which you should hang a wallcovering.

Water is an essential ingredient in stripping wallcoverings. Vinyls and washable wallcoverings are designed to withstand water, so they must be scored before they are soaked (unless you have a peelable vinyl). The same applies to a painted wallcovering.

If the covering isn't loose after a first soaking, try a second soaking. Or use a gel-type liquid wallpaper stripping agent, available at home centers.

Another choice is to use an electric steam stripper, which can be rented locally or bought at a home center. It has a tank to hold water, which takes from 30 seconds to 10 minutes to heat up before running for a few hours, depending on the model used. Never leave it sitting on an unprotected floor.

> ## Helpful hints
>
> Avoid soaking wallcovering around switches and outlets. If you can't remove the covering by peeling it away while dry, turn off the electrical power at the service panel, unscrew the face plate, and ease it away from the wall. Use as little liquid as possible.

USING A LIQUID STRIPPER

1 Use a wire brush or scoring tool to scratch the surface of non-peelable vinyls and other washable coverings. This allows liquid to penetrate through the covering to reach the adhesive. Do not allow the wire bristles to reach the plaster. Tiny pieces of metal from the brush can cause rust spots.

2 After scoring, apply a gel-type liquid wallpaper stripper to the wall with a sponge, roller, or brush. Start in one corner of the room and work your way around it. After 20 minutes, or by the time you get back to the start point, the stripper should have done its job.

3 Using a scraper, carefully work the wallcovering loose—it should bunch up and come away easily. If it doesn't, soak it with more stripper. Don't scrape too hard; this can gouge the wall. Leave small pieces for later. If you're stripping wallcovering from wallboard, note that this has a paper face that you don't want to strip off.

4 After removing most of the wallcovering, go around the room to soak and remove any small pieces or stubborn sections left behind. Once all the wallcovering has been removed, wash down the walls with a little detergent in a bucket of warm water.

USING A STEAM STRIPPER

1 Score washable coverings (see step 1, opposite page). Place the plate of the stripper (it has perforations through which the steam passes) against the wall; hold it in place from a few seconds to a minute, depending on the model and the thickness of the wallcovering.

2 Reposition the steam stripper onto the next section of wallcovering. At the same time, scrape away the loosened covering with the scraper as in step 3 above. Continue until all the paper is removed, and wash down the walls as in step 4 above.

PEELING AWAY VINYLS

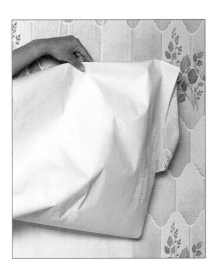

1 Some modern vinyls have been designed to simply peel off the wall. Try using your fingernail or the blade of a utility knife to lift a corner. If it comes up, simply pull the covering upward. If you're unlucky, you have a problem paper that requires scoring before you can strip it.

2 When you pull up a peelable vinyl, you'll discover a thin paper backing left behind. Simply soak and scrape it as for other wallcoverings— it will easily come off. If well stuck, it can be left in place and used as a lining paper.

REMOVING OTHER WALL DECORATIONS

YOU WILL NEED

Textured paint
Floor protection such as hardboard
Heavy work gloves, safety goggles, and respirator
Old paint brush
Poultice- **or** gel-type stripper
Scraper
Stiff brush
Trisodium Phosphate (TSP) **or** detergent
Bucket and sponge

Wall tiles
Wide cold chisel
Small sledgehammer
Safety goggles
Heavy work gloves
Heat gun and scraper

Sheet paneling
Wide cold chisel
Small sledgehammer

Tongue-and-groove paneling
Wide cold chisel
Small sledgehammer
Crowbar

SEE ALSO

Dealing with plaster cracks and stains pp.20–21
Washing down and preparing surfaces pp.30–31
Patching holes in walls pp.22–23

There are materials other than wallpaper (see pp.26–27) attached to walls as decoration. Whatever the decoration, it can be removed, but the walls may need repairing afterward.

TEXTURED PAINTS

With difficulty, textured paint can be removed from plaster walls, using a gel- or, preferably, poultice-type paint stripper. It cannot be removed from wallboard; the only solution is to cover it with a new wallboard. Because of the hazards of applying stripper to a ceiling, the ceiling should be covered with a suspended ceiling. Never sand off a finish; older paints contain asbestos, which must not be inhaled.

WALL TILES

Removing ceramic tiles creates a lot of work, perhaps for a professional, to provide the flat surface required for tiling or other decoration. Provided that they are flat and well fastened,

you can leave ceramic tiles on the walls and tile on top of them. Test for flatness by holding a long straightedge, such as a carpenter's level, across them vertically, horizontally, and diagonally. The odd loose tile can be refastened with tile adhesive. Old ones fastened with cement mortar will be more difficult to remove. Because fragments will be flying everywhere, you must wear a dust mask and safety goggles.

It may be easy to pry off cork and expanded polystyrene tiles, depending on how the adhesive was applied: in a few blobs on older tiles or spread all over, which is common on newer tiles.

PANELING

Individual boards are fastened to furring strips by nailing, screwing, or with clips. Panels fastened to furring strips are removed in the same way as boards. If panels sound solid when tapped, they were fastened to the wall with adhesive and will need prying off.

TEXTURED PAINT

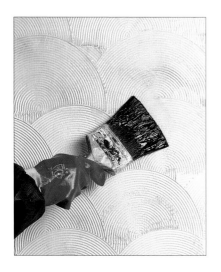

1 When using a stripper to remove textured (or normal) water-base paint, protect the floor (see p.32); wear gloves, a respirator, and goggles. Starting at top of the wall, apply a thick, even coat, dabbing it well into the surface. Leave for 3–8 hours, depending on the thickness of finish.

2 When the paint is soft (you may need to apply more stripper), use a scraper to remove it, starting from the bottom of the wall. Go over the wall with a stiff brush to remove any residue. Wash the wall down with Trisodium Phosphate (TSP) or detergent in warm water, then only water.

Wall tiles

1 Whether you want to remove one damaged tile or a whole field of tiles, position a wide chisel in the center of a tile and hit it hard with a small sledgehammer, which will shatter the tile. Insert the chisel into one of the cracks, gently tap it in, then use it to pry off the pieces of the tile.

2 To remove additional tiles, insert the chisel under one edge of an adjacent tile and gently hammer it in before prying off the tile. Some will come away whole, others in pieces. Continue to pry off the remaining tiles in the same way.

3 To remove the tile adhesive still on the wall, hold a heat gun 2 inches (50 mm) from the surface. As the heat gun softens the adhesive, follow behind with a scraper to remove it.

Sheet paneling

To remove sheets of paneling that were glued to the wall, insert a cold chisel into a vertical joint, hammer the chisel in, then pry off the board. The panels will split and come off the wall in pieces. You may have to sand off the adhesive, but first try a heat gun (see far left).

Tongue-and-groove paneling

1 Start by removing the dado cap, as well as any edge trim. Position the chisel behind the dado cap and tap down with a sledgehammer. Once it is wedged behind the rail, use the chisel to pry it off the paneling.

2 Use the hook end of a crowbar to remove each length of board. Bang it between the board and furring strip (but avoid damaging the wall), then pry the board away from the strip. Unscrew the strips, or pry them off with the crowbar, using a scrap of wood to protect the wall.

WASHING DOWN AND PREPARING SURFACES

YOU WILL NEED

Drop cloth and newspaper
Sanding block
Wet-or-dry sandpaper
Coarse-, medium- and
fine-grade sandpaper (if
required)
Trisodium phosphate (TSP)
or strong detergent and
warm water
Bucket
Sponge
Lint-free cloth
Pointed stick
Mineral spirits
Scraper (if required)
Putty knife (if required)
Tack cloth (if required)

MATERIALS

Spackling **or** wood putty
(if required)

SEE ALSO

Dealing with plaster cracks
and stains (pp.20–21)

Whether a wall, door, or wood trim has been stripped or is to be repainted, it must be washed down to ensure that all dirt, grease, or remnants of old wallpaper adhesive is removed. A dirty surface can lead to new wallpaper lifting or paint flaking.

Use plenty of newspaper on top of the drop cloth near the baseboards to soak up the water running down the walls. If you intend to repaint over old paint, wash walls from the bottom up so that dirty water will run down the wet wall and not leave dried streak marks. These can show through a new coat of latex paint. Always let a wall dry before redecorating.

SANDING AND FILLING

Gloss paint, which is normally used on woodwork, has a sheen that prevents new paint from adhering to it. Sanding it down will remove the sheen and leave the surface with a "key" so that the new paint will stick to it. Sanding can be done by hand, but you can use a power sander for a large surface. Whether you are sanding by hand or machine, wear a dust mask and safety goggles. After you sand, clean all the surfaces thoroughly—any dust will be picked up in the brush or roller and transferred to the new paint.

The final job is to remove flaking paint and fill any minor blemishes. Use wallboard spackling compound if the surface is to be painted. Where wood will show, use wood putty.

A WARNING ABOUT LEAD PAINT

Any home built before 1980 may contain lead paint, a dangerous health hazard, especially for children. Sanding and removing paint can create airborn, lead-bearing dust that may be inhaled. Unless you know paint in your home is lead-free, consult your local health department or lead-poison control center (listed in your phone book) for advice before beginning any work.

1 To take the sheen off gloss paint, wrap sandpaper around a sanding block and use a circular motion to roughen the surface. Work methodically, starting at the top and working down, to ensure the whole surface is sanded. If the surface is pitted, start with a coarse paper and finish with a fine-grade paper.

2 Whether or not you have sanded, wash the surface with trisodium phospate or detergent and warm water. If you plan to repaint the surface, work your way from the bottom to the top; otherwise, you can start from the top if you want, as long as the surface isn't too dirty.

3 To clean the nooks and crannies of intricate moldings, wrap a piece of lint-free cloth around a pointed stick, dip it in mineral spirits, and clean the debris from these places. Don't forget to clean the top edge of doors and windows, as well as the exterior edges so that dirt is not picked up on the brush.

4 If old paintwork has bubbled or is flaking off, push the scraper under the loose paint and lift it off, and scrape away any surrounding areas of loose and flaking paint.

5 Only mix up enough spackling or wood putty for the job in hand. Load up the putty knife with the filler and push it down into the damaged area. Press down and draw the knife across the repair before lifting it off.

6 Allow the filler to dry, then sand the filled area level with the surrounding paintwork, using fine-grade sandpaper wrapped around a sanding block.

7 Finally, use a lint-free cloth (cheese cloth is ideal) soaked in mineral spirits to clean off the dust from the filled area. Alternatively, use a tack cloth—a resin-coated dustcloth designed to collect fine dust.

Helpful hints

Mildew, recognizable as a covering of dark specks, can develop on a damp surface. Treat the cause of the dampness (see pp.12–13) before treating the mildew. To eradicate mildew, wash the surface with laundry bleach or a mildew killer available at home centers. Follow the directions on the container. Treat the area again and leave it for a few days.

Before redecorating, coat the wall with a stabilizing primer. If wallpapering, use an adhesive that contains a fungicide.

STRIPPING PAINT FROM WOOD TRIM

YOU WILL NEED

Using a chemical stripper
Overalls with long sleeves
Heavy-duty rubber gloves
Safety goggles
Dust mask
Plywood, hardboard, or
newspaper (to protect floor)
Chemical stripper
Old paint brush
Glass jar
Wide scraper
Shavehook
Plastic sheet
Sponge
Bucket and water **or** mineral
spirits
Steel wool
Medium wet-or-dry
sandpaper

Using a heat gun
Overalls with long sleeves
Plywood or hardboard
Bucket filled with water
Heat gun
Shavehook
Medium wet-or-dry
sandpaper

SEE ALSO

Removing other wall
decorations pp.28–29
Washing down and
preparing surfaces pp.30–31

When paint or varnish on wood trim is flaking, badly chipped, or cracked, or so thick that a door or window won't close easily, strip it to the bare wood before washing down and redecorating, only after you know it doesn't contain lead (see p.30).

You can sand small areas, but the more practical ways to strip paint are to use heat or chemicals. Always wear gloves, long sleeves, safety goggles, and a dust mask, and open windows or use fans to ventilate the room.

CHEMICAL STRIPPERS

Although powerful, chemical strippers are not economical for large areas, so they are best used for intricate work such as moldings. These strippers are also used around glass because of the risk of heat cracking it.

The chemicals come either as a gel, paste, or liquid, and most strip both paint and varnish. How many coats of paint or varnish will be removed in one go depends on the product; some require several applications. Always read the instructions carefully.

USING HEAT

By far the easiest and most economical way to strip paint or varnish is by using an electrically powered heat gun. It may look like a hair dryer, but a heat gun gets very hot and must never be used for anything other than its intended applications. When using a heat gun, never put your hand into the air stream, and switch off the gun when it is not being used. Never use a heat gun to remove lead paint.

Helpful hints

Avoid using a heat gun around an open window on a blustery day—the wind may dissipate the heat before it softens the paint. Remove curtains to keep them out of the way.
  Using a heat gun on paint can cause the paint to burn, so keep a bucket filled with water below the work area and drop the paint peelings into it (never use newspapers).

USING A CHEMICAL STRIPPER

1 The stripper can damage the floor, so make sure it is well protected; you can use a sheet of plywood or hardboard, or several layers of newspaper. Pour the paint stripper into a glass jar. Use an old brush to lay on a thick coat of stripper, starting from the top and moving down.

2 Follow the instructions from the manufacturer for how long to leave the stripper in place, which can be up to 45 minutes or so. When the paint has softened, use a wide scraper on the flat areas of the work to remove the paint, taking care not to dig into the wood.

3 To scrape the paint from moldings, corners, and other intricate areas, use the most suitable part of the shavehook, pulling it along the work to remove the paint.

4 Protect the floor with a plastic sheet (to prevent water seeping through to the floor). Wipe off the excess stripper with a sponge and water or with mineral spirits. Use steel wool to get into the crevices of the moldings. If some paint still remains in a crevice, you can use a folded edge of medium wet-or-dry sandpaper.

USING A HEAT GUN

1 Always protect the floor, using a sheet of plywood or hardboard. When switched on, the heat gun quickly produces a constant flow of hot air, so handle it with extreme care. To remove paint, hold the gun 2 inches (50 mm) from the surface of the work until the paint starts to bubble.

2 Before the paint congeals, use a shavehook to scrape off the softened paint. Continue to hold the heat gun over the work, but don't concentrate the heat on one spot as this can scorch it; instead, keep playing it across the surface.

3 Some types of heat gun have an integral scraper attachment, allowing you to heat and scrape off the paint in one movement. Other heat guns are equipped with metal deflectors to keep heat off sensitive surfaces such as glass panes in windows.

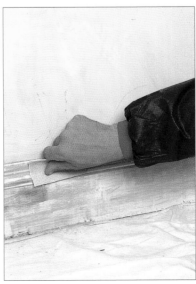

4 Whatever method used to remove the paint, there will always be traces remaining. Remove them with medium wet-or-drydry sandpaper. Fold the paper, insert an edge into the crevice, then sand back and forth.

STRIPPING AND PREPARING METAL

YOU WILL NEED

Safety goggles
Dust mask
Emery cloth
Wire brush
Power drill plus wire brush attachment
Rubber **or** wood sanding block
Putty knife
Sandpaper (if required)
Old, small paint brush
Small brush
Heavy-duty rubber gloves
Bucket and water
Soapy detergent (if required)
Mineral spirits **or** water
Steel wool

MATERIALS

Epoxy **or** acrylic filler
Poultice **or** gel-type paint stripper
Rust-inhibiting primer

SEE ALSO

Painting windows
pp.66–67

Lead-free paintwork (see p.30) on metal that is in good condition—whether a cast iron fireplace surround, steel window frame, or a radiator—may need only a wash with trisodium phosphate (TSP) or detergent to clean grime and a sanding to provide a key for the new paint. Additional preparation may only be a matter of sanding down drips flush with the surrounding area, but a buildup of paint obscuring details needs stripping.

TREATING RUST

Sadly, cast iron fireplace surrounds and steel-frame windows are often neglected. Rust can form in iron and steel where paint is chipped away, and, if left alone, the rust can eventually eat away at the metal, causing pitting.

The metal doesn't have to gleam, just be free of rust with no loose material remaining. A small area of rust can be removed with emery cloth, but larger areas may demand using an electric drill with a wire brush attachment. Always wear safety goggles and a dust mask to protect against flying particles.

To remove old paint and rust in detailed areas, use a poultice- or gel-type chemical stripper (a heat gun doesn't work well on metal); the poultice variety is peeled off after a few hours, bringing the paint with it.

If the rust has caused pitting in the surface, then fill this with an epoxy-base filler. After you remove the rust, apply a coat of a rust-inhibiting primer to the patches immediately—rust can return in less than a day.

Helpful hints

Aluminum used in window and door frames is not affected by rust, but a dull gray coat and white crystals can form on the surface. To restore it to a bright metal finish, use a fine wet-or-dry sandpaper lubricated with mineral spirits; then wipe the metal with a cloth and mineral spirits to remove any debris such as metal particles. After the metal dries, apply a coat of a rust-inhibiting primer.

1 To remove a small patch of surface rust, or rust near a molded area, fold a piece of emery cloth and rub the rust away.

2 Where there are large patches of chipped paint or rust, a handheld wire brush is a more efficient tool to use.

3 For large areas of loose, flaking paint and rust, you can use a powerful electric drill fitted with a wire brush attachment. A cup-shape brush is best for detailed molded areas; a wheel-shape one allows you to hold the drill at an angle. Remember to wear safety goggles and a dust mask.

4 To sand down paint drips, use emery cloth wrapped around a sanding block until the paint surface is flush with the surrounding area.

5 Fill in any pitted areas with a two-part epoxy or acrylic filler. (Removing old paint and rust will expose the pits.) Apply the filler with a putty knife; then use the blade of the knife to scrape off any excess until it is smooth with the surface, or leave it slightly protruding from the surface; rub it down with sand-paper once it is dry.

6 To remove paint in detailed areas, use an old paint brush to apply a thick layer of chemical stripper, and leave it in place the amount of time recommended by the manufacturer. (The poultice-type stripper will require a canvas backing placed in it, which is used to pull off the stripper and paint in one go.)

7 Once the paint has softened, it is ready to be removed. Use a small brush—an old toothbrush is ideal—to scrub away the paint from nooks and crannies. Some manufacturers suggest using soapy water.

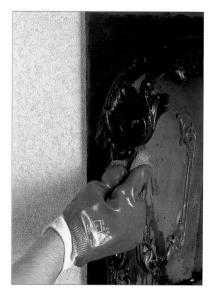

8 Finish the work by cleaning the metal with water or mineral spirits (depending on the brand of stripper used) to neutralize any remaining traces of the chemical. Use steel wool in intricate areas.

REMOVING BASEBOARDS AND OTHER MOLDINGS

YOU WILL NEED

Removing a baseboard
Utility knife
Wide cold chisel
Small sledgehammer
Pieces of wood
Crowbar
Panel **or** tenon saw
Work surface
Nail pullers **or** channel pliers

Filling a dent or hole
Flexible filler knife
Sanding block
Wet-or-dry sandpaper

Replacing a damaged section
Wide cold chisel
Small sledgehammer
Pieces of wood
Tenon saw
Wood chisel
Mallet
Plane

MATERIALS

Filling a dent or hole
Acrylic filler (one- or two-part)

Replacing a damaged section
Wood

SEE ALSO

Replacing baseboards
pp.38–39

In older houses, baseboards can be elaborate and up to 12 inches (300 mm) high, but a plain 4-inch- (100-mm-) tall molding is more likely to be used in newer homes. Baseboards are either nailed to wood blocks set into the brickwork behind them or into the studs behind a wallboard wall. New ones may be attached with panel adhesive.

One option when putting down a new flooring, such as laminated wood floorboards, is to remove baseboards, install the flooring, then replace the boards. Especially with old boards, avoid this because you can damage them. However, if you do remove the boards with the intention of refitting them, make sure you number them so that you can put them back in their original position. If the boards are already damaged, it is worth trying to do repairs or removing a damaged section to see if you can find a match at a local architectural salvage yard.

OTHER MOLDINGS

Crown molding is used to cover the joint between the ceiling and walls. Because this usually hides visible cracks, you should think carefully before you remove it. The method will depend on the way is was fastened to the walls. Pry off wooden crown molding with a wide chisel or crowbar. Use a putty knife to pry away crown molding made of plastic.

Picture and chair rail moldings were fixed to the wall with nails in older houses. Use a claw hammer against scrap wood (to protect the wall) to pry off the molding. Pull out nails that remain in the wall with nail pullers or channel pliers—if you leave them, rust will eventually stain the wall. Some moldings may be installed with screws—dig out the filler hiding the screw heads to remove the screws—or with a clip system in which moldings slip onto clips fastened to the walls.

REMOVING A BASEBOARD

1 Run a utility knife along the joint between the wall and baseboard to break a seam with the paint or wallpaper on the wall. Starting at an external corner or door, place a wide chisel behind the board and hit it with a sledgehammer. Wedge a piece of wood into the gap and remove the chisel.

2 Insert a crowbar into the gap, with a piece of scrap wood behind it to protect the wall. Gently pull the crowbar back; as the board comes away, move the crowbar and wood along about 3 feet (1 m) and repeat the process. Keep moving along until the board comes off the wall.

3 If the baseboard is proving difficult to loosen, hammer in a wedge of wood, then use the hook end of the crowbar to lever the baseboard away from the wall.

4 To remove a piece of board with a coped corner, pry it away from the wall with a wide chisel and hammer and insert a wedge into the gap. Rest the crowbar on a piece of wood and bang it in under the baseboard, then press down on the crowbar to lift up the baseboard away from the corner.

5 For a long board with ends covered at inside corners, use the wide chisel and hammer to open a gap between the wall and board; place a wedge at each side of the chisel. Use a panel saw to cut through the board at a 45° angle, drawing the saw upward. If you're not used to handling a saw, use a tenon saw with fine teeth.

6 If you plan to refit a baseboard, always remove the nails by pulling them through from the back to avoid damaging the front of the board. Clamp the baseboard onto a work surface. Grip the nail with pullers or channel pliers and firmly pull the nail down toward the board to lever it out.

FILLING A DENT OR HOLE

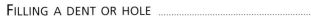

To fill in a dent or hole in a baseboard, mix up a small amount of acrylic filler, load up the filler knife, and push it into the damaged area. Press on it, pulling the knife toward you and away from the baseboard. After the filler dries, sand it level with the board.

REPLACING A DAMAGED SECTION

With the baseboard pried away from the wall (see step 5 above), make two diagonal cuts on either side of the damaged area with a tenon saw. Using a wood chisel and mallet, cut out the damaged piece. Glue a piece of wood into the area, then use a plane and wood chisel to shape it.

REPLACING BASEBOARDS

YOU WILL NEED

Miter saw **or** backsaw
Hammer
Work surface
Electric drill plus masonry bit
(if required)
Coping saw
Miter frame and saw **or**
miter box and tenon saw
Block plane
Stud detector (if required)
Nail set
Flexible putty knife
Pencil

MATERIALS

Baseboard
2½ inch (65 mm) finishing
nails
Hardboard quarter-round **or**
shoe molding (if required)
Brads
Wood putty

SEE ALSO

Removing baseboards
and other moldings
pp.36–37

Baseboards protect the walls from knocks caused by feet, vacuum cleaners, and other objects. If you're refitting old baseboards that were removed to install a new flooring, simply fasten the boards back into their original positions (see pp.36–37).

You may choose to replace baseboards because the old ones are damaged or because you want more attractive ones than the plain boards sometimes installed in newer homes. If you're replacing an older style of molding on plaster walls, make sure you buy new ones of a similar height. The plaster may not extend much farther beyond the top of the boards.

PLANNING AHEAD

Before installing new baseboards, make a sketch of the room and plan how the ends will have to be cut and the order of the installation. Butt the boards against any door casing. Avoid lengths that will require coping (see step 2, below) at each end. Where a length ends at two inside corners, butt one end to a wall and cope, or shape, the other end. A board with two mitered ends will require patience and skill as you test fit each joint individually; fit this board only after the adjacent ones have been installed.

The boards can be attached with nails. For masonry walls, if you don't want to use the original wood blocks, use a masonry bit in an electric drill to drill holes in the walls and insert wall anchors; then drive screws through the boards into the wall anchors. Another option is to use panel adhesive.

Helpful hints

Baseboards are available in different types of profile. However, if you don't find one to your liking, you can combine several types of molding to create your own style. Start with S4S (squared four sides) molding as the base, top it with a bead or other molding, and, if you want, finish off with quarter-round molding along its face.

1 For a long wall, two or more boards will have to be joined together. The best method for doing this is to make a scarf joint: cut each end at a matching 45° angle, using a miter saw or backsaw. Make sure you position the joint where you can fasten it to a stud behind a wallboard wall or to a wood block on a masonry wall.

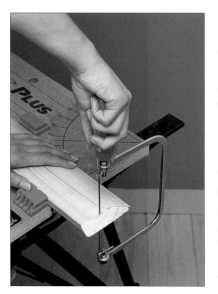

2 For an inside corner, you can fit the first length of baseboard butted against the adjacent wall. The second length, however, will have to be coped. First make a miter cut on the end of the board (see step 3), then use a coping saw held at a 85° angle to the work and follow the profile of the face of the cut end.

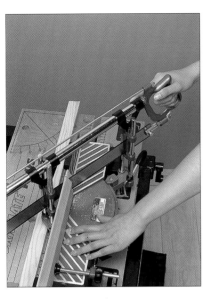

3 The boards will require mitering to fit an outside corner. Use a miter frame and saw or a miter box and tenon saw to make a cut at a 45° angle on each piece. Remember that the end of the board will project beyond the wall, so take this into consideration when measuring and marking the boards.

4 Many corners of walls are not truly square, so perfectly mitered boards may not fit snugly when in position. Do a test fit before fastening the boards—the chances are you may need to trim an end with a block plane. It's best to remove too little wood instead of too much—you can always go back to remove more wood.

5 Nail the boards to the walls—not the flooring—using 2½ inch (65 mm) finishing nails. On wallboard walls, drive the nails into the studs; use a stud detector (see p.229) to locate them. For masonry walls, mark the location of the wood blocks in the walls on the boards after you cut them to fit.

6 Use a nail set to drive each nail below the surface of the baseboard. Once all the baseboards are in place, use a putty knife to fill the nail holes with wood putty.

7 You can finish off the baseboard with quarter-round or shoe molding, which will hide any gaps between the baseboards and uneven floorboards. Fasten the molding to the baseboards with brads every 24 inches (600 mm); force the brads below the surface with a nail set and cover the heads with wood putty.

8 Alternatively, trim the baseboard if there is a short area that doesn't sit flush to the floorboards. Before fastening the board to the wall—but after cutting it to fit at corners if needed—pull a pencil along the floorboards to trace their contour onto the baseboard. Use a plane to trim the board to the pencil line.

REMOVING FLOOR COVERINGS

Floor coverings wear prematurely if there are defects in the subfloor below or the underlayment has become loose or begun to decay. The floor covering will have to be taken up and the floor prepared before a new material can be laid. Severely warped tiles, many loose tiles in a floor or crumbling adhesive beneath sheet vinyl flooring may also require the flooring being taken up. However, if the old covering is vinyl, wood, cork, ceramic, or quarry tile, and it is sound, flat, and fastened down well, you can leave it in place and lay the new covering on top. Carpets and carpet tiles must come up. The adhesives used for fastening new floor coverings will not stick to them.

If you suspect that the floor below is suffering from excess moisture or rot, the covering will have to be taken up and the problems underneath resolved. The same applies where dampness has been discovered in a concrete floor in an adjoining room.

PRIOR FASTENING METHODS

How the old covering was laid affects how it is removed. Carpets are nailed at the edges with carpet tacks, fastened to tackless strips, or loose laid. If tackless strips were laid with adhesive on concrete floors, you'll need a heat gun to soften the adhesive before you can remove them.

Sheet vinyl may be loose laid and stuck down at edges, doorways, and joints. If the vinyl doesn't easily come away at the edges, release it by using a utility knife to cut it 3 inches (75 mm) away from the walls. Tackle the strip left with a heat gun and scraper. If sheet vinyl was stuck down with an all-over adhesive, use a linoleum knife or sharp utility knife to slice the sheet into strips 12–18 inches (300–460 mm) wide before applying a heat gun.

Old sheet vinyl and hard plastic tiles may contain hazardous asbestos; call your local health department for advice before taking them up.

CARPETING

1 Old carpets may have been tacked down around door thresholds and along baseboards. Pulling up the carpet will remove some tacks, but others will remain. Using a tack puller, hook the V-shape end under the head of the tack and lever it up. Alternatively, you can use long-nose pliers.

2 To ease up a tackless strip from the floor, use a wide chisel and hammer; then insert a crowbar under the strip and pry it up. Move along the strip in a similar fashion until it is completely removed from the floor. Leave the strips in place if in good shape and laying down new carpet.

SOFT FLOOR TILES

Hold a heat gun 2 inches (50 mm) above a corner of a vinyl tile. As it softens the adhesive below, insert a scraper under the tile and start to pry it up. At the same time, move the gun over another part of the tile; continue prying. Use a long-handle tile scraper for a large area.

FLOATING WOOD FLOOR

To remove a floating wood floor, start at a door threshold. Hammer a wide chisel or crowbar under the strip of flooring. Once it is firmly wedged under the strip, pry it up. Continue across the room in the same way to remove the rest of the flooring strips.

PARQUET WOOD FLOOR

1 This method can be used to remove one block or as a first step to removing the whole floor. Wrap a piece of masking tape around a drill bit to indicate the depth of the wood block. Drill a hole at each end of the wood block along the same strip—don't go beyond the depth of the wood block.

2 Using a chisel and wooden mallet, cut a line to join the two drilled holes. Insert the chisel into this cut line and pry up a wood strip in the block. You can now pry up the rest of the block, and if you want, the remaining blocks on the floor.

CERAMIC AND QUARRY TILES

1 Place a wide cold chisel into the grout around a tile and hit it firmly with a sledgehammer. (Wear safety goggles and a dust mask.) Change the angle of the chisel and continue to hit it until the chisel goes under the tile and breaks it away. Hit the chisel under the remaining tiles.

2 It is a difficult, if not impossible, task to remove all of the tile adhesive from a concrete floor. Remove the high points with the cold chisel and hammer. Once the ridges have been knocked off, you can use a floor leveling compound to level the floor (see pp.50–51).

MAKING MINOR REPAIRS TO A WOOD FLOOR

The way a new floor covering performs is determined by the condition of the subfloor, and the best opportunity for exposing a subfloor for inspection and repair is when you remove an old floor covering to replace it with a new one.

INSPECTING THE FLOORBOARDS

Search the floorboards (or chipboard) for protruding tacks or other remnants left behind from the old floor covering (see pp.40–41). Look for protruding nails, which you should knock down into the joists below with a hammer. A protruding nail head could damage a new floor covering; or if you sand the floorboards before applying a finish, it will tear the sanding sheets used with the floor sander machine. However, in an upstairs room in an older house that has a lath-and-plaster ceiling, pull out a loose nail and replace it with a screw—the vibration of hammer blows could damage the plaster below.

A protruding or loose nail could be the reason a floorboard rocks as you walk on it, and it is often accompanied by an irritating squeak. As you make your inspection, walk around the room listening and feeling for noise and movement. A moving board is best secured with a screw. A nail could be forced out again at a later stage, but a screw will not pull out. If a board squeaks without discernable movement, it is rubbing against another board. You could puff talcum powder down between the boards, or lubricate glazier points with graphite and push them between the rubbing boards with a putty knife (if needed, tap them down with a hammer).

Gaps can be covered by a hardboard overlay, or in the case of a carpet, an underlay. However, if the floor is to be sanded and varnished, you'll have to fill them. If there are a lot of gaps, you may want to hire a professional to lift and relay all the boards.

FIXING A LOOSE BOARD

1 Before securing a loose floorboard in a bathroom, you may have to make sure that a pipe is not running through a notch made in the joist. On an upper floor, a metal detector will alert you if there is one—as long as it isn't a rigid plastic pipe.

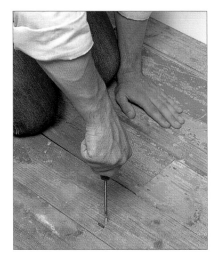

2 Alongside an exposed nail, drive down a screw through the floorboard and into the joist. Use a 1½ inch (38 mm) woodscrew, driving it in until the head sinks into the floorboard.

3 Use a nail set and hammer to drive any exposed nail heads below the surface of the floorboard.

4 Cover the holes over the screw head and over any previously exposed nails with a wood putty. If you plan to cover the floorboards with a floor covering, you can use an acrylic filler. However, you should use wood putty on floorboards that are to be sanded and finished.

REPAIRING A SPLIT BOARD

FILLING A LARGE GAP

Where a board has been split along the grain of the wood, you can hold the pieces together by driving down a nail into the subfloor on either side of the split. Angle the nails toward the split. If there is still a gap, fill it with an acrylic filler or wood putty (see step 4 above).

1 To repair a large gap, cut a piece of softwood slightly larger than the gap, using a tenon saw; then shave its sides with a block plane until it fits in the gap. Test-fit the wedge to make sure that it will fit snugly.

2 Apply a wood glue around the sides of the wedge and place it in the gap. Use a wooden mallet to tap down the wedge, working from one end to the other; leave it slightly protruding from the surface. Wipe off any squeezed-out glue with a damp cloth.

3 Once the glue has dried, use a block plane to shave the top of the wedge flush with the surface of the floorboard. If the floor is to be finished, you may need to stain the strip to match the surrounding boards.

REPLACING A DAMAGED FLOORBOARD

YOU WILL NEED

Wide cold chisel
Hammer
Crowbar
Circular saw, floorboard saw
or compass saw
Electric drill plus twist bit
(if required)
Jigsaw **or** padsaw
Screwdriver
Block plane **or**
woodworking chisel
Nail set (if required)
Flexible putty knife

MATERIALS

Floorboard
2 inch (50 mm) floorboard
nails **or** No. 8 screws
Acrylic filler **or** wood filler

SEE ALSO

Making minor repairs to a
wood floor pp.42–43

There are two types of floorboards: square edged and tongue-and-groove. A square-edge board, as the name implies, has square edges, which butt up against adjoining boards. A tongue-and-groove board has a tongue on one edge and a groove on the other; the tongue of one board slides into the groove of its neighbor.

Before removing a board, you'll have to know what type it is and whether you have a subfloor—older homes (as shown here) may not have one—the steps to remove them are different. Slide a knife down between the long edges of two boards. If the knife goes straight down, they have square edges and there is no subfloor; the knife will be stopped by the tongue of a tongue-and-groove board or farther down by subfloor if the board is square edged.

The board is nailed or screwed to joists below. A square-edge board can be pried up. Tongue-and-groove boards present a problem; if there is no subfloor, the tongue of the first board can be cut off before the board is pried up. If there is a subfloor, you have to drill a few holes no more than the depth of the floorboard across its width, then use a chisel to split the board down its length. (To remove a damaged section, drill two rows of overlapping holes beyond the damage.)

After the first board, other ones will lift up easily. Nails in floorboards may be rusty. Remove the nails from the board and dispose of them safely. Unless the board is replaced right away, cover any gap with plywood.

A NEW BOARD

If you can't buy boards of the correct thickness, get thinner ones and fasten plywood shims to each joist with finishing nails. You can use either nails or screws to fasten the board, but screws are preferred in upstairs rooms where hammering may cause damage to the ceiling below.

1 To pry up a square-edge board, insert a wide chisel near one end of the board—if necessary, carefully force the chisel in with a hammer. Pry up the board until the nails are released. Repeat on the other side of the board. Slip a crowbar under the board, then move to the next section and repeat the procedure.

2 Once you have lifted enough nails to get good leverage, with the crowbar under the board, step down on the free end of the board to release the next few rows of nails still secured to the joists. Move the crowbar along and repeat the process until the board is free.

3 To remove a tongue-and-groove board without a subfloor below, set a circular saw to cut ½ inch (12 mm) deep. Saw alongside the board to cut the tongue. You can now pry up the board in the same way as a square-edge board, as well as any successive boards.

4 Alternatively, you can cut through the tongue using a special hand-held floorboard saw, which has an adapted nose with teeth to allow you to start the cut from above. You can also use a compass saw, but you will have to first make a start hole with a suitable size drill bit.

5 To replace a short section of board, cut across it before you lever it up. Find the first joist beyond the damage (look for a line of screws or nails); drill a ⅜-inch-(10-mm-) diameter hole close to it. Insert a jigsaw or compass saw into the hole; cut across board. Repeat at the other end at the first joist after the damaged area.

6 Because the damaged board has to be sawn off flush with the joist, you'll have to create a nailing surface for the new board. Cut a piece of 1½ inch (38 mm) lumber just wider than the board, and fasten it with screws to the side of the joist. Make sure that the top of the strip is flush with the top of the joist.

7 While a square-edged board will slot neatly into the opening, a tongue-and-groove board won't. The simple solution is to use a block plane or chisel to remove the tongue. Position the board with its ends resting on the joists if there is no subfloor.

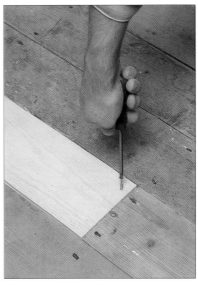

8 Attach the board along the end joists and at any intermediary ones (look for lines of nails across neighboring boards), using 2 inch (50 mm) floorboard nails or No. 8 screws. Drive nail heads below the surface with a nail set or countersink screw heads. If there is a subfloor, you can attach the board to it.

LAYING A HARDBOARD UNDERLAYMENT

Except for ceramic and quarry floor tiles, which need a thick plywood underlayment, the wearing power and appearance of any floor covering will be improved by first laying hardboard. It can provide a level surface where floorboards curl up at the ends, and it is useful for creating a smooth surface over damaged floorboards with may have gaps between them. Hardboard is inexpensive and easy to lay. You can lay plywood in the same way.

Standard hardboard and plywood are ⅛ inch (3 mm) thick and are ideal for most rooms. Use tempered hardboard on ground floors because it won't be affected by damp below. If a floor is uneven, use ¼-inch- (6-mm-) thick sheets. They come in 4 feet × 8 feet (1220 mm × 2440 mm) sheets, or they can be cut to custom sizes at the store.

Standard hardboard (not tempered) must be conditioned to the room's moisture content before being laid, otherwise the sheets can buckle later on. To form a perfect surface for the floor covering, make sure the sheets are butted up snugly before you secure them. Hardboard sheets are usually laid rough side up to provide a gripping surface for the adhesives used to lay the finished floor. To avoid a narrow strip at the edge of the room, lay out a dry run of sheets along two adjacent walls of the room and adjust the starting point of the first sheet.

You can fasten the sheets using ¾ inch (19 mm) annular ringed nails, panel nails, or staples, or you can use panel adhesive. Avoid longer nails, which can pierce any plumbing or cable under the floorboards.

Helpful hints

To ensure that a sheet of hardboard or plywood is in perfectly flat contact with the floorboards below it, kneel on the sheet before installing any fasteners. You should start the fasteners at the center of one edge of the sheet and work your way out to the ends and to the opposite side in a pyramid fashion.

1 To condition standard sheets of hardboard, brush water onto their rough sides. Use about 1 pint (600 ml) of water for each 4 square feet (1220 sq mm) of hardboard.

2 Stack the sheets rough side to rough side in the room in which they are to be used. Make sure that they are lying flat and leave them for 48 hours.

3 Secure the first sheet in a corner, spacing fasteners 4 inches (100 mm) apart along the edges and 6 inches (150 mm) apart in rows across the sheet. Butt the second sheet against the first and fasten it in place. Continue fastening the sheets until you reach the last full one in the row; do not secure it until the end one is trimmed.

4 To fit an end sheet, first use a wood block to scribe a line (see pp.200–201) along the end that will fit against the wall if the wall if uneven; trim it with a knife and straightedge (see step 8). Position the sheet, then place the neighboring one on top of it to act as a guide. Score along the bottom sheet with a utility knife.

5 Depending on the thickness of the hardboard, make several scores along the original one. Stand on one half of the sheet and briskly raise the other half to snap the sheet along the score line. Secure the previous sheet in place with the fasteners, then the end one.

6 Continue to secure the remaining hardboard sheets, staggering them in brickwork fashion to avoid joints aligning with each other. One method (which also reduces waste) is to use the second part of a trimmed sheet from a previous row to start the following one.

7 If you have to make a notch to fit around a pipe, simply use a utility knife to make a series of scores. For a larger obstacle, such as a basin pedestal, make a paper template to transfer the shape to the sheet (see pp.200-201). Then use the utility knife to make a series of scores.

8 At a doorway, roughly trim the board to the shape of the casing. You can use a profile gauge (see p.195) or a compass to transfer the shape to the sheet. To cut out the shape, use a utility knife to make a series of scores along a metal straightedge. An easier way to cut hardboard is to use a tenon saw or jigsaw.

MINOR CONCRETE FLOOR DEFECTS

YOU WILL NEED

Filling in a minor crack
Brush and dustpan
Work gloves
Safety goggles
Small sledge hammer
Cold chisel
Small paint brush
Bucket
Trowel
Wood straightedge **or** screed (if required)

Sealing in dust
Paint roller and thick-pile sleeve

Treating dampness
Bucket
Large disposable paint brush

MATERIALS

Filling in a minor crack
Latex bonding liquid
Cement and sand **or** dry-mixed mortar

Sealing in dust
Concrete floor sealer

Treating dampness
Crystalline waterproofing emulsion

SEE ALSO

The big issues pp.12–13
Leveling a concrete floor pp.50–51

Cracks in a solid floor are usually superficial, affecting only the thin, troweled layer of the concrete slab. However, if you find a deep crack or a long crack that runs across the room, you should call in a professional for advice.

If you have sand and cement left over from a previous job that is in good condition—not hard or lumpy—you can use it to make a mortar mix. If you don't have a supply on hand, then buy a bag or small container of dry-mixed mortar, which simply requires mixing with water.

A DUSTY SURFACE

Sometimes a concrete floor will continually give off dust no matter how often it is swept. The problem is often caused by the slab having been over-troweled, leaving it weak. The dust must be sealed in or any adhesive that is used to lay a floor covering will not adhere.

DAMPNESS

A wet patch on a concrete floor may be attributed to condensation or to dampness rising from the ground below. The two conditions are treated differently. To test for and cure condensation, see pages 12–13.

If dampness rising through the slab is the enemy, the slab probably lacks footing drain tiles or the tiles are clogged. If there are no drain tiles, the answer usually is to have a basement waterproofing specialist break through the slab around the perimeter (on the inside of the house) and install tiles or perforated drain hose. The trench is then covered with fresh concrete. Where drain tiles exist, the system can be professionally cleared with an auger. In severe cases, installing a sump pump may be necessary. If the condition is mild and the concrete is in good condition, try treating the floor with a crystalline waterproofing product recommended for basement floors.

FILLING IN A MINOR CRACK

1 To inspect the damage, first sweep away any dirt and debris with a brush. To ensure a good repair, also brush away any new debris created by following step 2.

2 Wearing work gloves and safety goggles, use a small sledge hammer and cold chisel to undercut (or open up) the crack by forming an inverted V-shape—with the point of the V at the top surface of the crack. This provides a better gripping surface for the mortar.

3 Prime the crack with a coat of latex bonding liquid. Follow the instructions from the manufacturer for diluting it, and use an old paint brush to apply it. The bonding liquid will help the mortar to grip the surfaces of the crack.

4 Use a trowel to mix one part of cement with three parts of sand mixed with bonding liquid instead of water (again, follow the manufacturer's instructions). The mix should be buttery, not weak—it is better to err on the dry side rather than having a runny mixture.

5 Using the trowel, press the mortar into the crack. Level it off with the surface of the floor, using the edge of the trowel. Skim off any excess before it dries. Leave the mortar to cure overnight, then brush away any loose dust.

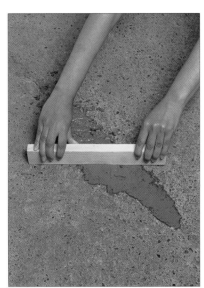

6 To fill a wide crack, instead of using the trowel to level the repair as in step 5, use a wood straightedge or screed—move it from side to side as you pull it toward you.

SEALING IN DUST

To bind the dust layer and seal it in, scrub the floor thoroughly with strong detergent and water and rinse it. Following the manufacturer's instructions, roll or brush a proprietary concrete floor sealer over the floor. The sealer is available from a concrete supplier or home center.

TREATING DAMPNESS

If dampness is mild and the surface is in good condition, you can try sealing the floor by brushing on a crystalline waterproofing emulsion, which is available from concrete suppliers and at home centers. Because dampness can spread beyond the treated area, it is best to treat the whole floor.

LEVELING A CONCRETE FLOOR

YOU WILL NEED

Paint brush
Bucket
Roller with extension handle
Trowel (if required)
Steel float
Watering can (if required)
Hammer (if required)

MATERIALS

Water
Strong powdered detergent
Self-leveling topping compound
Threshold strip (if required)
Nails (if required)

SEE ALSO

Minor concrete floor defects pp.48–49

A slab of concrete forms the bulk of a concrete floor. When it is covered with a layer of a sufficiently strong mixture of a cement mortar topping, it should remain flat. Hollows in a concrete floor are usually caused by an excessively weak topping layer. Sometimes there is a disparity in the floor, with some areas flat while others are hollow. This can occur because the topping has to be mixed in batches; as the work proceeds, too much water may be used in some of the batches, which weakens the mixture. The hollows can be as much as ½ inch (12 mm) deep at the center.

TOPPING

The best material for leveling the floor is a self-leveling topping compound. Because it is easy to mix and apply, it's suitable for anyone to use. The term "self-leveling" is exact. The compound is spread over the floor and levels itself after some assistance with a trowel—all float marks will disappear as the compound dries.

Although minor holes, cracks, and ridges in the topping can be caused by poor workmanship, cracks can also be due to shrinkage. Any holes or cracks deeper than ¼ inch (6 mm) should be filled with mortar (see pp.48–49). Shallow dents can be filled with the same compound used to level the floor.

While you may need to apply topping to only part of the floor, for a complete floor, start away from the door by which you will be leaving the room. The reason, of course, is that you don't want to be trapped by a carpet of wet compound between you and the door when the floor is done. If there is no raised threshold at the door and the compound is to be leveled there, you'll have to add a threshold.

A floor covering can usually be laid after 12 hours, but check the time recommended by the manufacturer of the compound that you are using.

1 First, sweep or vacuum the floor clean. Then scrub it with strong detergent, diluted according to the manufacturer's instructions. Rinse it off with plenty of water and leave it to dry for a couple of days. If the room is cold, put in temporary heating to ensure the floor dries completely.

2 Dents are best filled with a small amount of the self-leveling compound, which must be allowed to dry for 12 hours before you lay the all-over coat of compound.

3 Follow the manufacturer's directions for mixing the compound with cold water. A trowel is a good tool for mixing. Because the compound will start to dry after 10 minutes, at first mix only about an average-size bucket for each batch. As you start to work more quickly, you can make larger batches.

4 Just prior to using the compound, dampen the floor with water. This prevents the compound from drying out too quickly and possibly cracking at a later date.

5 Pour the mixture onto the floor, a bucket at a time. It will start to spread out in a puddle, so allow space for it to spread to any neighboring walls.

6 You can assist the compound in spreading by using a steel float. Hold the float parallel to the floor and move it in a semicircular motion. You should notice the float marks disappearing as the compound dries.

7 Should you not—at first—be able to use the float with complete success, then immediately sprinkle water onto the compound to prevent it from drying and try again.

DOOR THRESHOLD

When using the self-leveling compound at a doorway, first make sure there is a raised threshold that will prevent the compound from spreading into the adjacent room. If not, install a threshold strip, using masonry nails. A door that opens into the room may need trimming (see pp.76–77).

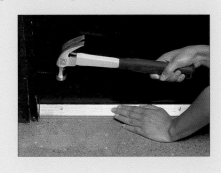

2

WINDOWS, DOORS, AND STAIRS

WINDOWS, DOORS, AND STAIRS DIRECTORY

TYPES OF WOOD WINDOWS

SEE PAGES 56–57

A description of hardwood and softwood windows— mainly casement and double-hung types—and how they work, with a look at some methods of glazing.

TYPES OF METAL AND PLASTIC WINDOWS

SEE PAGES 58–59

Metal (aluminium and steel) and plastic (PVC) are the alternatives to wood windows; they offer low maintenance, draft-proofing, and double glazing, as well as built-in locks.

REPAIRING DAMAGED WOOD WINDOWS

TIME FRAME 1 to 2 days
SKILL LEVEL Low to medium
SPECIAL TOOLS Wood chisel, router, bar clamp
SEE PAGES 60–61

How to replace wood damaged by wet rot and repair loose joints in old wood windows.

REPLACING SASH CORDS AND WEIGHTS

TIME FRAME 1 day
SKILL LEVEL Medium
SPECIAL TOOLS None
SEE PAGES 62–63

How to replace the cords that normally secure the sashes to the counterbalancing weights.

REPLACING A WINDOW PANE

TIME FRAME ½ day
SKILL LEVEL Medium
SPECIAL TOOLS Glazier's hacking knife or old chisel and tack hammer, putty knife
SEE PAGES 64–65

Glass is one of the most vulnerable materials in the home; if it breaks, it should be replaced immediately.

PAINTING WINDOWS

TIME FRAME 1 day per window
SKILL LEVEL Medium
SPECIAL TOOLS Paint brush
SEE PAGES 66–67

Old steel and wood windows need regular recoating with paint, or, for hardwood windows, preservative stain.

REPLACING OLD WINDOW HARDWARE

TIME FRAME ½ to 1 day
SKILL LEVEL Low to medium
SPECIAL TOOLS Wood chisel
SEE PAGES 68–69

Replacing handles and catches improves the appearance of a window. Replacing hinges is a more difficult job.

INSTALLING WINDOW SECURITY DEVICES

TIME FRAME Under 2 hours
SKILL LEVEL Low
SPECIAL TOOLS None
SEE PAGES 70–71

Burglars often gain entry to a home by breaking glass to reach through and open a window. Fitting security devices prevents them from opening the window.

TYPES OF INTERIOR DOORS

SEE PAGES 72–73

The choices for doors inside a home include panel, flush, glazed, and louvered doors. There's also advice on the standard sizes.

TYPES OF EXTERIOR DOORS

SEE PAGES 74–75

Thicker than interior doors, most exterior doors are paneled or glazed, but come in other materials and styles.

MAKING REPAIRS TO DOORS

TIME FRAME Under 2 hours to 1 day
SKILL LEVEL Low to medium
SPECIAL TOOLS Door trimming saw (rented), plane, wood chisel, large clamp
SEE PAGES 76–77

How to repair a binding door, a loose joint, and damaged wood, and how to trim a door to fit over new flooring.

REPAIRING DOOR FRAMES

TIME FRAME 1 day
SKILL LEVEL Medium
SPECIAL TOOLS Miter saw
SEE PAGES 78–79

A door frame may be loose or the hinge leaves in the frame may need repairing. You may want to replace the casing.

CORDLESS ELECTRIC DRILL

SPADE DRILL BITS

AWL

WOODWORKING CHISELS

TRY SQUARE

BLOCK PLANE

PAINTING DOORS

TIME FRAME 1 to 2 days
SKILL LEVEL Medium
SPECIAL TOOLS Paint brush
SEE PAGES 80–81

As with painting a window, it is the order in which you paint the door that is most important.

A NEW DOOR: INSTALLING HINGES

TIME FRAME 1 day
SKILL LEVEL Medium
SPECIAL TOOLS Circular saw, plane, wood chisel
SEE PAGES 82–83

Part one of hanging a door: how to measure up and fit the door to the opening and how to cut hinge recesses.

A NEW DOOR: HANGING IT AND INSTALLING HANDLES

TIME FRAME 1 day
SKILL LEVEL Medium
SPECIAL TOOLS Hacksaw, electric drill
SEE PAGES 84–85

Part two of hanging a door: hanging the door in the frame and fitting the door latches and handles.

CHANGING THE WAY A DOOR HANGS

TIME FRAME 1 day
SKILL LEVEL Medium
SPECIAL TOOLS Tenon saw, electric drill, chisel
SEE PAGES 86–87

Changing a door to open to the other side of a room or out of a room instead of into it.

CHANGING A HINGED DOOR TO A SLIDING DOOR

TIME FRAME 2 days
SKILL LEVEL Medium
SPECIAL TOOLS Carpenter's level
SEE PAGES 88–89

A sliding door frees space in the room into which the door previously opened. The light switch needs moving, which is best left to a professional.

INSTALLING A BI-FOLD DOOR

TIME FRAME ½ to 1 day
SKILL LEVEL Medium
SPECIAL TOOLS Electric drill
SEE PAGES 90–91

A bi-fold door is hinged in the middle so it projects only half-way into a room when opened.

INSTALLING SLIDING CLOSET DOORS

TIME FRAME 1 to 2 days
SKILL LEVEL Medium to high
SPECIAL TOOLS Jigsaw
SEE PAGES 92–93

Create a built-in closet by fitting sliding doors in front of a wall—either wall to wall or with an end panel; or attach them to a free-standing unit.

INSTALLING A CYLINDER RIM LOCK

TIME FRAME Under 2 hours
SKILL LEVEL Low to medium
SPECIAL TOOLS Electric drill plus spade bit, chisel, hacksaw
SEE PAGES 94–95

A common type of lock for the front door, a cylinder rim lock requires drilling to fit.

INSTALLING A MORTISE LOCK

TIME FRAME ½ day
SKILL LEVEL Medium
SPECIAL TOOLS Mortise chisel, brace or electric drill
SEE PAGES 96–97

The most secure lock on a front door is a mortise lock fitted into a slot in the door.

OTHER DOOR HARDWARE

TIME FRAME Under 2 hours to ½ day
SKILL LEVEL Medium
SPECIAL TOOLS Jigsaw, electric drill, hacksaw
SEE PAGES 98–99

How to install extra door locks and chains, a door viewer, and a letterbox.

REPAIRING STAIRS AND BALUSTERS

TIME FRAME Under 2 hours to 1 day
SKILL LEVEL Low to medium
SPECIAL TOOLS Tenon saw, electric drill, sliding T bevel
SEE PAGES 100–1O1

How to repair squeaky steps and mend broken balusters and stair nosings.

DECORATING STAIRCASE WOODWORK

TIME FRAME 1 to 2 days
SKILL LEVEL Low to medium
SPECIAL TOOLS Paint brushes, tack lifter
SEE PAGES 102–103

Preparing and painting or varnishing stair woodwork.

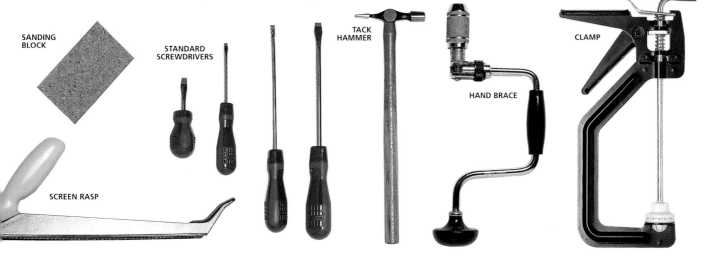

SANDING BLOCK

SCREEN RASP

STANDARD SCREWDRIVERS

TACK HAMMER

HAND BRACE

CLAMP

TYPES OF WOOD WINDOWS

Wood is a good insulator, so little heat escapes from the house through a wooden window frame. It is a common building material, so it blends in well with other wooden features such as doors and eaves. There are two main types of window—casement and double hung—and both come in solid wood or vinyl-covered wood.

In general, hardwoods are much better at resisting rot and insect attack than softwoods. Because hardwoods have a natural beauty, hardwood windows are normally protected with an exterior varnish or a preservative wood stain; softwood windows are painted with specific paints designed for outside use, including microporous paints that prevent water from getting into the wood but allow any trapped moisture to escape.

DOUBLE-GLAZED WINDOW
Two panes of glass with an air gap in between—a double-glazed window—reduces heat loss. Replacement windows have double-glazed sealed units (see p.59). To double glaze a window, install a stepped sealed unit (half fits into the rabbet and half fits on the frame) or secondary glazing, with a pane of glass or plastic fitted to the window or inside the reveal.

CASEMENT WINDOW
A wooden frame fitted with glass is either hinged on one edge so that it can be opened or fixed in a permanently closed position. If the window opens, it has a casement stay to provide ventilation and/or a handle to hold it shut. A typical arrangement is one large fixed casement and one large side-hinged casement. A larger window has a fixed casement in the center, with two side-hinged casements on the sides. Either may have small top-hinged casements above.

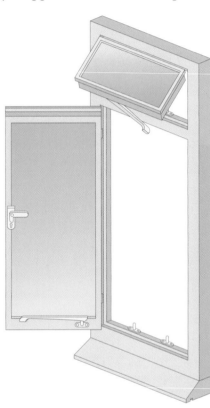

GEORGIAN WINDOW
This is the name given to an older type of wooden window, either casement or double hung, divided into a number of small panes of glass by glazing bars. It provides an attractive appearance when used on the right type of house and means that only small panes of glass need to be replaced when broken.

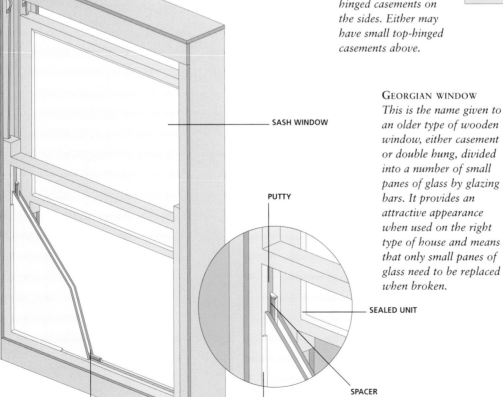

SASH WINDOW

PUTTY

SEALED UNIT

SPACER

DOUBLE-GLAZED WINDOW

BEADING

DOUBLE-HUNG WINDOW

Two frames, or sashes—which slide vertically, one behind the other—are used to form a double-hung window. Traditionally, double-hung windows are counterbalanced by sash weights at the end of sash cords. The cords are attached (nailed) to the sides of the sash and pass up over pulleys mounted in the window frame, where they are tied to large metal weights, which move up and down inside a concealed box.

Modern double-hung windows have springs or "spiral balances" instead of cords (a spiral balance is a twisting spring that counterbalances the weight of the window). Both methods of support allow the sashes to be tilted inward so that the outside pane can be cleaned from the inside.

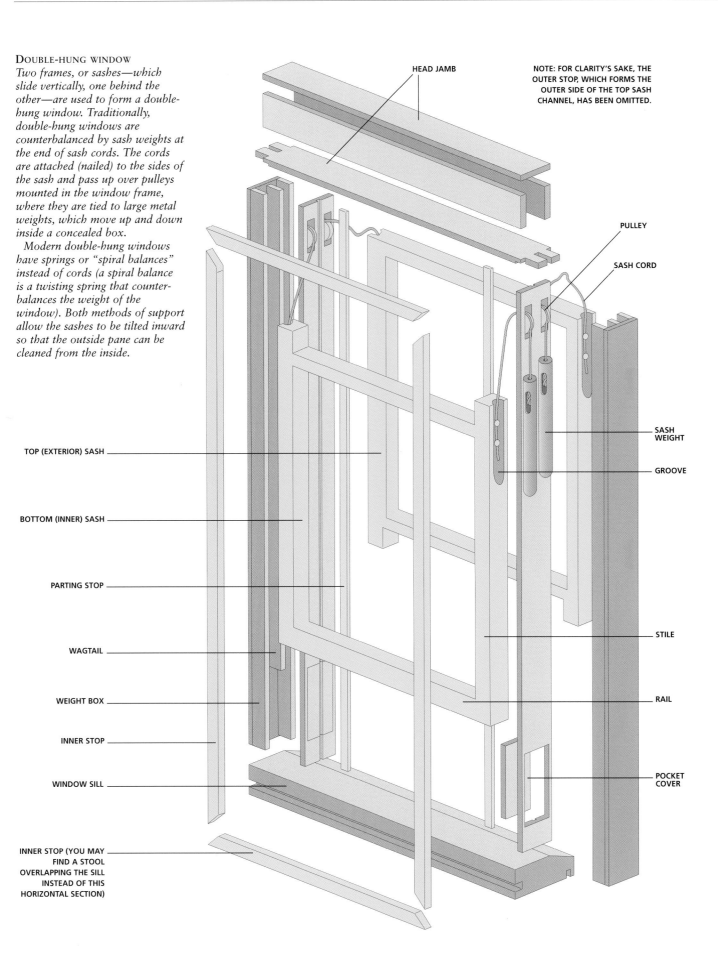

HEAD JAMB

NOTE: FOR CLARITY'S SAKE, THE OUTER STOP, WHICH FORMS THE OUTER SIDE OF THE TOP SASH CHANNEL, HAS BEEN OMITTED.

PULLEY

SASH CORD

TOP (EXTERIOR) SASH

BOTTOM (INNER) SASH

PARTING STOP

WAGTAIL

WEIGHT BOX

INNER STOP

WINDOW SILL

INNER STOP (YOU MAY FIND A STOOL OVERLAPPING THE SILL INSTEAD OF THIS HORIZONTAL SECTION)

SASH WEIGHT

GROOVE

STILE

RAIL

POCKET COVER

TYPES OF METAL AND PLASTIC WINDOWS

Modern metal and plastic windows are invariably double glazed and require virtually no maintenance. Steel windows were popular in the 1930s because they were relatively inexpensive, easy to install, and had slimline profiles, allowing plenty of light to shine through. A huge advantage of aluminum as a window material is that it can be fashioned into almost any shape and size, making it ideal for customizing a replacement window to fit most window frames.

Vinyl, or PVC (polyvinyl chloride), is the modern window material. It is ideal for replacing wooden windows because the window material is roughly the same thickness as the original, and vinyl is virtually maintenance-free.

ALUMINUM WINDOWS
The slim profile of aluminum windows can be formed into many shapes, including octagon or hexagon shapes for bay windows and curves for bow windows. Early replacement windows had a plain anodized finish, which not only had a boring, dull gray finish, but soon became pitted. Modern windows come with a factory-applied painted finish in a range of colors, and many have insulation built into the frame. Like many steel windows, aluminum windows are fitted into a wood frame.

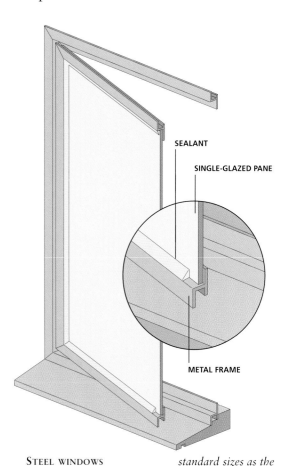

SEALANT

SINGLE-GLAZED PANE

METAL FRAME

PLASTIC WINDOWS
White or brown vinyl (polyvinyl chloridee) is used for plastic windows, which come in a range of styles, including a "tilt-and-turn" design—the window can be tilted inward from the bottom for easy cleaning. Once installed, maintenance is not necessary; however, the material can discolor in sunlight unless an ultraviolet (UV) light inhibitor was added to the material by the manufacturer.

STEEL WINDOWS
The original steel windows have drawbacks: they can rust, steel is a poor insulator (often giving rise to condensation on the inside of the window frame), and additional locks are difficult to add. Modern steel replacement windows— which are made in the same standard sizes as the originals—have largely overcome all of these problems. They come ready-painted from the factory (which provides a degree of insulation, as well as a maintenance-free finish) and usually come fitted with key-operated locks.

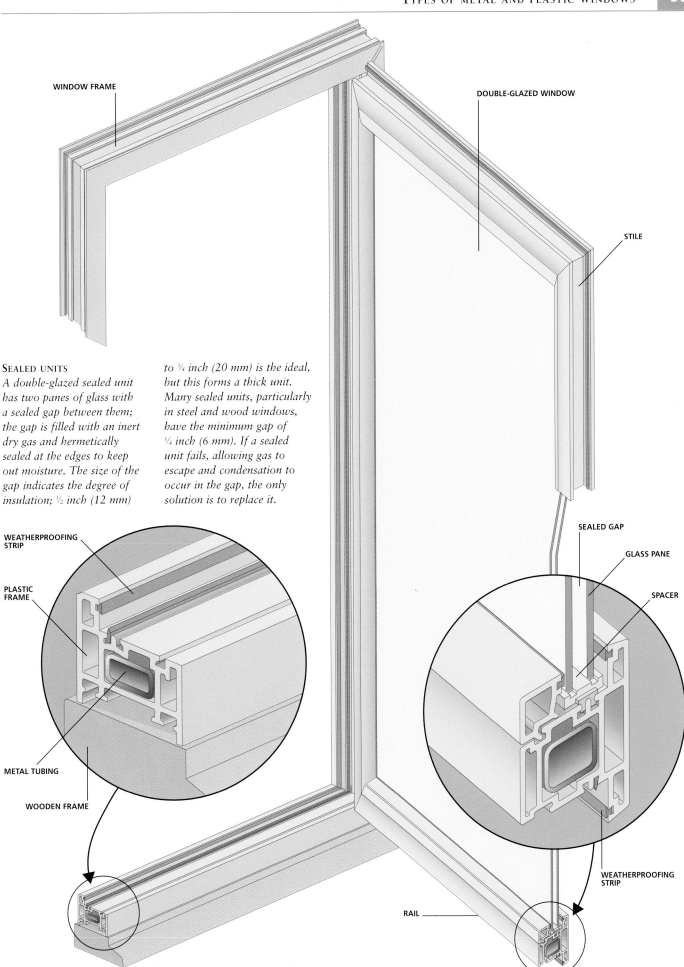

WINDOW FRAME

DOUBLE-GLAZED WINDOW

STILE

SEALED UNITS

A double-glazed sealed unit has two panes of glass with a sealed gap between them; the gap is filled with an inert dry gas and hermetically sealed at the edges to keep out moisture. The size of the gap indicates the degree of insulation; ½ inch (12 mm) *to ¾ inch (20 mm) is the ideal, but this forms a thick unit. Many sealed units, particularly in steel and wood windows, have the minimum gap of ¼ inch (6 mm). If a sealed unit fails, allowing gas to escape and condensation to occur in the gap, the only solution is to replace it.*

WEATHERPROOFING STRIP

PLASTIC FRAME

METAL TUBING

WOODEN FRAME

SEALED GAP

GLASS PANE

SPACER

WEATHERPROOFING STRIP

RAIL

REPAIRING DAMAGED WOOD WINDOWS

There are two particular problems that can affect the wood parts of windows; these are rot and failed joints in the window frame.

DEALING WITH ROT

Wet rot, which softens the wood (see pp.12–13), usually attacks window sills and the lowest frame member (rail) of softwood windows, where rainwater can collect. If the damage is serious, the only solution is to replace the frame; however, you can repair the damage if you catch it early by using a wood repair kit, which consists of a wood hardener, preservative and exterior filler. Dry rot (see pp.12–13) requires specialist help.

REPAIRING JOINTS

Most joints in wood windows—both casement and sash—are mortise-and-tenon joints. A joint can shrink as the wood dries out, causing the window to sag so that it binds at the top corner farthest from the hinge on a casement window and at the bottom edge on the same side. To do a proper job of repairing this damage, you'll have to remove the window so that it can be squared up while the joint is re-glued. Use bar clamps for doing this, as shown in *Repairing a large area* (opposite page).

If "wedged" mortise-and-tenon joints were used, the simplest way to repair a dried-out joint is to cut new wedges and insert them with as much waterproof glue as you can force into the joint; then clamp the work while the adhesive sets.

With non-wedged joints, drill holes across the joint, passing through both the mortise and tenon, using a brad-point twist drill bit; insert dowels plus PVA glue (with more glue squeezed into the exposed end of the joint), then clamp and allow it to set as before. Chisel off the excess length of the dowels once the glue has set.

TREATING A SMALL AREA

1 First determine the extent of the damage by poking the rotten area with a sharp pointed tool such as an awl. This will go easily into rotten areas. Use a chisel to remove all the affected wood until you reach solid wood (this ensures that all the rotten wood is removed).

2 If the wood is still damp, use a heat gun to dry it out, but keep it away from the glass to avoid cracking it. Brush on a wood hardener (follow the manufacturer's instructions); let dry. If necessary, apply a second coat. Some wood hardeners contain a preservative; work it into the wood.

3 If the kit provides preservative pellets, drill holes in the sound wood. The holes should be the same diameter and slightly longer than the pellets. Insert the pellets into the holes, pushing them just below the surface. Fill the holes with an exterior filler (see step 4), allowing it to slightly protrude from the surface.

4 Whether or not you use pellets, mix together the resin-base wood filler and its hardener; apply it with a putty knife, leaving it just raised from the surface. You may have to apply the filler in two layers; mix a little at a time, and wait for the first layer to set before applying the second one. When it has dried, sand it flush with the surface.

REPAIRING A LARGE AREA

1 For a large area, draw a pencil line 2 inches (50 mm) beyond the rotten area. Clamp a wood straightedge along this line to guide a router. Set the router's blade to a depth just greater than the rot, and hold it firmly against the guide as you cut away the rotten wood.

2 In the corners at each end—where the router cannot reach—cut out any rotten wood with a chisel. Cut a piece of wood the correct length to fit in the gap. Use waterproof glue on the sides and ends of the piece, and push it into the cut-out area.

3 On a window frame, squeeze waterproof glue into the joints and insert wedges (or dowels) in each side of the frame; clamp the frame with a bar clamp, putting blocks of wood between the clamp's jaws and the work to avoid harming the frame. Tighten the bar clamp gently—tightening it too much will break the glass.

4 After 24 hours, remove the bar clamp, then use a small block plane to plane down the wood insert flush with the surrounding surfaces of the frame. Apply a finish to match the surrounding frame. Treat the repaired area with a primer, then apply a top coat over the complete window frame (see pp.66–67).

REPLACING SASH CORDS AND WEIGHTS

If your sash windows tend to crash down—or rise slowly when not secured—the cords may have broken or the wrong size weights may be attached to them. Replacing the cords or weights is not a job to undertake lightly. It is best to do it with a helper, because the individual sashes (which must be removed) are both heavy and awkward to handle.

It is impossible to do this job without causing considerable damage to the paintwork—and you may well damage some parts of the window as well. Allow plenty of time for the job, including time for painting (avoid getting paint on the new sash cords). For security reasons, limit the time the sashes are out of their frame to the absolute minimum.

BUYING REPLACEMENTS

Check the size and type of sash cord you'll need to replace the damaged ones; you can take a piece of the original cord to the store as an example. The weights should exactly balance the weight of the window, including the glass. If thicker, or thinner, glass has been used as a replacement for the original glass, the existing weights could no longer be the correct size and will need replacing. You can purchase replacement sash weights at larger hardware stores and at builders' supply stores.

1 Before removing the inner stop molding on each side of the frame, run a utility knife between the molding and frame to break the skin of the paint. Pry off the molding with an old chisel, starting from the center. It is common to destroy the molding in the process; simply buy replacement molding at the lumberyard.

2 Pull the top edge of the bottom sash away from the frame. Cut through any remaining sash cord with a utility knife. Tie a length of string to the cord attached to the weight and gently lower it to the bottom of its box. Now remove the bottom sash from the frame.

3 Before removing the top sash, pry out the parting stop that divides the two sashes from each side of the frame, starting at the bottom of the frame. Lower the top sash; cut the cords and lower the weights as in step 2. You can now remove the sash from the frame.

4 Unscrew the cover of the weight boxes at the bottom of each side of frame. Carefully lift each weight up slightly before pulling it out. Make a sketch of how the weights are tied to the cords.

5 Work out how much sash cord you need (use an old one as a guide). When the window is in its lowered position, the weight should not quite reach the top; in the upper position, the weight should be just above the bottom of its box. Attach a length of string to the new cord.

6 Starting with the outer sash, feed the cord through the pulley and down inside the box. Pull the cord through and thread it through the weight; tie it in the knot previously noted in step 4. Return the weight to its box, and screw the cover back in place.

7 After you replace the outer sash window (use the procedure described for the inner sash in step 8) replace the old parting stops (or cut new ones to length) and push them into place on both sides of the frame. Fasten the stops to the frame with finishing nails, and use a nail set to drive them below the surface.

8 Fit the inner sash; pull the weights until they are just below the top of their boxes. Hold the sash in its lower position, place the cords in the groove at each side of the sash, and fasten them with box nails. If needed, cut off the cords at the grooves. Fit the sash into the frame; replace the stop moldings, using brads. Paint the work.

REPLACING A WINDOW PANE

Replacing cracked or broken glass is a common do-it-yourself job. It isn't difficult, but it takes time and great care is needed—particularly when removing the old glass—to avoid cutting yourself. If you doubt your ability to do the job, have a professional glazier do it for you. Provided you can cover the opening securely (for example, with plywood), you can remove the window from its frame and take it to a hardware store or glazier for replacement panes. Even if you feel capable of replacing the pane yourself, have the glass cut to size where you buy it.

THE RIGHT TYPE OF GLASS?

Normally, you should replace glass with the same type as the broken pane; for most home windows, this will be $5/32$ inch (4 mm) glass. Only small windows—or panes in, say, interior "Georgian" glazed doors with several panels—can be glazed with

$1/8$ inch (3 mm) glass, while large windows will require $1/4$ inch (6 mm) or $3/8$ inch (10 mm) glass.

Some glass in "vulnerable areas" (glazed exterior doors, large panels next to these doors, large "picture" windows, and low-level glazing) must be glazed with safety glass, either toughened or laminated. Toughened glass is five times stronger than glass and breaks into harmless fragments when struck. Laminated glass consists of a sandwich of two sheets of glass surrounding a plastic interlayer, which holds all the glass in place if either surface is broken. Unlike toughened glass, it is relatively burglar-proof.

Helpful hints

If the putty has too much linseed oil in it, it can stick to your hands and be difficult to use. The answer is to roll it around on newspaper, which will absorb the excess oil, until the putty is the correct consistency. If the putty has dried out, make it more pliable by adding linseed oil. You can clean putty off glass with paint thinner.

1 Remove the window from its frame, and lay it down (exterior side up) on a worktop covered with a protective cloth. Using a chisel or a glazier's knife, remove the old putty. You'll come across glazier's points holding the glass in place; remove them with a hook scraper. Wearing thick gloves, pull the glass from the frame.

2 Wearing safety glasses to protect your eyes, use a chisel and mallet to remove the remaining large pieces of old putty from the bottom of the rabbets in the frame—make sure you avoid cutting into the wood.

3 Use the scraper to clear the thin residue of putty from the frame rabbets. When completely clean, carefully gather up and dispose of the old broken glass. Give the rabbets a coat of wood primer. Measure for the new pane of glass, allowing ⅛ inch (3 mm) clearance on each side for both dimensions—width and height.

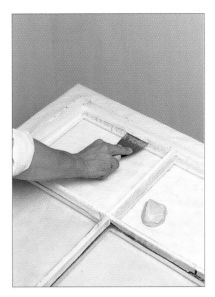

4 When the primer has dried, check that the new glass pane is the correct size. Knead the putty in your hands until it is pliable; run a bead ⅛ inch to ¼ inch (3 mm to 5 mm) thick around the bottom of the rabbets. Use a putty knife to press it down flat and smooth it out, trimming off any excess putty that hangs over the edge.

5 Insert the glass into the frame, leaving an ⅛ inch (3 mm) gap all around. Gently press the glass firmly into place along its edges—never the center—until putty squeezes out of the inside of window. If the frame is in place (vertical), first insert matchsticks across the the lowest horizontal rabbet to create an equal gap all around.

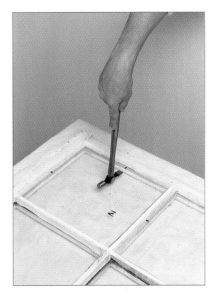

6 Use glazier's points to secure the glass in place. Using the flat end of a tack hammer, a putty knife, or the back of a glazier's knife, press the points into place (do not hit them as you would nails).

7 Knead the putty as before, and roll it into a thin sausage shape. Starting at one corner, lay the putty down and push it against the sides of the rabbets in the frame. Move along the frame, laying down the putty and pushing it into place, and continue in this way completely around the frame.

8 To make a smooth bevel in the putty, hold a putty knife at a 45° angle, with its straight edge on the putty, and pull the knife along. To miter each corner, place the knife diagonally in the center, and pull it away from the corner. Use the knife to remove any putty left on the glass. Allow the putty to dry for at least a week before painting.

PAINTING WINDOWS

The best results were acheived on this window by removing all its hardware before it was painted.

B efore painting a window, especially one made of wood, carry out any needed repairs, replace damaged glass (let new putty harden for a week before painting), and remove flaking paint. Sand down the surfaces with fine sandpaper and thoroughly clean them, and apply primer to any bare wood. If a window has been painted too often, it can bind on its frame. To avoid this, plane or sand the edges before priming and painting.

If you have removed a window to repair joints or replace sash cords, it will be easier to paint it before putting it back in its frame—the frame will also be easier to paint. Whether the window is in or out of the frame, remove all window hardware, such as handles and stays, before painting.

A simple way to avoid getting paint on the glass is to apply low-tack masking tape; you can remove it once the paint has set. The alternative is to forget about getting paint on the glass and to remove it once it has dried, using a special window scraper. You may well need this anyway to remove spots of splattered paint on the glass.

PAINTING A CASEMENT WINDOW

1 To paint the inside of a casement window, wedge the window slightly open. If you prefer, stick lengths of painter's masking tape onto the glass; leave a $5/64$ inch (2 mm) gap between the glass and frame so the paint can seal the joint between the two—this helps to block moisture.

2 Using a narrow trim brush, paint the glazing bars (including the rabbets). Use the brush with a dabbing motion to get paint into the corners. It doesn't matter if the paint goes onto the tape, but try to avoid getting any paint on the glass.

3 Adjust the window to open it slightly more. Paint the top and bottom horizontal rails, then paint the vertical stiles of the window.

4 Open the window fully and paint the inside closing edge of the window, brushing down from the top. With the window still fully open, paint the frame. Just before the paint has dried completely, carefully pull the tape back on itself and away from the window—if allowed to dry, the tape can pull off paint as it is peeled away.

PAINTING A SASH WINDOW

1 To paint the inside of a sash window, push the inner sash to the top and pull the outer sash to the bottom. Using a narrow trim brush on the upper sash, paint the bottom rail, followed by the vertical stiles as far as you can reach. Paint the inside of the frame at the bottom.

2 Paint the lower rail of the inner sash, using the narrow trim brush to paint up to the glass; then paint the sections of the vertical stiles that are within reach.

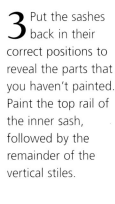

3 Put the sashes back in their correct positions to reveal the parts that you haven't painted. Paint the top rail of the inner sash, followed by the remainder of the vertical stiles.

4 Slide the outer sash down, and paint its top rail and the unpainted areas of the vertical stiles. Paint the remainder of the inside of the frame and, finally, paint the window frame casing.

REPLACING OLD WINDOW HARDWARE

One common reason for replacing old window hardware, such as handles and catches, is to create a new style—perhaps using brass or bronze hardware in place of aluminum, or exchanging a plain design for an ornate one. Another reason is to replace an existing handle or catch with a lockable one for security reasons (see pp.70–71). Unfortunately, it is unlikely that the mounting holes for the new hardware will be in the same position as the old ones, so there will be filling to do, as well as drilling, before you can install the hardware.

Handles and catches are available in hardware stores, home centers, and building supply stores; you'll also find them at mail-order and specialist suppliers, especially ornate brass and wrought iron hardware.

REPLACING HINGES

Casement-type windows can pivot in and out of the window frame because they are attached with hinges. A stiff or squeaky hinge will simply need a squirt of a household lubricating oil. However, hinges may need replacing if they are worn or badly rusted, or if they are covered by so much paint that they can no longer function properly. Hinges are available in standard sizes, so unless you are replacing one size of hinge with a larger one, there is a good chance that the screw holes for the new hinges will be in the same place as those for the old ones.

Brass hinges can be left unpainted, but steel hinges must be primed and painted to prevent them from rusting. When fitting the hinges, use screws of a matching metal.

RELEASING A STUCK WINDOW

A sash may stick in a window because it has been painted shut, debris has accumulated in the sash channels or wooden stops or jambs have become warped. To break a paint seal, run a utility knife around the sash, then carefully pry it at several points with a putty knife. For dirt buildup, after scraping it away, lightly sand the jambs, stops, and parting strips, then lubricate them with paraffin wax.

If paint or dirt is not jambing the window, try prying it open from the outside, using a pry bar against a block of wood for leverage. If warped stops are causing the window to bind, you can tap a block of wood $\frac{1}{16}$ inch (2 mm) wider than the channel between the stops and parting strip; or lightly sand the stops.

REPLACING HINGES

1 Unscrew and remove the old hinges, starting with the screws holding the hinges to the frame. If they are encrusted with paint, use a utility knife to remove the paint from the slots and around the sides of the screw heads.

2 Check if the new hinges fit the recesses in the frame and window. To deepen, widen, or lengthen a recess, center a new hinge over the recess, and score around it with a utility knife to mark its position. Cut along the scored line with a chisel, then pare away wood from the recess.

3 Fit the new hinge in the recess, then check that the holes line up. If they do, use screws a little longer than the old ones. If they are misaligned, even slightly, drill out the old holes, glue in dowels and, if needed, trim them flush to the surface. Drill pilot holes for the screws. Refit the window as you would hang a door (see pp.86–87).

SASH LOCK

To fit a sash lock, correct alignment is important—the sashes must be in their closed positions. Screw the receiving bracket into the center of the bottom rail of the outer sash. Place the other part on the top rail of the inner sash, turn its disc so it locks into the bracket, and screw it down.

SASH LIFTER

Measure and mark the positions of the sash lifters, one on each side of the bottom rail of the inner sash. They should be equidistant from the sides and the bottom. Drill pilot holes and screw the lifters in place. (Alternatively, fasten one larger-style lifter to the center of the bottom rail.)

HOPPER WINDOW

Hinges at the bottom of the sash allow it to open from the top, usually inward. Hardware in the form of bars or chains are installed on each side of the sash—they restrict how far the window can be opened. A latch at the top keeps the sash closed.

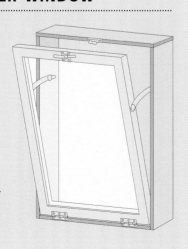

FITTING WINDOW SECURITY DEVICES

YOU WILL NEED

Electric drill plus twist bits
and spade bits (for larger
holes in wood windows) **or**
HSS bits (high-speed steel
bits for metal windows)
Screwdriver
Pencil
Chisel (if required)

MATERIALS

Window locks and screws

SEE ALSO

Replacing old window
hardware pp.68–69

To reduce the risk of burglary, all accessible windows in a house should have secure locks, including second floor windows reachable from a garage roof and all downstairs windows. In fact, some insurance companies insist on security devices.

Three types of locks for casement windows are a lockable handle, which replaces the existing handle; a locking stop to prevent the existing handle or casement stay from being operated without a key; and a separate lock to hold the window shut. The two main types for sash windows are a dual screw, which holds the two sashs together, and a sash stop, which prevents the inner sash from being lifted up. There is a special lock for patio doors, which can also be used on sash windows.

Most locks require the window to be shut before it can be locked; but some have a second position, allowing the window to be left ajar for ventilation.

SECURITY CONSIDERATIONS

Few burglars will climb through a broken window—they break the window to get at the catches to open it. Locks will prevent this, but only if the key for the lock is not left on the window sill. Where possible, you should always fit two locks on all but very small windows.

If you live in an area where burglary is common, you may want to either fit laminated glass (see pp.64–65) or attach a grille to the window.

FITTING THE LOCKS

Most window locks are easy to fit, requiring only pilot holes to be made for the screws. This is simple for wood windows, but you'll have to drill holes and use self-tapping screws on metal windows. Some locks require you to drill larger holes, others need small recesses cut with a chisel. There may be a trade-off between the ease of fitting the lock and its obtrusiveness.

DUAL SCREW SASH LOCK

1 To fit a screw lock, with the windows closed, drill a hole for the screw thread into the inner sash's top and the outer sash's bottom rail. Drill a hole the size of the lock body into the top rail of the inner sash, using the hole already drilled as a pilot. Screw the lock body into the second hole.

2 Reverse the sash windows and place the brass receiving plate over the hole on the bottom rail of the outer sash, then draw a pencil line around the plate. Cut a recess for the plate with a chisel (see step 5, p.83) and screw the plate in place.

WINDOW HARDWARE

A variety of hardware is available to operate casement windows, depending on the age and style of the window. Newer windows have a crank-style operator that moves an extension arm along a track to open and close the window. Older casement windows use sliding rods held in position with a thumbscrew. Some hopper windows (see p.69) have a crank-style operator with scissor arms. All parts should be lubricated with oil every year.

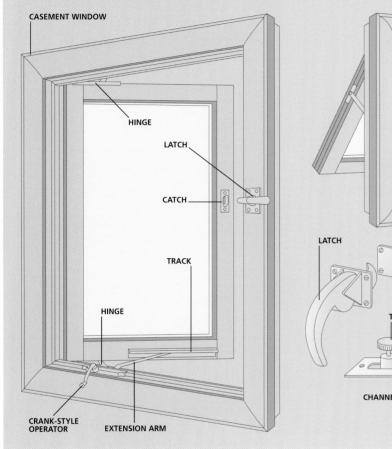

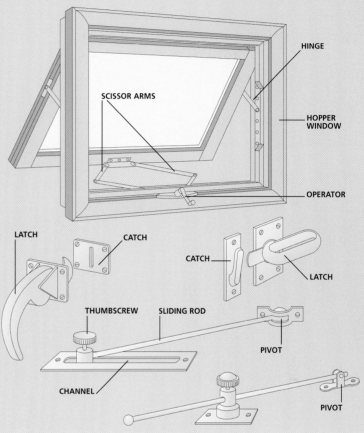

SASH STOP

To leave a window slightly ajar but still secure, fit a sash stop to the outer sash. Drill a hole the same diameter and depth as the ferrule provided in the vertical stile. Push the ferrule into the hole, then put the arm of the stop into it and screw the stop in with a key.

TWO-PART SASH LOCK

A two-part sash lock can be fitted at the center point of the top rail of the inner sash and the bottom rail of the outer sash by drilling pilot holes and screwing the two parts in place. It comes with a key to lock it.

TYPES OF INTERIOR DOORS

There are three main types of interior door for access between rooms: panel, glazed, and flush. The traditional type is a panel door, which consists of a solid wooden frame (hardwood or softwood) with, typically, two, four, or six panels of a lighter material. A glazed door is similar to a panel door, but glass is used instead of the panels. A flush door is less expensive than a panel door, and it is lighter and easier to install. The core material may be a honeycombed paper, laminated wood, wood rails, or a solid fire-resistant material.

DOOR SIZES

Interior doors are made in standard sizes, which is usually in "imperial" (inches). Imported doors, which are rare, are in "metric" (millimeters).

Common sizes are (by height, then width):

Imperial

6 feet 6 inches × 2 feet (1981 mm × 610 mm)
6 feet 6 inches × 2 feet 3 inches (1981 mm × 686 mm)
6 feet 6 inches × 2 feet 6 inches (1981 mm × 762 mm)
6 feet 6 inches × 2 feet 9 inches (1981 mm × 838 mm)

Metric

2040 mm × 626 mm (6 ft 8¼ in × 2 ft ½ in)
2040 mm × 726 mm (6 ft 8¼ in × 2 ft 4½ in)
2040 mm × 826 mm (6 ft 8¼ in × 2 ft 8½ in)
2040 mm × 926 mm (6 ft 8¼ in × 3 ft ½ in)

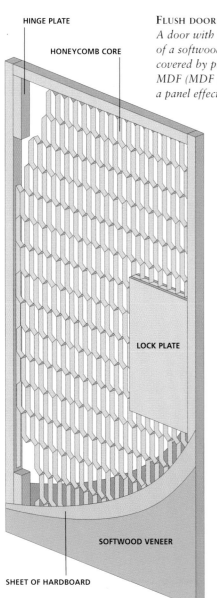

HINGE PLATE

HONEYCOMB CORE

LOCK PLATE

SOFTWOOD VENEER

SHEET OF HARDBOARD

FLUSH DOOR
A door with flush surfaces consists of a softwood frame with a core covered by plywood, hardboard, or MDF (MDF may be molded into a panel effect), then a wood veneer.

LOUVERED DOOR
Slats are fitted into the frame of a louvered door. It is ideal for a closet (it allows ventilation). You can use narrow ones as a bi-fold door—a pair of doors hinged in the center.

GLAZED PANEL DOOR
The frame is wooden, but the "panels" are made of glass in this type of door. A glazed door can have from 1 to 15 glass panels, each of which fits into a rabbet held in place by a glazing strip. A single-pane glazed door and the lower half of a double-pane glazed door should be fitted with safety glass (see pp.64–65).

THE ANATOMY OF A DOORWAY

A doorway between interior rooms consists of five main parts: the door frame, which is made of 1 in × 4 in (25 mm × 100 mm) lumber and secured to the vertical studs of a wallboard wall or to the masonry of a solid wall; the door stop, narrow strips of wood against which the door closes; the door itself (a panel door, below), fitted with hinges to hang it on the frame; the casing, which covers the gap between the wall and the door frame; and the door "hardware" (handles, locks, and latches) fitted to holes cut in the door and the door frame. You can replace any or all of the parts.

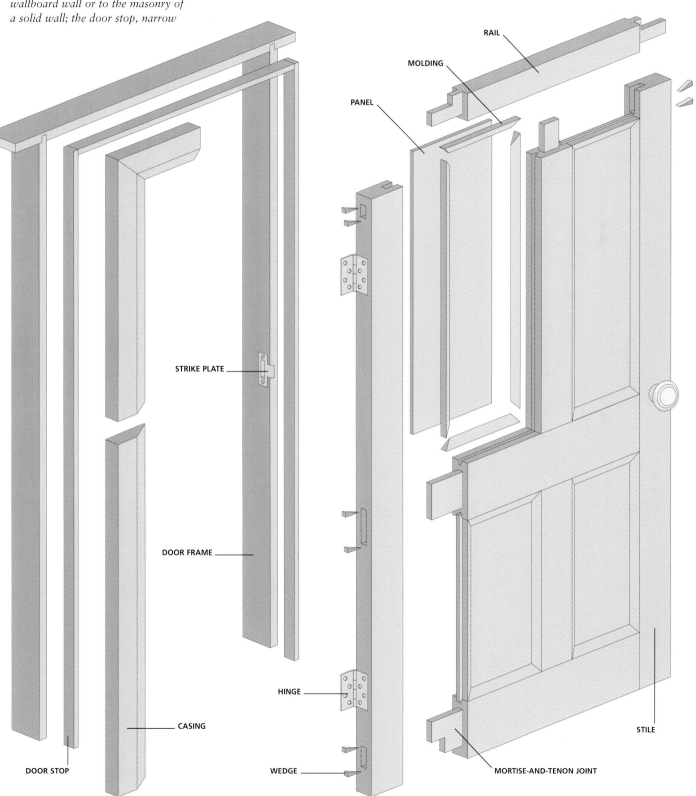

RAIL

MOLDING

PANEL

STRIKE PLATE

DOOR FRAME

HINGE

CASING

DOOR STOP

WEDGE

MORTISE-AND-TENON JOINT

STILE

TYPES OF EXTERIOR DOORS

Exterior doors are bigger, heavier, and thicker than interior doors and come in a wider range of styles and materials. You can fit a new exterior door into the existing frame, but if you are replacing a painted softwood door with a hardwood door (to be varnished or stained), the door frame will probably need changing, too.

Installing a new front or side door is similar to installing an interior door, but it's more awkward to move and you'll have more work to do on the door itself—for example, installing door locks.

EXTERIOR DOOR SIZES

Doors for outside use are thicker than interior doors, usually 1¾ inches (44 mm) thick, and larger. They are almost always in "imperial" (inch) sizes, but if you have an imported door, it will be a "metric" (mm) size.

Common sizes are (by height, then width):
Imperial
6 feet 6 inches × 2 feet 3 inches (1981 mm × 686 mm)
6 feet 6 inches × 2 feet 6 inches (1981 mm × 762 mm)
6 feet 6 inches × 2 feet 9 inches (1981 mm × 838 mm)
6 feet 8 inches × 2 feet 8 inches (2032 mm × 813 mm)

Metric
2040 mm × 726 mm (6 ft 8¼ in × 2 ft 4½ in)
2040 mm × 826 mm (6 ft 8¼ in × 2 ft 8½ in)
2000 mm × 807 mm (6 ft 6¼ in × 2 ft 7¼ in)

FLUSH DOOR
An exterior flush door is stronger and heavier than an interior flush door. The core is of a more solid material, such as waferboard, and the door usually has an exterior-quality plywood facing.

SOLID WAFERBOARD CORE

LETTERBOX PLATE

LOCK PLATE

PLYWOOD

VENEER COVERING

FRENCH DOORS
A pair of glazed doors forms what are known as French doors. Each door has from 1 to 10 glazed panes. They fit into a standard frame; wider frames are available if matching side lights are fitted. The most common size is 6 feet × 3 feet 10 inches (1828 mm × 914 mm) or the metric size of 2000 mm × 1106 mm (6 ft 6¼ in × 3 ft 7½ in).

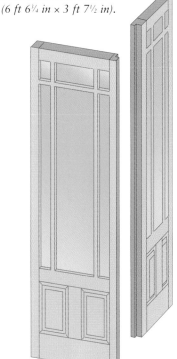

BOARDED DOOR
Softwood tongue-and-groove boards are secured to horizontal ledgers and angled braces to form this door, which is known as a "board-and-batten" door. It's suitable only as a door for storage areas indoors and outside.

ANATOMY OF AN EXTERIOR DOOR FRAME AND PANEL DOOR

An exterior door frame has a rabbet cut in it for the door to close against and a built-in door sill (threshold). There is a huge range of exterior panel doors, made in both softwood and hardwood. Many are solid—typically with six panels—but they can also be single or double glazed. The glazing can vary from one small glazed panel to the top half divided into up to nine panels, with a range of options in between. Fanlights (glazed panels in a curved shape) are also common.

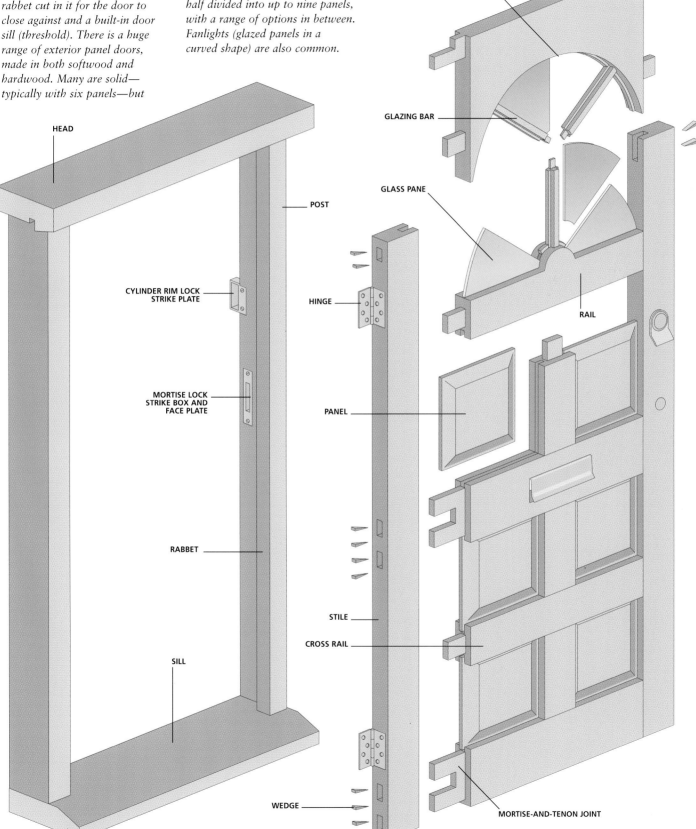

HEAD

POST

FANLIGHT

GLAZING BAR

GLASS PANE

CYLINDER RIM LOCK STRIKE PLATE

HINGE

RAIL

MORTISE LOCK STRIKE BOX AND FACE PLATE

PANEL

RABBET

STILE

CROSS RAIL

SILL

WEDGE

MORTISE-AND-TENON JOINT

MAKING REPAIRS TO DOORS

YOU WILL NEED

Hammer
Nail set
Door trimming saw
Dust mask, safety glasses, and ear protectors (if required)
Electric drill plus twist bits
Screwdrivers
Block plane
Large plane
Bar clamp
Mallet
Chisel
Flexible putty knife
Sanding block

MATERIALS

Wood wedges
Rising butt hinges
Dowels
Softwood
Wood filler
Fine-grade sandpaper

SEE ALSO

Stripping wood trim pp.32–33
Painting doors pp.80–81
A new door: installing hinges pp.82–83
A new door: hanging it and fitting handles pp.84–85
Changing the way a door hangs pp.86–87

Most door repairs are simple and require few tools. For a door to work, a repair may have to be made to the frame (see pp.78–79).

Too much paint on the closing edges of a door can cause it to stick. Strip off the paint and apply a thinner layer. As a wood door's moisture content changes, the door can change in size; it may bind in damp weather and go back to normal when it dries out. You may have to plane or sand it. If you can, wait until dry weather when the door is at its minimum moisture level, and paint the edges to ensure that no more moisture can get in.

A door that binds at the bottom may be caused by the door swelling or by loose hinges (see pp.78–79); or the glue in the mortise-and-tenon joints (which holds the rails to the stiles) may have dried out and the joints loosened. You will have to remove the door to reinforce a loose joint with wood dowels.

Where you have leveled a solid floor or changed a floor covering, a door into the room may bind at the bottom, scraping on the floor as it opens. You can remove the door from the frame and plane a small amount off the bottom; use your plane from the edges toward the center of the door to prevent the wood from splitting, or rent a door trimming saw. Or replace the existing hinges with rising butt hinges, which lift the door as it opens.

Helpful hints

To remove a door, prop it open (see below). If the door has loose-pin hinges (most do), simply use a hammer and a nail set to knock out the hinge pins from below. Start with the bottom hinge. With fixed-pin hinges, undo the screws holding the hinges to the frame (see pp.68–69), removing all but one of the screws from the top hinge, then taking all the screws out of the bottom hinge (and, if fitted, the middle hinge). With a helper supporting the door, remove the remaining screw from the top hinge and pull the door away. You may have to pry heavily painted hinges out of their recesses.

PROPPING A DOOR FOR REPAIRS

When removing, hanging, or making repairs to a door, hold it firmly in position with a wedge. Open the door at a right angle to the frame. Position a wedge at the side or end of the door, and give it sharp taps with a hammer until it stops moving.

USING A DOOR TRIMMING SAW

To use a trimming saw, prop the door open with a wedge at each side and set the depth of the trimming saw. Wearing a dust mask, safety glasses, and ear protectors, start cutting the door at the open end; hold the saw firmly against the door. Move the wedges as the saw cuts along the door.

FITTING RISING BUTT HINGES

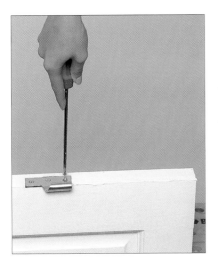

1 Choose rising butt hinges for either a lefthand or righthand door. Secure the door with the hinged edge upright, then position the sleeve parts on the door and mark the screw holes. Drill out the holes, then screw the hinges in place. Fasten the pivot part of the hinges to the door frame.

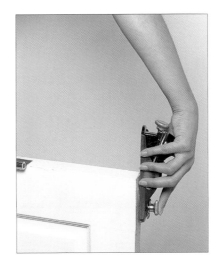

2 Before hanging it, chamfer (bevel) the top edge of the door to enable it to close into the frame, using a small plane. Make the chamfer near the hinge end of the door, and taper it down to the face of the door that opens into the room.

TRIMMING A BINDING DOOR

If a high moisture content causes a door to bind, take it off its hinges and support it with the door-latch edge upright. After removing the latch (see pp.84–85), use a large plane to trim the edge. (Increase the depth of the recess to refit the latch.)

REPAIRING A LOOSE JOINT

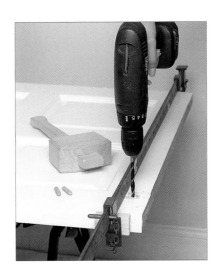

Position a clamp at a loose joint and tighten it, keeping the door square. Drill two holes the diameter of a dowel into the joint. Apply glue to the dowels; insert them into the holes, tapping them in with a mallet. Let the glue harden before removing the clamp, then trim the dowels with a chisel.

REPLACING DAMAGED WOOD

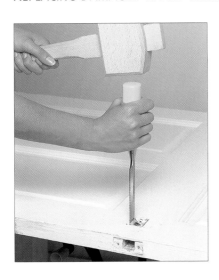

1 Lay the door flat on a worktop, then use a chisel and mallet to mark an oblong shape around the damaged area. Continue to cut out the damaged area with the chisel and mallet, going down to about half the depth of the door.

2 Cut a piece of wood to fit the cut-out area, and chamfer (bevel) the bottom half of each side. Add glue, then push it into the hole, level with the surface of door. Let the glue dry; sand the repair level with the door. Fill any gaps with wood filler; after it dries, sand and paint.

REPAIRING DOOR FRAMES

YOU WILL NEED

Replacing the casing
Utility knife
Pry bar
Adjustable square and pencil
Mitre frame and saw **or** miter box and tenon saw
Hammer
Nail set
Flexible putty knife
Sanding block

Other frame repairs
Electric drill plus countersink and twist bits
Screwdrivers
Hammer
Chisel
Flexible putty knife

MATERIALS

Replacing the casing
Case molding
Finishing nails
Fine-grade sandpaper
Wood filler

Other frame repairs
3-inch- (75-mm-) long screw
PVA glue
Dowels
Cardboard

SEE ALSO

Making repairs to doors
pp.76–77

Most repairs to internal door frames are usually simple. For example, a rattling door can be repaired by moving its strike plate. If the frame is loose, first try tightening or replacing any existing screws; if the frame has been nailed in place, add a few screws. In a masonry wall, you could try tightening any existing screws, but you'll also need to add wall anchors.

If the hinge screws are loose, try tightening them; if they won't hold, fit bigger screws—either the same gauge but longer or, if the hinge holes are big enough, a larger gauge of the same length. If you can't get the screws tight, drill out the holes and add dowels. If too large a gauge of screw had been used, it may protrude beyond the hinge, preventing the door from closing properly; replace it with a smaller, longer screw. The recess of the hinge may not be deep enough (see pp.82–83) or it may too deep.

New door casing, with a coat or two of paint, can improve the overall look of a tired door frame.

Old case molding, or casing, that surrounds a door may eventually need replacing. When buying new casing, remember to measure each length to the end of the mitered corner.

TIGHTENING A LOOSE FRAME

If the frame is fitted to a partition wall, drill and countersink a hole into the door stop. Have a helper hold the frame in place; drill a smaller diameter hole through the frame into the stud, then drive in a 3-inch- (75-mm-) long screw. Cover the screw head with wood filler; once dry, sand and paint it.

REPAIRING A LOOSE HINGE

If the screws of a hinge are loose, take them out; redrill each hole the diameter and depth of small lengths of dowel. Apply glue to the end of the dowels and to the edge of each hole, then tap a dowel into each hole. Drill pilot holes into the dowels to take new screws for the hinges.

BUILDING UP A HINGE RECESS

A door may bind if the hinge is recessed into the door frame too deeply. To rectify this, so the door hangs farther away from the frame, remove the door from the frame (see pp.76–77). Cut a piece of cardboard the same size as the hinge leaf and insert it into the recess; then rehang the door.

FIXING A RATTLING DOOR

If the door rattles in its frame, reposition the strike plate of the door latch. Unscrew the plate; then use a chisel to enlarge the width of the recess on the side closest to the door stop. Drill out the screw holes and glue in dowels; after the glue dries, drill new pilot holes and screw in the plate.

REPLACING THE CASING

1 Insert the tip of a utility knife blade between the casing and door frame. Slowly pull the knife down to break the skin of the paint. Repeat on the other pieces of casing. Use a pry bar to pry off the molding. Clean the exposed area with sandpaper.

2 Mark a right angle ¼ inch (6 mm) away from top corner of the frame. Align a length of molding at the vertical line, with its end above where the horizontal length will be. Make a mark on the piece at the point where the two pencil lines meet. Repeat at the other side of the frame.

3 Use a miter frame and saw to cut miters at the marks—they indicate the lowest end of the miter. Nail the lengths in place. Hold a length of molding across their tops. With a ruler at the outside edge of one vertical length of molding, mark the top of the horizontal length. Repeat at the other side; use these marks to cut miters.

4 As with the vertical lengths, drive nails through the front of the horizontal length and into the frame. To hold the corners together, nail down through the top of the horizontal length into the vertical one at each side. Drive the nail heads down with a nail set, and cover them with wood filler. After it dries, sand and paint the casing.

PAINTING DOORS

YOU WILL NEED

Painting a flush door
3-inch- (75-mm-) wide paint brush
Narrow trim paint brush

Painting a paneled door
Narrow trim paint brush
3-inch- (75-mm-) wide paint brush
1-inch- (25-mm-) wide paint brush

MATERIALS

Painting a flush door
Paint **or** varnish
Preservative stain (if required)
Paint brush cleaner (if using solvent-base products)

Painting a paneled door
See above

SEE ALSO

Washing down and preparing surfaces pp.30–31
Stripping paint from wood trim pp.32–33
Replacing a window pane pp.64–65
Making repairs to doors pp.76–77
Repairing door frames pp.78–79
Changing the way a door hangs pp.86–87

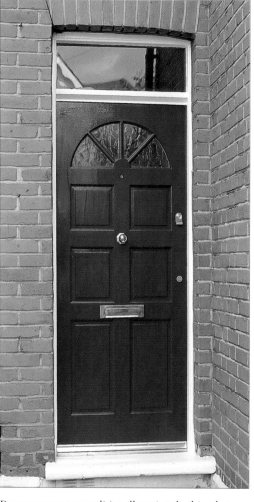

Doors were once traditionally painted white, but now there is a huge range of colors to choose from.

When painting or varnishing a door, choose an appropriate finish. Inside, try a low-odor, quick-drying water-base paint. Outside, use a weather-resistant paint: either a two-coat system (primer and top coat) or a "micro-porous" paint, which may also act as a primer.

With hardwood or pine doors, you can allow the beauty of the wood to show through. Use ordinary varnish or polyurethane for interior doors. Exterior doors need a durable yacht varnish with a UV prohibitor; a preservative stain is also an option.

Before you start, remove the door hardware and make any repairs. With a new door, sand down all its surfaces; with an existing door, remove all loose and flaky paint. If necessary, strip the old paint off the door. Paint or varnish a new glazed interior door before installing the glass with molding; glaze a new exterior door (allow a week for the putty to dry) before it is painted.

PAINTING A FLUSH DOOR

1 To ensure that the paint "edge" never dries out (this will leave a line that is difficult to remove), paint the door in blocks. Start in the top lefthand corner. Apply the paint horizontally until the brush is empty. Continue painting horizontally until the first block is filled.

2 To remove the horizontal brush strokes in this first block, lightly load the brush with paint and, starting at the top, brush down in vertical strokes until the block is complete. Now quickly move on to block two—alongside the first block.

3 Start block three, by painting upward into the bottom edge of block one, using short vertical strokes. Then turn the brush around to create horizontal strokes to fill up the block. Eliminate brush strokes from this block with vertical strokes as before. Continue painting each block in this manner until the door is painted.

4 Paint the opening edge of the door. Using a narrow trim brush, start at the top and paint to the bottom of the door. Paint the top and bottom edges of an exterior door. For an interior door, if the top of the door can be seen from the stairs, paint that edge. Finish off by painting the frame, working from the top down.

PAINTING A PANELED DOOR

1 If the door is glazed, start at the top, and use a narrow trim brush to paint the glazing bars. Do not overload the brush with paint, and avoid getting more than a thin band of paint on the glass (see pp.66–67).

2 Move to the topmost panel, and paint the moldings that surround the panel before painting the panel itself. Repeat on the other panels of the door, working from top to bottom.

3 When all the panels are complete, paint the horizontal cross rails, starting at the top. Work down the door, painting each cross rail in turn.

4 Paint the vertical stiles on each side of the door (and in the center, if there is one), from top to bottom. Paint the opening edge of the door, as well as the top and bottom edges if it is an exterior door or the top edge if it can be viewed from stairs above. Finally, paint the door frame: start at the top and work your way down.

A NEW DOOR: INSTALLING HINGES

YOU WILL NEED

Tape measure
Square
Circular saw **or** panel saw
Block plane
2-inch- (5-cm-) wide
paint brush
Clamps (if required)
Power plane **or** bench plane
Utility knife
Chisel and mallet
Electric drill plus twist bits
Marking gauge (if required)
Screwdriver

MATERIALS

Hinges (unless old ones
are used again)
New door
¼ inch (6 mm) wood
wedges
Primer
Screws

SEE ALSO

Repairing door frames
pp.78–79
Painting doors pp.80–81
A new door: hanging it and
installing handles pp.84–85
Changing the way a door
hangs pp.86–87

You might want to replace a door because the old one is damaged, or simply because you want one that is more attractive, durable, or in keeping with the style of the house. Whatever your reason, new wood doors come without any hinge recesses or holes for locks, latches, or door handles—you'll have to create them yourself, and make holes for the strike plates of locks and latches in a new door frame.

On these two pages are the first two stages of installing a new door: laying out and cutting recesses for the hinges. On the following two pages are details on how to hang the door and install the latch. Before you start, make sure the door frame is secure and the hinge side of the frame is vertical.

LAYING OUT

Start by determining the size of your existing door (see pp.72–75). If you're replacing a door in an old house, it could be a nonstandard size; you may have to find a secondhand door from an architectural salvage yard (which will have recesses and lock holes, but not necessarily in the correct places); otherwise, order a door to be made to your dimensions.

Measure the existing door frame (not the door); remember that you can trim most panel doors down to size. Allow for a gap of ⅛ inch (3 mm) at the top and sides of the door for clearance, and ¼ inch (6 mm) at the bottom.

Because the frame may not be square, check the size in at least two places for the height and at least three places for the width. Double-check the thickness, too. An exterior door must be the correct thickness to fit the rabbet; with an interior door, you can move the door stop if necessary. Allow the door, unwrapped, to acclimatize for a few days before hanging it.

An interior door needs two 3 inch (75 mm) hinges; an exterior door requires three 4 inch (100 mm) ones.

1 Hold the door against the frame, supported on wedges (see p.67), and mark where it is larger than the frame, allowing for the correct clearance (see above). To reduce a panel door in height, divide the excess between the top and bottom, and use a panel saw or a circular saw fitted with a rip guide to cut the ends at the marks.

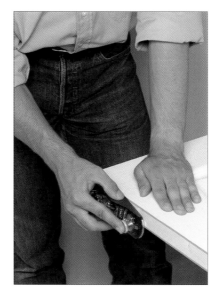

2 Each end of the door will be rough, so use a block plane to smooth the surfaces. To avoid chipping the ends, start from each edge and work to the center. Alternatively, you can clamp a piece of scrap wood flush with the edge of the door—it will take the damage instead of the door. Seal the ends with a primer.

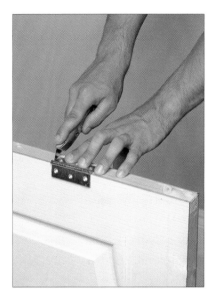

3 To reduce a panel door in width, use a power plane or bench plane, working along the whole length and following your marked lines; take equal amounts off each side and ensure that the hinge side, in particular, is straight. A slight bevel on the strike side will help the door close more easily.

4 Lay the door on its opening edge and clamp it in place. Mark the position of the hinges on the door (see box, below). Place a hinge at its mark; align the center of the pin with the edge of the door. Score around the hinge with a utility knife, then score the depth of the hinge on the face of the door. Repeat the process for any other hinges.

5 Tap the chisel blade along the marked lines, bevel facing in; then chop out the wood with a series of short strokes, using a mallet. Take care not to go beyond your marked lines. Clean up the bottom of the recess, using the chisel held horizontally and bevel facing downward.

6 Check the fit of the hinge in the recess; the inner surface of the hinge should be exactly flat with the surrounding door edge. If you need to, deepen the recess, using the chisel, bevel facing upward.

7 After making sure the hinges fit, make pilot holes for the screws and fit the hinges to the door, using just one screw per hinge. You're now ready to hang the door (see pp.84–85).

Helpful hints

If the door frame already has hinge beds and you're reusing old hinges or the new ones fit, hold the door in place on the wedges and transfer the positions of the hinges on the frame to the door. If new hinges don't fit, fill in the recesses and make new ones (see pp.86–87). If you have a new frame, the hinges should be about 7 inches (175 mm) from the top and 10 inches (250 mm) from the bottom, with the third hinge for exterior doors centered between the other two.

If you have a marking gauge, it will be the most accurate tool to measure the depth of a hinge for the recess.

A NEW DOOR: HANGING IT AND INSTALLING HANDLES

YOU WILL NEED

Tape measure
Square
Awl
Pencil
Electric drill plus spade and twist bits
Utility knife
Chisel
Mallet
Vise **or** adjustable workbench
Hacksaw
Screwdriver
Tenon saw
Hammer
Carpenter's level

MATERIALS

Door handles and latch kit
Masking tape
Door stop (if old one is damaged during refit)
Nails

SEE ALSO

A new door: installing hinges pp.82–83
Changing the way a door hangs pp.86–87

With the door measured and trimmed and the hinges fitted on a new door (see pp.82–83), you can hang the door. Prop it up on wedges, with the hinges by their final positions, then slide it into place so that the hinges are in their recesses. With your helper steadying the door, insert one screw into each hinge in the frame, driving it home. Check that the door swings properly, without binding, and closes properly. Remove the door and reshape the hinge recesses if necessary; insert the remaining screws when it operates smoothly. You may need to refit or replace the door stop.

INSTALLING A DOOR LATCH

On interior doors, all you need is a simple spring latch operated by a handle on each side of the door, with a strike plate in the door frame. On exterior doors, you'll need a secure cylinder rim lock (see pp.94–95) or mortise lock (see pp. 96–97), or both.

Choose a door to match the style of the room that it will be most prominent in—don't forget that the style of the handles will be just as important.

1 Measure and mark the height of the handle on the edge of the door, half way up the door. Use a spade bit the same diameter as the latch body, and put masking tape on its shaft to indicate the length of the latch body. Bore out the hole, keeping the bit vertical.

2 Insert the latch body into the hole, position the face plate parallel with the edges of the door, and score around it with a utility knife; remove the latch body. Cut along the scored lines with a chisel, bevel face in, and mallet before chopping out a recess to the depth of the face plate (see step 5, p.83).

3 Place the latch body on the face of the door, with its face plate flush with the edge of the door. Use a pencil to mark the position of the spindle hole through the latch body. Repeat on the other side of the door. Using a drill bit the same diameter as the spindle, bore out the hole from both sides. Test-fit the latch and spindle.

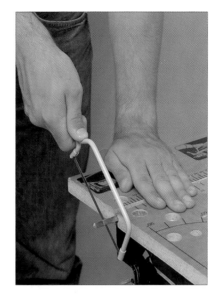

4 It may be necessary to reduce the length of the latch spindle on a thin door. After inserting the spindle in the hole and fitting on the handles, mark the amount to be cut off the spindle. Clamp the spindle in a vise or workbench, then use a hacksaw to cut it to the correct length.

5 Fit the latch body into the edge of the door and screw it in place. Insert the spindle and mount the handle—make sure it's facing the correct way. Position the sides of the handle's face plate parallel with the door's edge. Drill pilot holes and screw the face plate to the door.

6 Turn the door over and slide the other handle over the exposed spindle. Position the face plate of the handle as in step 5, drill pilot holes, and screw the face plate to the door. You can now hang the door (see main text).

7 Mark the top and bottom of the latch bolt on the door frame. Center the strike plate at these marks, and score around it with a utility knife. Cut a recess for the plate with a chisel and mallet; use the chisel to pare the last layer. Fit the plate in the recess; mark and bore the hole for the bolt. Refit and screw the plate in place.

8 Close the door and mark it's position on the frame near the strike plate. Cut the door stop to length. Position the stop against the mark, and nail it in place at the plate; use a level to check that it is vertical, then nail the remainder of the stop to the frame. Repeat on the other side, then nail on the horizontal piece.

CHANGING THE WAY A DOOR HANGS

YOU WILL NEED

Screwdrivers
Utility knife
Metal straightedge
Backsaw
Chisel
Mallet
Tack hammer
Nail set
Block plane (if required)
Flexible putty knife
Pencil
Electric drill plus twist bits
Carpenter's level

MATERIALS

¼ inch (6 mm) wood wedges
Pieces of softwood
Brads
Wood glue
Wood filler
Nails

SEE ALSO

A new door: installing hinges pp.82–83
A new door: hanging it and installing handles pp.84–85
Changing a hinged door to a sliding door pp.88–89

A door is often hinged to swing away from the window so that when you open it you see a blank wall; but you may prefer it the other way around to show a different view of the room as the door is opened. You might also want to have the door opening outward instead of inward to create more useful space within a room. This means there are three ways you can change the way in which a door is hinged: left to right (or vice versa); in to out (or vice versa); in to out and left to right (or vice versa).

You'll have to refit the strike plate into which the door latch goes and make new hinge recesses in the door frame and door and fill in the old ones (you can reuse the old hinges unless they are "handed" such as rising butt hinges). When changing from in to out (or vice versa), you'll have to move the door stop against which the door closes. The other tasks you might have to do are refitting the door handles and moving a light switch. When changing the side on which a door is hinged, you can avoid doing some of these by reversing the door; however, the door may have warped and might not fit, and it may need painting. The instructions here are for changing a swing from in to out. To fill recesses when changing from left to right (or vice versa), see page 88.

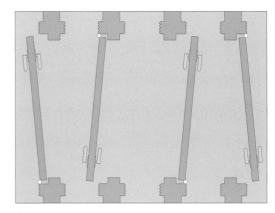

SITING YOUR HINGES
There are four positions in which a door may be hung, depending on whether you want it to swing into or out of the room and to the left or right. Most hinges can be used in any position. However, rising butt hinges are "handed," either right or left; their positions are designated by their hand.

1 Wedge the door open (see p.76). Knock out the hinge pins (see p.76), or remove all the screws from the bottom hinge and all but one from the top hinge. With a helper holding the door, remove the last screw; pry the hinges out of the recesses in the frame. (Fill the recesses if you move the hinges to the other side of the frame).

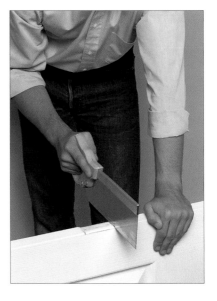

2 Stand the door on its opening edge and secure it in place. With a utility knife and metal straightedge, score across the door edge at the hinge recesses, then score a line along the front face to the depth of the recess. Use a backsaw to cut along the scored lines across the edge, cutting to the line that indicates the depth.

3 Chisel out the area of the new recess, bevel facing up. Fit the hinge in and mark its position. Remove the hinge and cut a piece of wood to fill the leftover recess. Glue and insert the wood into the recess; secure it with brads and drive them in with a nail set. Let the glue dry, then plane the wood level and fit the hinges.

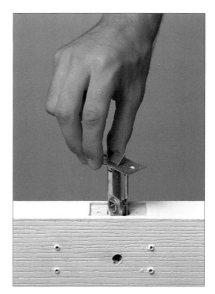

4 Rotate the door latch so its bevel will go into the strike plate. Secure the door with the latch end facing up. Remove the door handles. Unscrew the face plate of the latch, lift the latch out of its hole, and turn it 180°. Push it back in the hole and screw in the face plate; drill new pilot holes if needed. Refit the door handles.

5 Remove the strike plate from the frame and cut a piece of wood to fit into the hole in the recess. Glue it in place, and allow the glue to dry before filling the rest of the recess with wood filler. If the block of wood is raised above the surface, level it with a chisel or block plane.

6 Position the hinge side of the door vertical and at right angles to the door frame, raised on the wedges. Mark the position of the hinges on the frame. Score along these lines with a utility knife and cut out the recess with a chisel and mallet (see step 5, p.83), finishing by paring the last layer with the chisel.

7 After hanging the door (see p.84), close it and mark the position of the latch on the face of the frame. Center the strike plate at these marks; score around it with a utility knife. Drill two holes for the latch bolt; use a chisel to finish the hole for the bolt. Cut a recess for the strike plate (see step 7, p.85), and screw it in place.

8 To reposition the door stop, pry the stop away with a chisel (it may snap and need replacing). Close the door, with a playing card between the door surface and inside edge of the stop; mark its position on the door frame at the strike plate. Nail the door stop back to the frame (see step 8, p.85); then fasten the other pieces.

CHANGING A HINGED DOOR TO A SLIDING DOOR

YOU WILL NEED

Utility knife
Old chisel
Tape measure
Tenon saw
Tack hammer and nail set
Block plane
Small paint brush
Putty knife
Panel saw
Hammer
Screwdriver
Carpenter's level
Electric drill plus twist bits

MATERIALS

Pieces of softwood
PVA glue
Brads
Wood primer
Joint compound
2 inch (50 mm) common nails
3 inch (75 mm) softwood
Sliding door kit
¼ inch (6 mm) wood wedges
Softwood and hardwood **or** plywood (for valance to cover door track)
Door handles

SEE ALSO

Patching holes in walls pp.22–23

If there is room on the wall to one side of the door, converting a hinged door to one that slides can save space in the room into which the door opens.

Using a kit, you can convert an existing door to a sliding door, but there will be a lot of work to do on it similar to that involved in changing the way a door hangs (filling recesses and holes; see pp.86–87). Kits are available for double closet doors, and kits may vary from the one shown here. It may be better to buy a slightly wider, lightweight door so that it completely covers the door opening.

MOVING LIGHT SWITCHES

If a light switch will be covered by the sliding door when it's opened, the switch has to be moved to the other side of the door or to the other room. Moving the switch to the other room is simple for an electrician if it is to be at a matching position on the other side of the wall; moving it to the other side of the door involves rewiring. With either method, you have the choice of filling the hole taken up by the old light switch box or simply fitting a blank cover plate over it.

1 After removing the door from the frame (see p.86), score along the seams of the casing and door stops with a utility knife to break the film of paint. Remove the door stop, prying it away from the frame with an old chisel; then remove the casing, prying it off the frame with the chisel.

2 Cut pieces of wood the same size as the hinge recesses. Glue and nail them in place with brads, knocking the heads down with a nail set. Once the glue has dried, plane the wood level with the frame and brush on a coat of wood primer.

3 Fill any gaps between the wall and the frame with joint compound and allow it to dry. Fit lengths of 3 inch (75 mm) wood, the same thickness as the baseboard, to each side of the door frame, using common nails; then fit another piece, the length of the track, across the top of the frame.

4 Secure the door on its side and position the door hangers onto the top of the door at either side, following the manufacturer's instructions; screw them in place. Hold the door against the door frame, raised ¼ inch (6 mm) on wood wedges, to mark the position of the track.

5 Screw the left-hand side of the track onto the top of the frame. Place a carpenter's level on top of the track to level it; then mark the position of the screw holes, drill pilot holes, and screw it in place. Mount the sliding piece of the track.

6 Hang the door on the track, engaging one end, then the other. Tighten the nuts at the top of the bolts to secure the door to the sliding section and level it. Then fasten the door stop and door guide to the floor, following the instructions from the manufacturer.

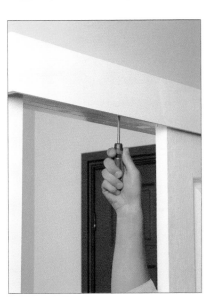

7 If a valance to hide the track is not provided with the kit, you can make your own from softwood and hardboard or plywood. To attach the valance, rest it on the track, then drill holes through the track—from the top or bottom—into it; then screw the valance in place.

8 Fit a handle on each face of the door. You can use surface-mounted handles, which are screwed through the door. Decide on their position, and drill the holes for the screws before attaching them. On a flush door, you can create blind holes in the door, using a hole saw in an electric drill, then fit in recessed pulls.

HANGING A BI-FOLD DOOR

A bi-fold door consists of two narrow doors hinged together. You can buy them already made or make them yourself from a pair of narrow louvered doors.

Bi-fold doors project only a small distance into the room when open. They can be used singly or in pairs and are popular for built-in closets, but you can also use them in large doorways (where double doors are fitted) and on free-standing wardrobes. Most bi-fold doors have a top track along which the door slides (the hardware might be different); others are hinged to the side of the door frame. Allow ⅛ inch (3 mm) clearance at each side and between the doors.

Adequate ventilation can be a problem in insulated houses; without it the result is condensation, which can lead to mold. This can be a problem in closets (particularly those built against an exterior wall). Bi-fold louvered doors will allow air to flow and reduce the condensation.

Multi-fold, or "accordion" doors have several sections and are fitted with a top track; they normally come in pairs. The doors are screwed to the sides of the door frame, and they need little space in the doorway or in the room when they are open.

1 Measure the width at the top of the closet and cut a length of track to this size, using a hacksaw. If this involves cutting off one of the pre-drilled securing holes, you'll have to drill a hole at the cut end. Clamp the cut length securely, measure and mark the position of the new hole, then drill it out using a twist drill bit.

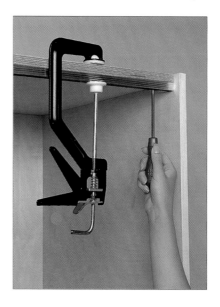

2 Clamp the track onto the under edge at the top of the closet. Using the holes in the track as a guide, drill holes into the underside. Screw the track into place, and screw the receiving catch into the lefthand side of the track. Check the fit of the doors—they may need trimming with a plane so they fit (see pp.76–77).

3 Mark the position of the pivot on the top, lefthand side of the door, following the manufacturer's instructions. Using a drill bit the same diameter as the pivot, bore into the end of the door to the depth of the fitting. Push the pivot into the hole, leaving its top exposed. Fit the bottom pivot in the same way.

4 Screw the pivot plate into position at the bottom, lefthand corner of the closet. After the doors have been hung, align them vertically and horizontally by using a wrench (provided with the kit) to adjust the bottom pivot and the retaining screws in the pivot plate.

5 Follow the instructions to mark the position of the guide on the top, righthand side of the door. Using a spade bit, bore out a hole the same diameter as the guide fitting, insert it into the hole, and push it in, leaving the guide exposed.

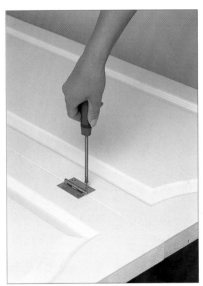

6 The hinges are screwed onto the backs of the doors. Lay them down next to one another, with a (⅛ inch (3 mm) gap in between. Place the three hinges equally spaced along the doors, mark the position of the screw holes, and drill them out. Reposition each hinge and screw them into place.

7 To fit the doors, fold them and insert the bottom pivot into the receiving plate at the bottom of the closet. Once in position, place the top pivot and guide in the top track and push the top of the door against the side of the closet until the top pivot clips into the receiving catch in the track.

8 The door handle, fitted before the doors are hung (see pp.238–239), should be positioned in the middle of the right-hand door – this allows the door to fold and slide along in one movement when the door handle is pulled.

INSTALLING SLIDING CLOSET DOORS

YOU WILL NEED

Tape measure
Combination square
Screwdriver
Hacksaw
Metal file
Electric drill plus twist bits
Hammer
Nail set
Flexible putty knife

MATERIALS

Sliding closet door kit
Common nails
Wood fillet (if required)
2 inch x 4 inch (100 mm x 50 mm) wood studs (if required)
Plywood, particleboard, **or** wallboard (if required)
Wall ancherss (if required)
Wood filler

SEE ALSO

Building a partition wall pp.170–171

In confined areas with no room for a closet door to swing open, a sliding door is the answer.

You can fit sliding doors on a closet, or create your own built-in closet by fitting sliding doors in a frame stretching the length of a wall. The doors themselves can be normal flush doors or louvered doors—they are fitted in the same way. A sliding door kit contains all the fittings you'll need, but you may have to create the correct opening width by fitting an end panel or spacer against one wall (see pp.234–235) or by reducing the opening height. If the size of your door kit is within 6 inches (150 mm) of the distance between the two walls, reduce the width by adding a wood "fillet" on one or both sides. Screw it to the wall using wall anchors.

For a larger gap, create a side panel by using 2 inch × 4 inch (50 mm × 100 mm) studs to create a frame, adding a horizontal support in the middle, and covering it with plywood, particleboard, or wallboard. Secure the frame to the wall, floor, and ceiling. Use the same methods for reducing the height. Where you want to stop short of a door or window, construct an end panel at right angles to the back wall.

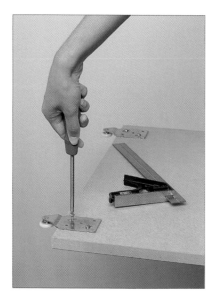

1 Use an adjustable square to position the roller plates equidistant from each side of the door. Mark the center point of the two diagonal slots on each roller plate, drill out these marks, and screw the roller plates in place.

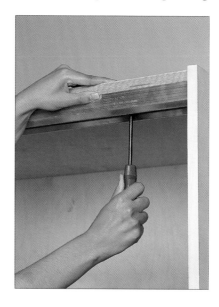

2 Measure the dimension of the closet opening and cut a length of roller track to this size, using a hacksaw, then file it smooth. If screwing it onto the underside of the closet, hold the front flush with the top edge of the closet. (On ceilings, make sure you screw through the wallboard into solid wood.)

3 Measure and mark out an oblong hole for the handle. Drill a ⅜ inch (10 mm) hole into each corner, then insert a jigsaw into one of the holes and carefully cut out the shape. You can insert the handle after the door has been painted.

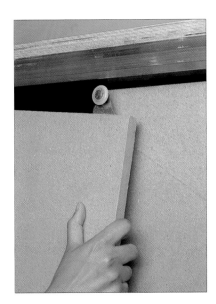

4 Hang the first door by hooking it onto the back runner track. In the same way hook the other door onto the front runner track. The doors can be aligned vertically and horizontally. Loosen the screws in the diagonal slots of each roller plate, reposition the doors, and mark the new position of the plates on the doors.

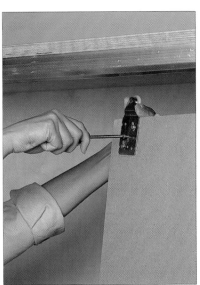

5 Take the doors down and use the new marks to reposition the plates. Screw down the diagonal slot screws, drill out the remaining holes, and screw the roller plates down before rehanging the doors. Mark the position of the bottom of each door on the side of the closet, then, once again, take the doors off.

6 Transfer the marks to the center of the bottom of the closet—they are for fitting the door guides in place. In general (see the manufacturer's instructions), screw the back guide down first, rehang the back door, and screw down the next guide. Fit the third guide in place, rehang the second door, and screw down the last guide.

7 Screw the door stop onto the bottom, lefthand side of the closet. (On solid concrete floors, use wall anchors to fit the stop and door guides.)

8 Finally, fit the removable fascias to the top and bottom of the closet. Use a nail set to drive the nailheads below the surface of the fascia, then cover them with wood filler.

INSTALLING A CYLINDER RIM LOCK

YOU WILL NEED

Tape measure
Pencil
Combination square
Awl
Electric drill plus twist and spade bits
Hacksaw
Locking pliers
Screwdriver
Utility knife
Wood chisel
Mallet

MATERIALS

Cylinder rim lock

SEE ALSO

Installing a mortise lock
pp.96–97
Other door hardware
pp.98–99

The security provided by a rim lock varies from a simple surface-mounted "night latch" to a cylinder rim lock that passes through the door. A deadlocking rimlock can be as effective as a good mortise lock. The security of a rim lock depends on the number of "tumblers" it has—five is the minimum for a secure lock. Rim locks all have a knob position to keep the door from locking when all you want to do is walk in and out.

The effectiveness of a rim lock depends on how well it is attached to the door and, particularly, to the door frame. The lock and its housing sit on the surface, held in place only by their screws. For extra security, use longer screws than the ones supplied, but of the same diameter.

One size of cylinder rim lock fits all the door sizes, but the lock will be "handed"—that is, suitable for left-hand or righthand hinged doors. A deadlocking cylinder rim lock has a

Unlike an ordinary rim lock, a cylinder rim lock has a key-operated cylinder that passes through the door, making it more secure.

lock bolt that can be operated only with a key. Before installing any type of lock, make sure the door and door frame are secure (see p.96); otherwise, the door can simply be kicked in.

1 Measure and mark both sides of the door one-third of the way from the top. If the lock comes with a template, use it to mark the center point of the hole for the cylinder. Or follow the manufacturer's instructions to find the center point, using a combination square. Drill a pilot hole through the door at the center point.

2 Bore into the pilot hole, using a spade bit the same diameter as the cylinder; however, to prevent damage to the surface of the door, drill only until the point just appears at the opposite side. Turn the work over and finish drilling the hole.

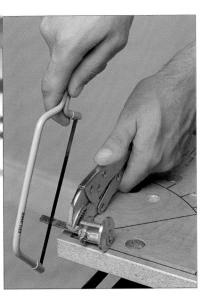

3 From the front of the door, place the cylinder and retaining ring into the hole; hold the lock mounting plate in position. The cylinder connecting bar should project ½ inch (12 mm) beyond the mounting plate. Mark the amount to be cut off; holding the bar firmly with the locking pliers, cut it to the required length with a hacksaw.

4 Reinsert the cylinder, with the retaining ring, place the lock mounting plate over the connecting bar and use long screws to secure the plate to the cylinder. As you tighten the screws, adjust the plate so its front edge is flush with the door's edge. Drill pilot holes for the smaller screws and drive them in place.

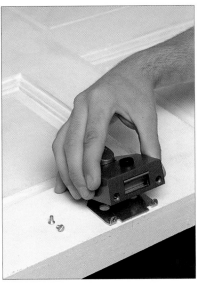

5 Move the button on the lock case to bring the latch to the unlocked position; then position it on the mounting plate, lining up the connecting bar with the slot on the back of the lock case. Slide it in place, and use the small screws to attach the lock case to the mounting plate.

6 Using the button to move the latch to its locked position, close the door toward the door frame and mark the position of the top and bottom of the latch on the frame. Place the strike plate on these pencil marks, and score around its flange with a utility knife.

7 Cut along the scored lines with a chisel and mallet, holding the chisel at a right angle to the surface, with its bevel side facing in. Make cuts inside this area, then remove wood to the depth of the flange on the strike plate. To finish, use a chisel, bevel side down, to pare out the remaining wood in the recess.

8 Fit the strike plate in the recess and close the door to ensure that it receives the bolt of the lock when in the closed position—if necessary, pare out more of the recess. When the lock works efficiently, drill pilot holes for the striker plate and screw it into the recess.

INSTALLING A MORTISE LOCK

YOU WILL NEED

Tape measure
Try square
Pencil
Metal straightedge
Utility knife
Brace and bit **or** electric drill
plus twist and spade bits
Mortise **or** firmer chisel
Mallet
Wood chisel
Combination square
Awl
Screwdriver

MATERIALS

Mortise lock
Masking tape
Shimming material such as
cardboard (if required)
Wood filler (if required)

SEE ALSO

Types of exterior doors
pp.74–75
Installing a cylinder rim lock
pp.94–95
Other door hardware
pp.98–99

On a front door, a mortise lock is normally installed in addition to a rim lock. This requires making a slot, or mortise, in the door to take the lock's body. A similar operation has to be carried out on the door frame to take the strike plate into which the lock bolt shoots. The security provided by a mortise lock is determined by the number of "levers" the lock contains; a seven-lever lock is the most secure, but five-lever locks are adequate.

Because mortise locks come in different sizes, measure the width of the door stile before you go shopping. There is no point in fitting a mortise lock to a weak door. The door itself must be at least 1¾ inch (44 mm) thick and mounted in a secure frame.

Decide where you want the lock to be. If it's fitted with a rim lock, place it one-third of the way up the door; if a mortise sash lock is being installed in a back or side door, fit it at a convenient handle height. If you

A mortise lock, which fits into the body of the door, is the best way to make a front door secure.

positioned the strike plate incorrectly, you can extend its recess and use shims, such as cardboard strips, inside the hole to compensate. Use wood filler to repair any oversized recesses.

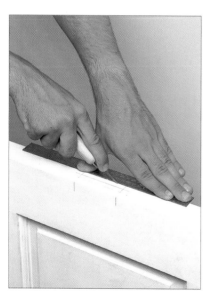

1 Hold the lock to the door and mark the position of its body on the door. Square lines across the edge of the door with a try square. Between these two lines draw a line down the center of the door; mark out half the thickness of the lock body on each side of the center line. Score along these two lines and the top and bottom lines.

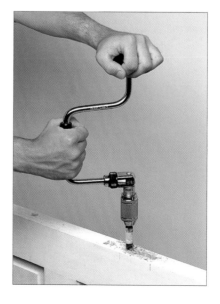

2 Using a brace fitted with a bit that fits between the marked lines (or an electric drill and spade bit), start at one end and bore along the center line within the scored rectangle to the depth of the lock's body—do not overlap the holes. Use a piece of tape on the bit as a gauge to indicate the depth of the hole.

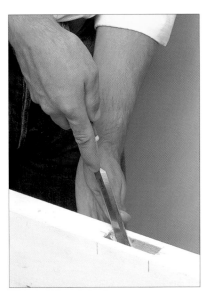

3 Make a vertical cut at each end of the rectangle with a mortise chisel, bevel side in, using a mallet. Then go along each side, carefully paring down vertically. Lever out the waste wood from the slot, and continue until the body of the lock fits snugly in place.

4 Put the lock in place, with its bolt in the locked position so it can be pulled out. Place the face plate on top, and score around it with a utility knife. Remove the lock; make vertical cuts with the chisel along the scored lines. Remove enough wood to make a recess the thickness of the face of the lock's body and the face plate.

5 Measure and mark the position for the cylinder on either side of the door, following the maker's instructions, using a combination square or template. Drill a pilot hole through the door at the mark. Bore a hole, using a spade bit, until the bit just appears on the opposite side; turn the work over and finish drilling the hole

6 Drop the body of the lock into the slot, pushing it down until its plate fits flush to the door's edge. Ensure that the key operates smoothly before screwing the lock into the recess. Screw on the face plate.

7 With the bolt locked, close the door and mark the position of the bolt on the side of the door frame. Center the strike plate at these marks, then mark the position of the strike box on the frame; score along these lines with a utility knife. With a brace and bit, drill to the depth of the box, then a chisel to cut out the wood.

8 Insert the box into the slot and score around its face plate with a utility knife. After cutting along the scored lines with a chisel and mallet, pare away the wood in the recess to the depth of the plate. Replace the strike box and plate, and check that the lock operates properly before screwing it in place.

OTHER DOOR HARDWARE

YOU WILL NEED

Fitting a letter box
Tape measure
Straightedge and pencil
Electric drill plus twist bits
Jigsaw
Hacksaw (if required)
Screwdriver

Fitting a door viewer
Pencil
Electric drill plus twist bits
Screwdriver

Fitting a deadbolt
Pencil
Electric drill plus twist bits
Utility knife
Chisel and mallet
Screwdriver

Fitting a door chain
Pencil
Screwdriver

MATERIALS

Door hardware (depending
on your preference)

SEE ALSO

Painting doors pp.80–81
A new door pp.82–85
Installing a cylinder rim lock
pp.94–95
Installing a mortise lock
pp.96–97

You can fit your front door with a door chain, door viewer, and letter box, or any combination of a variety of other hardware.

A mortise lock and cylinder rim lock on their own (or together) may keep the door locked, but they may not be sufficient for your safety. There are other devices you can fit on a front door where you may have unknown visitors. These include a door viewer, which allows you to see

who is outside before opening the door, and a door chain (or door limiter), which allows you to open the door partially to check the credentials of the person, such as a cable installer, before you open the door completely. You may also want to fit a letter box.

Back doors and side doors can be fitted with additional door locks, such as a deadbolt, that operate from the inside, but these will only be effective on the front door at night or when you are in the house.

It is important that any locks you fit to your doors are not accessible from the outside. Large letter boxes (and cat flaps) may allow access to the main door lock—never hang a spare key near them on the inside. Any glazed doors, particularly French windows, are vulnerable if access to the locks is possible by breaking the glass.

FITTING A LETTER BOX

1 Lay the door on a work surface (remove it from the door frame if needed). Measure and mark the opening of the letter plate on the door, centered from the sides. Drill a hole into each corner; insert the blade of a jigsaw into one hole, and cut along the lines to cut out the rectangle.

2 Check the length of the threaded rods against the door's thickness; to cut them, use a hacksaw. Mark and drill holes on each side of the opening. (Hang and paint the door if needed.) Hold the letter plate to its front, thread the rods in from the back, then add the nuts. Screw on the back plate.

FITTING A DOOR VIEWER

1 Mark the position of the peephole in the center and at eye level on the door (unless there are steps to the door). After drilling a pilot hole, drill a hole from both sides of the door (see step 2, p.94) the same diameter as the outer sleeve of the peephole fitting. (Hang and paint a new door.)

2 Unscrew the two sections of the viewer and, from the outside, insert the lens through the hole in the door. From the inside, insert the viewing barrel and, holding the lens in place, screw the barrel part onto it. Finish off by tightening the viewer with a large screwdriver or coin.

FITTING A DEADBOLT

1 At the center of the door's edge, drill a hole the size of the bolt. Put the bolt in the hole; score around its face plate with a utility knife. Chisel a recess for the plate (see pp.96–97). Place the bolt on the door, aligning its face plate with the door's edge and the recess. Mark the keyhole's position.

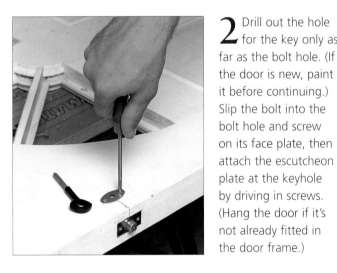

2 Drill out the hole for the key only as far as the bolt hole. (If the door is new, paint it before continuing.) Slip the bolt into the bolt hole and screw on its face plate, then attach the escutcheon plate at the keyhole by driving in screws. (Hang the door if it's not already fitted in the door frame.)

3 Close the door and operate the bolt, so it leaves a mark on the door frame. Drill a hole at the mark the same depth and diameter as the bolt. Center the strike plate over the hole; score around it with a utility knife. Cut a recess for the plate (see step 7, p.95). Fit the plate into the recess and screw it in place.

FITTING A DOOR CHAIN

Position the chain bracket on the door frame; mark and drill screw holes. Screw the bracket in place. Insert the chain into the receiving plate, and position it on the door; mark and drill screw holes. Screw the receiving plate in place. Use the longest screws possible (buy them separately).

REPAIRING STAIRS AND BALUSTERS

YOU WILL NEED

Fixing a squeaky step
Electric drill plus twist and countersink bits
Screwdriver
Hammer **or** putty knife
Wood chisel

Fixing a damaged nosing
Jigsaw and backsaw
Screwdriver
Block plane **or** wood rasp

Securing a loose baluster
Hammer and nail set
Flexible putty knife

Repairing a split baluster
Utility tape

Replacing a baluster
Sliding T bevel and pencil
Backsaw
Hammer

MATERIALS

Fixing a squeaky step
Wood screw and wood plug
Wood glue

Fixing a damaged nosing
Wood for patch
Wood glue and screws

Securing a loose baluster
Finishing nail and putty

Repairing a split baluster
Wood glue

Replacing a baluster
Baluster and finishing nails

The staircase and its accompanying balustrade is the most complex piece of carpentry in the house, and, as time goes by, it can develop a variety of faults, primarily caused by daily wear and tear. A step that creaks is one of the most common and annoying defects. The problem is caused by the joint between the tread (the part you step on) and the riser (the vertical part) working loose, with each part rubbing against the other as you walk up or down the flight.

The tread itself can be damaged, especially along the overhanging front edge, which is known as the nosing. This is often caused by careless movement of furniture, with heavy items being rested or dropped onto a tread as they are carried up or down the stairs. Lastly, the balustrade may be damaged and loosened by accidental impacts—a fault that needs immediate attention if the staircase is to remain safe to use.

ASSESSING THE DAMAGE

Inspect your staircase to get an idea of how it has been constructed and to assess its need for repair. The treads and risers are supported at each side of the flight by two parallel "stringers." In a close-stringer staircase, the treads and risers fit into grooves that are cut into the faces of the stringers; an open-stringer staircase has the outer stringer cut in a zig-zag fashion so the outer ends of the treads can rest on the cut-outs. The inner stringer against the wall is always closed.

If you cannot access the underside of the stairs, remove any carpet and make the repairs from above.

Helpful hints

If you can get underneath the stairs, to stop a squeak, check that the wedges holding the treads and risers into their grooves are driven home. Glue and drive in any that are loose and replace any missing ones. Glue and screw blocks of wood into the angles between treads and risers to stop them moving against each other.

FIXING A SQUEAKY STEP

1 If you cannot get below the stairs, drill a pilot hole smaller than the screw through the tread and into the top of the riser. Next, drill a larger clearance hole into the tread for the shank of the screw, then countersink the top of the hole to accept the screw head. Install the screw in the hole.

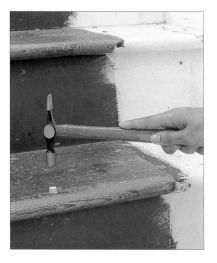

2 You can use a store-bought wood plug to cover the screw head, or make one yourself—use a bit specifically designed to cut plugs. Dab some wood glue onto the plug and tap it into place; then chisel it flush with the tread. Alternatively, use wood putty to fill the hole.

FIXING A DAMAGED NOSING

1 Mark out the area to be removed, making sure the back edge is parallel with the nosing but does not reach the riser. Using a jigsaw, cut into the nosing and, to release the strip, along the back edge. Then use a backsaw to make cuts at right angles to the back edge.

2 Cut a patch of replacement wood, with the grain running lengthwise, to fit the shape of the cut-out, then glue and screw it into place, countersinking the screws. Using a block plane or wood rasp, shape the patch to match the profile of the nosing.

SECURING A LOOSE BALUSTER

If a baluster is loose, you can tighten it by toe-nailing. Drive a finishing nail into the stringer below or handrail above at a 45° angle. Use a nail set to sink the nail below the surface. Cover the nail head with acrylic filler if the repair will be painted or wood putty if it will be varnished.

REPAIRING A SPLIT BALUSTER

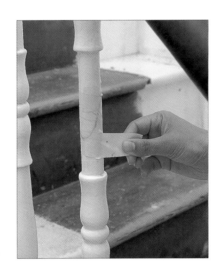

A strong impact is usually responsible for cracking a baluster. To repair it, open up the split and squirt in some wood glue. Then bind the split firmly by wrapping utility tape around it. Leave the tape in place for 24 hours, until the glue is dry.

REPLACING A BALUSTER

1 Pry out the two broken sections. Using a sliding T bevel, transfer the angles of the stringer and handrail to the new baluster. Finding one that matches can be difficult. If a mismatch will be noticeable, remove one from a less conspicuous area, but first make sure it will fit in the new site.

2 Trim the baluster along the marks with a backsaw. Then work it carefully into place and toe-nail it to the stringer and handrail (see *Securing a loose baluster*).

DECORATING STAIRCASE WOODWORK

How you choose to decorate your staircase woodwork may depend on what decorative finish it has at present. The stairs in a relatively new house are usually finished with varnish, either clear or tinted, in keeping with recent appreciation for exposed woodwork in the home. Stairs in an older home will probably have been painted several times over the years.

You can revarnish wood that has already been varnished, perhaps in a darker shade, or paint over it. If the old finish is paint, it is usually easier to repaint the staircase—you must first strip off all the old paint if you want to varnish it. A staircase that has been covered with several layers of old paint may also require stripping before repainting. No matter the finish, the sequence will be similar.

Before painting or varnishing, inspect the balustrade to ensure that it is sound. Make sure you have good light to work in, especially if the

An ordinary balustrade is made more elegant by painting the balusters and finishing the handrail.

stairwell normally has little light. The order of painting will depend on your staircase, but it is usually best to start at the top and work your way down.

1 If the stairs are carpeted, pull the material up, and make sure you remove any carpet tacks with a tack puller. If you must strip off the old finish—either paint or varnish—follow the instructions from the manufacturer of the stripper for applying and neutralizing it. However, first make sure any paint is lead-free (see p.30).

2 Give the stairs a good clean to remove any loose debris. Now is the time to check for and make any repairs (see pp.100–101). As you inspect the work, fill in any small holes.

3 Provided the paint does not contain lead (see p.30), key the wood by sanding it with fine-grade sandpaper, giving it a surface to which the finish can adhere. Wipe away any sanded material with a tack cloth. Apply masking tape along wall surfaces where they meet the parts of staircase that you plan to paint or varnish.

4 It is generally best to tackle the balustrade first. You should paint or varnish the underside of the handrail, working carefully between the individual balusters to avoid a buildup of the finish, then finish the rest of the handrail. If you're using two different finishes, wait for the handrail to dry before moving on to the balusters.

5 Paint the outer stringer after the balusters. Work carefully along the stringer, painting the base rail and the fillets between the balusters first, then tackling the vertical surfaces. If the area below an open outer stringer is closed in, paint this part (which is called the spandrel) after finishing the outer face of the stringer.

6 Apply the paint to the closed stringer adjacent to the flanking wall. Instead of applying masking tape, you can use a small brush to paint near the wall if you're confident that you have a steady hand.

7 If the stairs will be covered by a carpet runner, paint the treads and risers where they will be exposed at either side of the runner and 2 inches (50 mm) beyond. Alternatively, paint the treads and risers completely if the stairs won't be carpeted. Remind the occupants that the paint is wet by placing a sign by the stairwell.

VARNISHING THE WOODWORK

To stain and finish part of or all of the staircase, follow the steps for finishing a floor—a stain, then a few coats of varnish or polyurethane (see pp.182–183)—but follow the painting sequence, starting with the balustrade and ending with the steps.

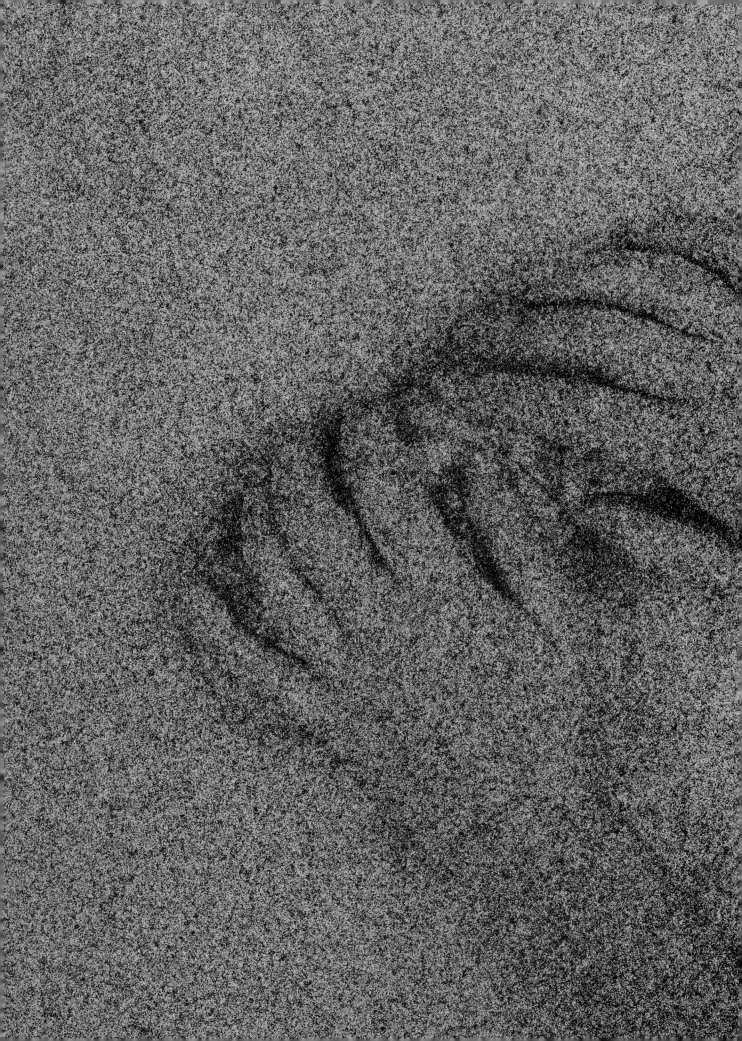

3

WALLS AND CEILINGS

WALLS AND CEILINGS DIRECTORY

INTERIOR DESIGN TRICKS

SKILL LEVEL Low
TIME FRAME ½ day
SPECIAL TOOLS Paint color cards, wallpaper and fabric samples, paint test cups, magazines for ideas
SEE PAGES 110–111

Before decorating, plan a scheme of color and patterns for the room. It helps to have an understanding of how color affects a room, creating rooms that are warm and welcoming or cool and relaxing. Color and pattern can also change a room's proportions, making high ceilings seem lower or narrow rooms wider.

PAINTING OPTIONS

SEE PAGES 112–113

If you choose paint as the basic material for your color schemes, you can use it as a plain color on walls and ceilings or create one of a number of decorative paint effects that can look eye-catchingly different.

PAINTING BASICS

SKILL LEVEL Low
TIME FRAME Under 2 hours
SPECIAL TOOLS Paint bucket, nylon fabric
SEE PAGES 114–115

How to determine the amount of paint you'll need for a room, and guidelines for the order in which to apply paint to the various surfaces in a standard room, including the wood trim. Also, instructions for protecting unpainted surfaces, ladder safety, and hints for preparing the paint.

USING PAINT BRUSHES

SKILL LEVEL Low
TIME FRAME ½ day per room (depending on room size)
SPECIAL TOOLS Paint brushes of various sizes, paint bucket
SEE PAGES 116–117

Paint brushes are often used for painting walls and ceilings, and they are the usual option for painting paneled doors and wood trim such as casing. Also included is how to apply textured paints.

USING PAINT ROLLERS

SKILL LEVEL Low
TIME FRAME ½ day per room (depending on room size)
SPECIAL TOOLS Paint roller, sleeve, paint roller tray
SEE PAGES 118–119

Using a paint roller is a quick way to apply paint to large unobstructed areas, but it can create messy paint splashes if not used carefully.

USING PAINT PADS

SKILL LEVEL Low
TIME FRAME ½ day per room (depending on room size)
SPECIAL TOOLS Large paint pad, edging or small paint pad, paint pad tray or paint roller tray
SEE PAGE 120

Paint pads are an alternative to paint brushes and rollers for applying paint.

USING A SPRAY GUN

SKILL LEVEL Low
TIME FRAME ½ day per room (depending on room size)

SPECIAL TOOLS Airless spray gun, strainer, safety glasses, respirator
SEE PAGE 121
Spraying paint with a spray gun can be considered in rooms completely stripped of furnishings and fittings.

PAINT EFFECTS: COLORWASHING

SKILL LEVEL Low
TIME FRAME 1 day per room
SPECIAL TOOLS Paint bucket, paint brush
SEE PAGE 122

A paint effect created by applying a top coat with random brush strokes onto a base coat of a different color.

PAINT EFFECTS: DRAGGING

SKILL LEVEL Low
TIME FRAME 1 day per room
SPECIAL TOOLS Paint bucket, paint brush
SEE PAGE 123

Dragging a translucent coat of paint over a lighter color

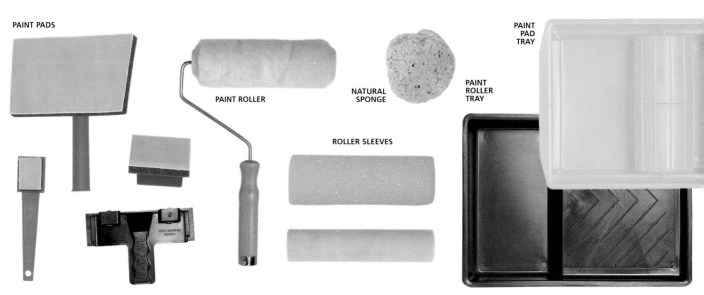

PAINT PADS

PAINT ROLLER

NATURAL SPONGE

ROLLER SLEEVES

PAINT ROLLER TRAY

PAINT PAD TRAY

base coat creates a striped paint effect.

PAINT EFFECTS: SPONGING

SKILL LEVEL Low
TIME FRAME 1 day per room
SPECIAL TOOLS Paint bucket, paint tray, natural sponge
SEE PAGE 124

A broken effect is created by adding a top coat of glaze with a sponge, either dabbing it on or sponging it off.

PAINT EFFECTS: STIPPLING

SKILL LEVEL Low
TIME FRAME 1 day per room
SPECIAL TOOLS Paint bucket, paint brush, stippling brush or paint roller with mohair sleeve
SEE PAGE 125

Points of color from the base coat appear through the top glaze, giving a speckled effect.

PAINT EFFECTS: RAGGING

SKILL LEVEL Low

TIME FRAME 1 day per room
SPECIAL TOOLS Paint bucket, paint brush, lint-free fabric
SEE PAGE 126

After brushing a top coat of glaze over a base coat, wads of fabric are randomly dabbed into the wet paint, creating areas of broken color.

PAINT EFFECTS: RAG-ROLLING

SKILL LEVEL Low
TIME FRAME 1 day per room
SPECIAL TOOLS Paint bucket, paint brush, lint-free fabric
SEE PAGE 127

Similar to ragging (see above), but the fabric is crumpled into a cylinder shape and rolled.

PAINT EFFECTS: STENCILING

SKILL LEVEL Low to medium
TIME FRAME 1 day per room
SPECIAL TOOLS Stencil, stencil brush, carpenter's level, palatte
SEE PAGES 128–129

How to add a patterned border to a room. Also, using a stamp to make your own random pattern.

WALLCOVERING OPTIONS

SEE PAGES 130–131

If you prefer wallcoverings for your walls and ceilings, you have two main design elements to consider—pattern and texture—of which there is a huge variety. The covering may require pasting or it may be prepasted.

WALLPAPER BASICS

SKILL LEVEL Low
TIME FRAME Under 2 hours
SPECIAL TOOLS Dust cloth, wallpaper brush
SEE PAGES 132–133

Once you decide what type and design of wallcovering to use, you have to measure and estimate how many rolls you'll need for the job.

CUTTING, PASTING, AND FOLDING WALLPAPER

SKILL LEVEL Low
TIME FRAME 5 minutes per length
SPECIAL TOOLS Paste table, paste bucket, paste brush
SEE PAGES 134–135

The secret to successful wallpapering lies in preparing each length correctly. After cutting a length slightly long, brush paste onto it, section by section, then fold it accordian fashion to transport it. Soak prepasted types in water.

HANGING AND TRIMMING WALLPAPER

SKILL LEVEL Low to medium
TIME FRAME 1 day
SPECIAL TOOLS Paperhanging brush, paperhanging scissors, seam roller
SEE PAGES 136–137

Basic techniques for hanging and trimming wallpaper for one wall, as well as details for hanging lining paper.

PAPERING AROUND CORNERS

SKILL LEVEL Low to medium
TIME FRAME 1 to 2 days
SPECIAL TOOLS Paperhanging brush, paperhanging scissors, seam roller
SEE PAGES 138–139

Additional details to help you tackle corners in rooms that are seldom perfectly square.

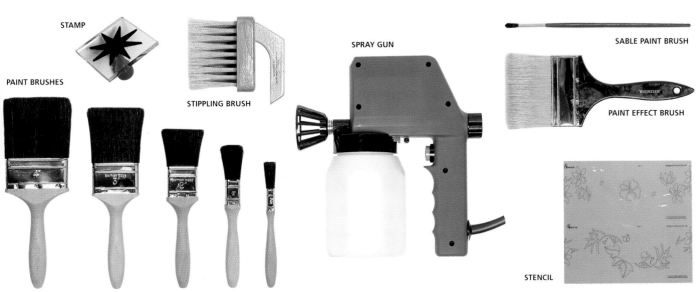

STAMP

PAINT BRUSHES

STIPPLING BRUSH

SPRAY GUN

SABLE PAINT BRUSH

PAINT EFFECT BRUSH

STENCIL

PAPERING AROUND DOORS AND WINDOWS

SKILL LEVEL Low to medium
TIME FRAME 1 to 2 days
SPECIAL TOOLS Paperhanging brush, paperhanging scissors, seam roller
SEE PAGES 140–141

How to paper around door and window openings to get the best results.

PAPERING AROUND OBSTACLES

SKILL LEVEL Low to medium
TIME FRAME Under 2 hours per obstacle
SPECIAL TOOLS Paperhanging brush, paperhanging scissors, seam roller
SEE PAGES 142–143

Papering around obstacles such as light switches, arches, and fireplace mantels.

PAPERING A CEILING

SKILL LEVEL Low to medium
TIME FRAME ½ to 1 day

SPECIAL TOOLS Paperhanging brush, paperhanging scissors, seam roller
SEE PAGE 144–145

Once you have taken down any light fixtures, the only problem lies in handling long lengths of pasted wallpaper, and in obtaining suitable access equipment.

USING FRIEZES

SKILL LEVEL Low
TIME FRAME Under 2 hours to ½ day
SPECIAL TOOLS Pasting brush, carpenter's level, utility knife, metal straightedge, paperhanging brush, paperhanging scissors, seam roller
SEE PAGE 146

Friezes are wallpaper strips hung just below ceiling level or near picture or chair rails.

FRAMING WITH BORDERS

SKILL LEVEL Low
TIME FRAME 2 hours to ½ day
SPECIAL TOOLS Pasting brush, carpenter's level, metal straightedge, paperhanging brush,

paperhanging scissors, seam roller
SEE PAGE 147

Borders are narrower than friezes and are used to frame doors and windows or to make decorative panels on walls.

PUTTING UP CROWN MOLDING

SKILL LEVEL Low to medium
TIME FRAME 1 day
SPECIAL TOOLS Miter box, tenon saw, glue spreader
SEE PAGE 148

Crown molding is fitted in the angle between the walls and ceiling. Modern crown molding is made from wood or foamed plastic.

INSTALLING PICTURE AND CHAIR RAILS

SKILL LEVEL Low to medium
TIME FRAME 1 day
SPECIAL TOOLS Miter box, tenon saw, coping saw, electric saw plus twist, countersink, and masonry bits, carpenter's level
SEE PAGE 149

Picture rails are wood moldings attached to walls

above head height and used to hang pictures; chair rails are installed at chair height to protect walls from furniture.

TILING OPTIONS

SEE PAGES 150–151

You can choose ceramic wall tiles with plain colors or with patterns, mix the two together, or finish off half-tiled areas with borders. Tiles are used in kitchens and bathrooms, where their water resistance makes them ideal for splashbacks, shower stalls, and other areas likely to be in contact with water.

TILING BASICS

SKILL LEVEL Low
TIME FRAME Under 2 hours
SPECIAL TOOLS Softwood strips, tile spacers
SEE PAGES 152–153

Careful planning of the tile layout is essential for the best results. Plan to center the tiles on each wall, then finish off with cut tiles of equal width at each side. Once you have planned the layout, count how many tiles you'll need.

PASTE TABLE

HAMMER

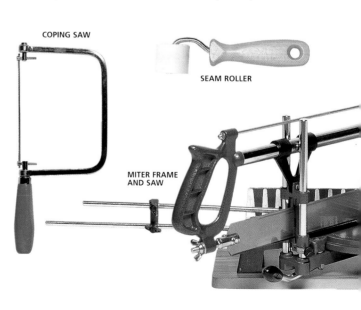

COPING SAW

SEAM ROLLER

MITER FRAME AND SAW

TILING A WALL

SKILL LEVEL Low to medium
TIME FRAME 1 to 2 days
TOOLS Notched adhesive spreader, tile cutter, carpenter's level
SEE PAGES 154–155

Once you have attached guide strips to the walls to help keep the tiles properly aligned, work across the wall, row by row, to position all the whole tiles. Then remove the strips and cut and fit edge tiles to complete the wall. Details are included for sheets of mosaic tiles—small tiles fixed to a backing sheet.

TILING AT CORNERS, WINDOWS, AND DOORS

SKILL LEVEL High
TIME FRAME 1 to 2 days
SPECIAL TOOLS Same as for *Tiling a wall*, plus tile saw, tile nippers, tile file
SEE PAGES 156–157

Unless you are tiling just a simple backsplash, you'll have to fit tiles round inside and outside corners, doors, and windows. Careful cutting will ensure that tiles fit neatly.

TILING IN BATHROOMS AND KITCHENS

SKILL LEVEL Low to medium
TIME FRAME 1 to 2 days
SPECIAL TOOLS Notched spreader, platform tile cutter, tile saw, tile file, tile nippers, profile gauge
SEE PAGES 158–159

Tiling a limited area in a bathroom or kitchen, such as a backsplash, calls for slightly different instructions. For example, tiling over a kitchen countertop may not require using guide strips.

GROUTING AND SEALING

SKILL LEVEL Low
TIME FRAME 1 day
SPECIAL TOOLS Grout spreader, grout finisher or dowel, caulking gun
SEE PAGES 160–161

Once the adhesive holding the tiles to the walls has hardened, grout must be applied between tiles, and the joints between tiles and other surfaces must be sealed to make the area completely waterproof.

PANELING OPTIONS

SEE PAGES 162–163

Tongue-and-groove wood boards are nailed to strips on the walls and varnished or painted. An alternative to natural wood is hardboard or plywood sheet paneling with a decorative finish. These are attached to strips or glued directly to the wall.

PREPARING WALLS FOR PANELING

SKILL LEVEL Medium
TIME FRAME 1 to 2 days
SPECIAL TOOLS Carpenter's level, electric drill, tenon saw or jigsaw
SEE PAGES 164–165

Before installing the paneling you must attach supporting wood strips to the wall (unless you glue sheet cladding to the walls). At the same time, add insulation for soundproofing or draftproofing if needed.

INSTALLING TONGUE-AND-GROOVE PANELING

SKILL LEVEL Medium
TIME FRAME 1 to 2 days

SPECIAL TOOLS Carpenter's level, try square, tenon saw or jigsaw, padsaw, plane
SEE PAGES 166–167

Details for installing tongue-and-groove boards to strips by blind nailing through the tongues or using clips.

INSTALLING SHEET PANELING

SKILL LEVEL Medium
TIME FRAME 1 to 2 days
SPECIAL TOOLS Panel saw or jigsaw, profile gauge
SEE PAGES 168–169

Instructions for nailing sheet paneling to supporting strips or gluing them to the wall.

BUILDING A PARTITION WALL

SKILL LEVEL High
TIME FRAME 2 days
SPECIAL TOOLS Panel saw or jigsaw, carpenter's level, electric drill, filling knife
SEE PAGE 170–171
You can divide a room by erecting a partition wall. Build the wooden frame, including a door opening, then cover it on both sides with wallboard.

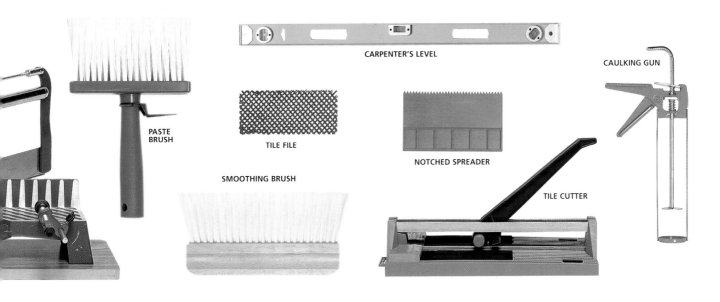

PASTE BRUSH

SMOOTHING BRUSH

TILE FILE

CARPENTER'S LEVEL

NOTCHED SPREADER

TILE CUTTER

CAULKING GUN

INTERIOR DESIGN TRICKS

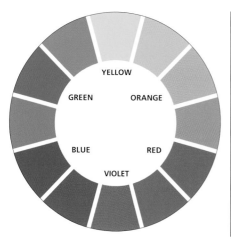

Interior designers use a host of tricks to give individual rooms distinctive moods and to alter the way they appear to the viewer. To understand how they do this, it helps to know a little about how color works. Every color is derived from three primary colors: red, blue, and yellow. These three colors, plus black and white, can be blended together in different proportions to make an infinite range of colors. If you mix two primary colors, you get one of the three secondary colors: orange (red plus yellow), green (yellow plus blue), and violet (blue plus red). Continue mixing, this time adding a primary color to a secondary color, and you'll get six tertiary colors. Mix these further to create even more colors.

▲ The color wheel is based on the basic primary, secondary, and tertiary colors. You can add white to create paler tints of these colors or black to create darker shades. Any three neighboring colors on the wheel are referred to as "related." They work together well and create a harmonious effect in a room. Colors on opposite sides of the wheel are complementary colors—when used together, one provides contrast for the other, creating dramatic and eye-catching color schemes.

▼ ▶ The same room has been decorated in different schemes. The complementary colors of orange and blue (right) create a warm, exciting effect; the neutral colors with touches of blue (below) create a cool, calming effect.

▶ Paint a high ceiling in a darker color than the walls and it will seem lower. Conversely, paint a low ceiling in a lighter color than the walls and it will appear higher, especially if you change the color at picture-rail level.

◄ Highlight room features (such as paneling, window frames, and baseboards) by using tints of one color or related colors for a subtle effect, or use complementary colors to create a bold look.

▶ Strong dark colors can provide a sense of coziness, especially when a subtle wallpaper pattern breaks it up. Mirrors make small rooms seem larger.

◄ The neutral colors, which do not appear on the color wheel, are white, black, gray, and pale tints that contain a lot of white, including cream and beige. These colors are a perfect backdrop for stronger, more vibrant colors.

▼ The strength of a color is important. Light-colored surfaces reflect light better than darker ones, making rooms seem larger and more open. You can hide unattractive objects, such as a radiator, by painting them the same color as the wall behind (use a matte latex or alkyd finish).

◄ Warm colors contain yellow and red. They make wall and ceiling surfaces seem to advance toward the viewer, and make rooms appear intimate and welcoming. Cool colors, based on blues and greens, have the opposite effect, making walls and ceilings recede and rooms seem cool and airy.

PAINT OPTIONS

POSSIBLE MATERIALS

MATTE

SATIN

ENAMEL

GLOSS

MASONRY

BLACKBOARD PAINT

STENCIL PAINTS

ARTIST'S OIL COLORS

TRANSPARENT OIL GLAZE

SCUMBLE GLAZE

TEXTURED PAINT

Paint is the most popular decorative finish for walls and ceilings. It is inexpensive, easy to apply, and simple to replace when you want a change of color scheme. You can apply it to sealed plaster or wallboard, or use it over a textured finish or wallcovering.

When buying paint, which comes in an almost infinite range of colors, consider the type of finish you want—for example, matte (non-reflective) or satin (a shiny sheen)—and the surface it will be covering. Water-base paint is often the choice for walls, while solvent-base paint is sometimes preferred for wood trim.

▷ Most rooms are painted in one relatively bland color, but strong colors can be effective when used on only one wall. Here, the related colors of yellow and orange (see pp.110–111) are cleverly juxtaposed in a room where the rest of the walls are painted white.

◁ Stippling creates a delicate effect, achieved by lifting off a colored glaze with a short-bristle stippling brush.

▽ Ragging is a variation on the technique of sponging, but uses crumpled-up cloth to remove the color.

▲ The star motif stamped randomly around this room is an elegant way to break up the large expanse of colorwash on walls. Stenciling is another way to add pattern to walls.

▲ These dark walls provide the perfect backdrop for brightly colored furniture, but such rooms need a lot of natural light.

▶ Textured paint is the appropriate choice for covering up less-than-perfect walls. Patterned roller sleeves designed for textured paint will help create a sophisticated but rugged look.

◀ Sponging is one of the easiest broken-color paint effects to use. The second color can be either sponged on or sponged off the base color.

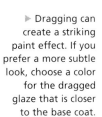

▶ Dragging can create a striking paint effect. If you prefer a more subtle look, choose a color for the dragged glaze that is closer to the base coat.

PAINTING BASICS

YOU WILL NEED

Ladder **or** other access equipment
Low-tack masking tape
Fabric drop cloth
Nylon pantyhose or tights
Polythene bag **or** aluminum foil

SEE ALSO

Preparation pp.18–35
Painting techniques pp.116–129

ORDER OF WORK

The numbers indicate the order in which to paint a room. Start with the ceiling so that any splashes of paint that land on the walls can be painted over. On a ceiling, paint in rows 10 square feet (1 sq m) at a time. On walls, covering the same size areas, start at the top and work down. If you are right-handed, start at the right-hand corner; if you are left-handed, the left one. This allows you to rest your non-painting hand against an unpainted surface as you work.

Once you have done all the necessary preparation work on the walls and ceilings and have chosen the paint you want, your next task is to figure out how much paint you'll need and to plan the order of work.

ESTIMATING QUANTITIES

On previously painted surfaces, most water-base, or latex, paint covers about 400 square feet (40 sq m) per gallon. On rough surfaces the coverage rate may be only half that amount—200 square feet (20 sq m) per gallon. New wallboard and plaster are especially absorbent, so coat those surfaces first with a primer designed for the purpose before applying the finish paint. This economizes on paint costs and ensures that the final coat doesn't contain blotchy areas. Diluting latex paint with water to make your own "primer" is not recommended. The method of applying the paint—

for example, by brush or spray gun—can also affect the paint coverage.

To work out the area of the walls in a room, measure the wall height, add together the lengths of all the walls, then multiply the two sums. Similarly, work out the area of windows and doors in the room, then subtract this from the overall area. To work out how many gallons of paint to buy, divide this figure by the expected coverage per gallon. Measure the floor to find the dimensions for the ceiling.

To save money, always buy paint in the largest containers appropriate to your needs. You can then decant paint into a smaller paint bucket as you work. This will also ensure that paint color is the same—even paint mixed by computerized machines can vary.

PROTECTING SURFACES

Unless you are confident that you have a steady hand, it always pays to mask off surfaces next to those you'll be painting. This means sticking lengths of masking tape to window frames, door casings, and baseboards, as well as to wiring accessories such as light switches and wall outlets (unless you remove them, see pp.18–19). The tape should stay in place until the paint is touch dry. Use only low-tack masking tape; any other type will damage the surface to which it is stuck.

Protect flooring with a drop cloth. If you have carpet in the room, consider taking it up—it's the only sure way to avoid getting paint on it.

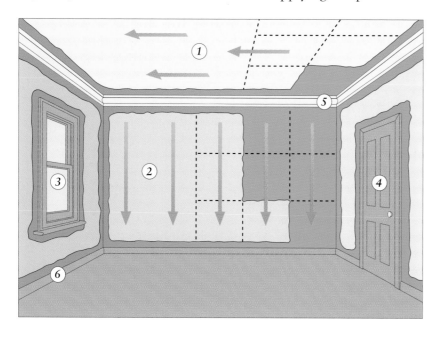

Helpful hints

It is never a good idea to use paint straight from the container it comes in, unless you plan to use the entire contents in one painting session. The main reason for this is that the paint may become contaminated by loose bristles from paint brushes and by dust, fluff, and other particles picked up by the brush during the painting session.

In any case, if you have purchased your paint in large, economical containers, they will be too heavy to hold comfortably. Instead, pour the paint into a paint bucket or roller tray, depending on which implement you'll be using to apply it.

LADDER SAFETY

Whether painting your ceiling or walls, you'll need a ladder for areas above your reach. Always make sure the feet of the ladder are steady on the floor and the braces are securely locked down before getting on a ladder.

When standing on a ladder, always lean toward it. Never extend beyond a comfortable reach, which could cause the ladder to tip over.

1 To protect adjacent surfaces, such as wood trim, that you don't want covered with paint, apply masking tape in short lengths—they are easier to handle and apply than longer ones. Firmly press down on the edge next to the surface you are painting to prevent paint from seeping underneath it.

2 Tape drop cloths to baseboards to stop them from creeping and exposing floor coverings to splashes. Start with vertical strips to hold the cloth in place, then apply the tape horizontally so paint doesn't drip behind it. Use fabric drop cloths that absorb paint splashes, instead of polythene ones, which do not.

3 If the can of paint has already been partly used, strain the remaining paint through old nylon fabric such as a pair of pantyhose stretched across the mouth of the bucket. If you are using a freshly opened can of paint, simply pour the paint directly into your bucket.

4 Be prepared for pauses in your painting by having plastic kitchen wrap, a polythene bag, or aluminum foil handy. Simply wrap the roller sleeves or brush bristles in the plastic or foil to stop the paint from drying out. A paint tray can be protected in the same way.

USING PAINT BRUSHES

Most people instinctively reach for a paint brush when they want to paint a wall or ceiling. It's a familiar tool that is easy to control, and it gives excellent results with a minimum of skill. Choose a brush with plenty of long, thick bristles in a size to match the strength of your hands. A 4-inch- (100-mm-) wide brush will suit most people; a larger brush will be tiring to handle unless you do a lot of painting and have developed strong wrists.

You will also need a smaller brush— a 1½ inch (38 mm) size is ideal—for painting neatly into internal corners and angles and for painting around obstacles such as light fixtures, switches, and outlets.

Depending on the smoothness and porosity of the surface, you'll normally need a half a gallon of paint to cover 150 to 200 square feet (15 to 20 sq m) of surface. Before you start the job, make sure you protect both any surfaces not to be painted and the contents of the room. Paint should be thoroughly mixed before pouring it into a bucket for application.

BRUSH CARE

To clean a brush after using it, first remove any excess paint by brushing it against newspaper, avoiding areas that become covered with paint in the process. Use hot water and liquid dishwashing detergent to clean latex paint from a brush; or use mineral spirits for oil-base, or alkyd, paint, followed by liquid detergent and water. Once the brush is clean, shake out any excess water, wipe it on a paper towel, and store it wrapped in clean paper to help retain the shape of the bristles.

Helpful hints

Work the bristles of a new brush back and forth across the palm of your hand to dislodge loose bristles and dust. Wipe off the top of the paint container before opening it so that dust and other debris do not fall into the paint.

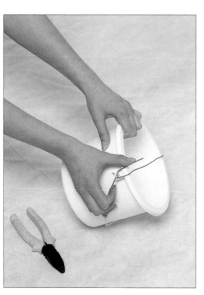

1 To scrape off excess paint after loading your brush— without drips running down the sides of the paint bucket—attach a length of wire across the opening. Hook the ends around the handle and snip off the excess with wire cutters. Or use a piece of clean, lint-free string. You can also use the wire or string as a brush rest.

2 Load your brush by dipping the bristles into the paint to no more than half their length. Then draw it against the wire or string scraper to remove any excess paint, which will drip straight back into the paint bucket.

3 At internal angles, such as between the ceiling and a wall, use the small brush to create a neat edge, unless you are painting both areas the same color. Either angle the bristles or hold the brush on edge, with the end of the bristles on the surface and the narrow edge leading the way. Alternatively, use masking tape.

4 Apply the paint to the surface in two or three parallel vertical strips, each slightly overlapping its neighbor. Brush across the strips at right angles to blend them together, and finish with gentle, vertical brush strokes. Move to the next section, blending the work together.

5 To avoid a build-up of paint at external corners, brush the paint out toward the edge and let the brush run off the wall at right angles.

6 To reach into crevices and other hard-to-reach areas, use the end of the bristles to apply the paint by holding the brush perpendicular to the work and moving it in a dabbing, back and forth motion.

TEXTURED PAINTS

To create a random, stippled texture, use a large painter's sponge inside a plastic bag and dab it into the wet paint.

One way to create a three-dimensional effect on a surface is to use textured paint. After applying it to the surface with a wide brush or roller, you can give it a random or regular pattern. Among the tools for texturing are a sponge (left), a comb (right), and a molded roller.

Before painting the walls, make sure you prepare them as you would for a traditional paint. The paint comes in white, but once it dries you can apply a color by using latex paint.

You can use a comb to create a variety of effects. To create these arches, start at the top and work your way down.

USING PAINT ROLLERS

The quickest way of painting walls and ceilings is with a paint roller. Most paint rollers for do-it-yourself use are 9 inches (230 mm) wide. (A wider roller would require more effort to push it). Some rollers are 4 inches (100 mm) wide or smaller for painting trim areas and touch ups. There are also rollers molded into special shapes for painting corners and pipes.

Select the cover to suit the surface you're decorating. You'll need a short-pile cover for smooth surfaces and a longer pile for textured surfaces and relief wallcoverings. Covers are also available to create textured finishes.

Depending on the smoothness and porosity of the surface being covered, you'll need one gallon of paint for every 300 to 400 square feet (30 to 40 sq m) of surface. You're not limited to covering surfaces with one color. You can use rollers (and brushes) to create stripes or blocks of color next to each other (see box, facing page).

Before you begin painting, make sure you protect surfaces not to be painted, as well as the room's contents. You cannot apply paint in internal corners or near obstacles such as light switches with a roller, so you'll also need a small paint brush to tackle these areas.

CLEANING UP

Remove excess paint from a roller by running it over the ribs in a paint tray, then along newspaper (avoid areas on the paper as they are covered by paint). If possible, pull the cover off the cage. Wash it in hot water and soap for latex paint or mineral spirits for alkyd paint (wear rubber gloves if you use mineral spirits). Squeeze out any excess liquid and wrap the roller in aluminum foil or paper to store it.

Helpful hints

Before adding paint to the roller tray, you can line it with aluminium foil or plastic food wrap to make cleaning up quick and easy.

1 Pour paint into your roller tray to a depth of about ¾ inch (20 mm). Run the roller down the slope of the tray and into the paint. Then roll it up and down the slope across the ribs a few times to load the cover and disperse the paint evenly through the pile.

2 To reach high walls or ceilings, you can use an extension pole fitted to the handle of many paint rollers. (First cut in at the edges; see step 3.) To avoid paint spatters, take care not to overload the roller, press it too hard, or roll it too quickly. Consider wearing a hat to protect your hair, especially if you use an oil-base paint.

3 Because a roller cannot reach right into internal angles, use a paint brush about 2 inches (50 mm) wide to paint a border around the wall (or ceiling) that you are working on. Also use the brush to paint around outlets, switches, light fixtures, and other obstacles.

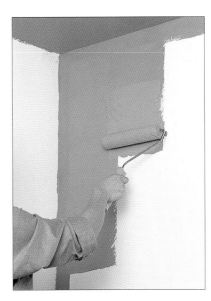

4 Start applying the paint by running the roller over a wall from top to bottom, letting each pass overlap the previous one. Cover an area of 10 square feet (1 sq m) at a time, starting in a corner.

5 Without reloading the roller, run it over the paint just applied, this time rolling it at right angles to the original direction. This helps to spread the paint evenly and fill in any uncovered patches, especially on uneven or textured surfaces.

6 Reload the roller and paint the next area, blending it in with the previous one. Paint a whole length of a wall or ceiling at a time. Once you have a length completed, go over the work to smooth out the paint, gradually lifting the roller at the end of the pass. Reload and repeat the process to complete the surface.

PAINTING ALTERNATIVES

To make straight lines between areas of paint, align low-tack masking tape along a pencil line and paint up to it. After the paint dries, move the tape and paint the second color.

You can use horizontal lines to create a mock chair rail or to frame a stencil applied around a room (see pp.128–129). Create stripes with vertical lines, either of equal widths or by mixing wider stripes with narrower ones. Use them on the full length of the wall or below a chair rail.

To draw a horizontal line, balance a torpedo spirit level on top of a metal straightedge or use a standard spirit level.

For vertical lines, hook one end of a chalk line on a nail tapped into the wall, hold the other end taut and snap the line.

USING PAINT PADS

A nontraditional way of applying paint to walls and ceilings is by using paint pads. These consist of pieces of short-pile, mohair fabric mounted on foam plastic and stuck to metal or plastic handles. They are available in a range of sizes. You will need the biggest pad for fast coverage of large areas, plus a smaller one for painting clean edges and for touching in around obstacles such as lighting fixtures, switches, and electrical outlets. Some manufacturers offer specialty pads, including a wall/ceiling pad that has built-in edging wheels, which are designed to guide the pad precisely along the corners created where the walls meet the ceiling.

One benefit of using a paint pad is that paint coverage is generally a little higher than with brushes and rollers. This is because the paint pad applies a thinner film of paint to the wall. The disadvantage is that the adhesive holding the parts together can dissolve after prolonged use.

You can load the pad simply by dipping it into the paint, but it is easier to use a special tray with a roller. The design of this tray guarantees that the pad is evenly coated with paint every time.

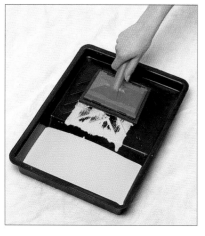

1 If you are using an ordinary roller tray to load your pad, pour about ½ inch (12 mm) of paint into the tray. Dip the pile of the pad into the paint and remove any excess paint by wiping the pad across the ribbed slope.

2 If you have a special tray for the pad, fill it with paint to the depth recommended by the manufacturer. Draw the pad across the roller, which transfers paint from the tray to the pad; then draw it along the back edge of the tray to scrape off any excess paint.

3 Start painting a room by creating a border around the perimeter of the walls by the ceiling. Use a pad with edging wheels, or stick short lengths of masking tape on the adjoining surfaces and paint up to them. You can use a small pad to paint around obstacles.

4 Pull a large pad across 10 square feet (1 sq m) of wall or ceiling in a series of parallel and slightly overlapping passes. Then run the pad across the painted area at right angles to the first passes. Finish off by making light passes, then move on to the next section.

Using a spray gun

YOU WILL NEED

Airless spray gun
Strainer
Safety goggles
Respirator

MATERIALS

Latex paint
Water **or** mineral spirits
(if required)

SEE ALSO

Painting basics pp.114–115

Small, electrically powered, airless spray guns are worth considering for painting walls if you have several completely empty rooms that require painting—for example, when moving into a new house. However, they are not suitable for spraying ceilings. Although a spray gun can apply paint quickly, the fine overspray it produces means you must completely mask all doors, windows, wood trim, and floor coverings before using one. Spray guns are also difficult—as well as time-consuming—to clean, so you should carefully consider if using one is the right choice for you.

Runny types of paint generally work better in a spray gun than nondrip formulas. In fact, the paint may require thinning before you can use it; follow the manufacturer's recommendations. Make sure you strain the paint (see p.115), which will avoid blocking the nozzle on the gun.

You must wear a respirator and safety goggles to avoid inhaling the paint mist or getting it in your eyes while you work. You must also make sure that the room is well ventilated; however, avoid painting on windy days when open windows can create drafts crossing the room.

1 Airless spray guns all have slightly different performance characteristics, so it is a good idea to first practice on an out-of-the-way surface in order to establish your gun's spray pattern and optimum spraying distance.

2 On flat surfaces, you must keep the gun nozzle the same distance from and at right angles to the wall as you move it from side to side. Do this by flexing your wrist as you complete each side-to-side pass. Make sure you do not spray in an arc.

3 At an external corner, spray the flanking wall to within about 6 inches (150 mm) of the angle. Then stand in front of the end of the wall and paint across it, using short side-to-side passes of the gun as you work your way down. Repeat for the adjacent wall.

4 When painting an internal corner, spray each flanking wall first, again to within about 6 inches (150 mm) of the angle. Then fill in the corner by pointing the gun into the angle and moving it from top to bottom in one pass.

PAINT EFFECTS: COLORWASHING

Because colorwashing is extremely easy to execute, the technique is an excellent introduction to the varied and interesting world of paint effects. Simply paint your wall or ceiling with a plain base coat, then apply a random broken wash of a second color over it, allowing the color of the base coat to occasionally show through.

Well-thinned oil-base paint was used as the wash coat in traditional colorwashing. Today, however, most people rely on ordinary latex paint mixed with a water-base glaze. You can protect your work with a final coat of varnish.

Pale color combinations work best for all-over decorating, but darker shades can be used to create a dramatic effect on smaller self-contained panels.

1 Apply the base coat and let it dry. Then make up the colorwash—one part flat latex paint to four parts glaze—and use a small brush to mix it thoroughly. About 1¾ pints (1 liter) of colorwash is enough for two coats in an area of 30 square feet (3 sq m).

2 Brush on the first coat of the colorwash mixture, using a series of random brush strokes to cover an area of about 10 square feet (1 sq m). Work all the paint out of the brush.

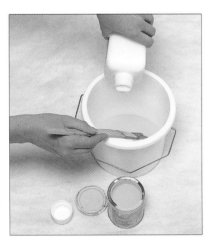

3 Break up the damp colorwash with the edge of the brush bristles, using a jabbing action. Move on to the next section. Repeat step 2, and, again, break up the wash with the edge of the bristles. Continue until the complete surface is covered with the wash.

4 After the coat of colorwash dries, repeat steps 2 and 3 to apply a second wash coat over it. This will build up the depth of color. When the second wash is dry, you can apply a clear flat varnish to make the surface washable and more durable.

PAINT EFFECTS: DRAGGING

YOU WILL NEED

Bucket for glaze
4-inch- (100-mm-) wide
paint brush
Small paint brush

MATERIALS

Flat alkyd paint for
the base coat
Proprietary oil glaze
Mineral spirits
Universal pigments such as
artist's oil colors
White alkyd undercoat

SEE ALSO

Painting basics
pp.114–115
Using paint brushes
pp.116–117
Using paint rollers
pp.118–119

A thin, translucent coat of paint, known as a colored glaze, is applied over a lighter color base coat to create dragging. Because you have to maintain even pressure throughout each continuous top-to-bottom brush stroke, it can be one of the more difficult paint effects to create. If you fail to apply pressure properly, you may leave telltale brush marks and denser color at the start and finish of each stroke.

It is a good idea to work with a partner. The dragger should create each vertical strip in the glaze as soon as the painter has applied it.

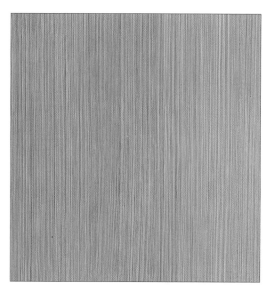

The use of dragging on walls (it is rarely used on ceilings) creates a finely striped effect. It evolved from the technique of graining wood.

1 Apply the base coat and let it dry. For about 1 pint (½ liter) of the glaze, mix one part oil glaze, three parts mineral spirits, a tablespoonful of undercoat, and pigment, if required— but first use a small brush to mix the glaze with the pigment on a white tile or saucer.

2 Brush a thin coat of the glaze onto the wall in overlapping, vertical strokes, then horizontal ones; end in light, vertical strokes. From top to bottom, aim to cover an area about 18 inches (460 mm) wide.

3 Drag a dry paint brush down the wall in one continuous stroke, using even pressure. It helps to start work alongside a vertical edge such as a corner or door frame. At regular intervals, use rags or paper towels to wipe off the buildup of paint on the brush.

4 Repeat the process to drag the next series of lines parallel with the first ones before the glaze dries, and continue until the surface is completely covered. The dried finish is durable, but you can give it a coat of clear varnish if you wish.

PAINT EFFECTS: SPONGING

YOU WILL NEED

Paint bucket
Paint tray
Natural sponge
4-inch- (100-mm-) wide
paint brush for sponging off

MATERIALS

Latex paint (sample cups
are ideal for second
colors) **or** satin-gloss alkyd
paint for base coat,
proprietary oil glaze, and
universal pigments such as
artist's oil colors
Mineral spirits (if required)

SEE ALSO

Painting basics pp.114–115
Using paint brushes
pp.116–117
Using paint rollers
pp.118–119

You can create an almost infinite variety of looks by sponging. The final result will depend on the color combinations you choose, the texture of the sponge you use and the actual painting method.

Sponging can be applied in two ways. The first is called sponging on, and it involves taking up paint or glaze on a sponge and dabbing it onto a wall or ceiling that has been given an overall base coat. The second method is called sponging off. Here the color coat of glaze is brushed out over the base coat, then a clean, damp sponge is used to dab some of the color off.

You can add depth to a sponging finish by adding a second color over the first one. For the best results, apply the darker color first.

1 Apply the base coat and let it dry. Use latex paint if you intend to sponge on diluted latex colors, or satin-gloss alkyd paint if you'll be using tinted oil glaze (see p.126 for preparing the paint). To sponge on, load a little paint onto the sponge from a roller tray.

2 Dab the sponge on the wall, aiming to create an even, overall pattern. Vary the spacing of the dabs if you want a more random effect, and repeat the process with a second color after the first layer has dried.

3 For sponging off (this technique doesn't work with latex paint), mix the tinted glaze (see p.126 for preparing the paint) and brush it on evenly but thinly over the base coat. Work on an area of 10 square feet (1 sq m) at a time so that the glaze stays workable.

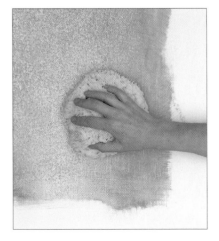

4 Soak the sponge in mineral spirits and wring it out. Then dab it on the surface evenly, lifting off some of the glaze. When the sponge becomes saturated with glaze, wash it in mineral spirits, and follow up with dishwashing liquid—it will then be ready for re-use.

PAINT EFFECTS: STIPPLING

YOU WILL NEED

Paint bucket for glaze
4-inch- (100-mm-) wide
paint brush
Stippling brush **or** paint
roller with mohair cover
Rags **or** paper towels

MATERIALS

Satin-gloss alkyd paint for
base coat
Proprietary oil glaze
Mineral spirits
Universal oil pigments such
as artist's oil colors

SEE ALSO

Painting basics pp.114–115
Using paint brushes
pp.116–117
Using paint rollers
pp.118–119

One of the most delicate of paint effects, stippling is created by brushing a colored glaze over a satin-gloss alkyd base coat, then dabbing the wet surface with a large flat, short-bristled stippling brush. This lifts off specks of the glaze, depending on how much pressure is applied.

This can be a difficult technique to execute well, and if using the stippling brush, it is easier if tackled by a two-person team—one applying the glaze and the other stippling the wet surface. On large areas, a quick alternative technique is to use a short-pile mohair paint roller to stipple the surface.

In stippling, tiny points of color from the base coat appear through the top glaze, creating a subtle grainy or speckled effect.

1 Apply the base coat and let it dry. Then mix up and tint the glaze (see p.126), and brush it onto the wall in a thin even layer over an area of no more than 10 square feet (1 sq m).

2 Use the stippling brush to dab the wet glaze firmly and evenly area by area, just letting successive dabs overlap. (If you are working with a partner, he or she can apply the glaze to the next section as you do the stippling.)

3 Periodically, you should remove the buildup of glaze from the bristles by wiping the brush on clean rags or paper towels.

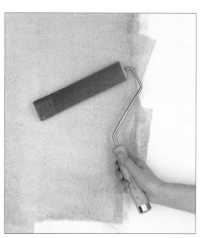

4 To stipple with a short-pile mohair roller, run it up and down in a series of parallel lines, then across them at right angles. Don't let the roller skid—this wipes off the color instead of texturing it. Make light vertical passes over the glaze to remove any lines.

PAINT EFFECTS: RAGGING

One way to create a broken color effect is ragging, which produces a coarser look than sponging. This simple technique involves brushing a colored glaze onto the base coat, then lifting it off by pressing a crumpled ball of clean fabric against the surface in overlapping dabs.

The effect you achieve depends on how tightly the fabric is crumpled and on its absorbency. Natural fabrics absorb more paint then synthetic ones. It is easier to rag a wall or ceiling as a two-person team, with one person applying the glaze as the other one follows and rags it.

For the best results when ragging, use colors in tones that are close to each other, with the darker color applied on top of the lighter one.

1 Apply the base coat: use latex paint as the base if you intend to use latex paint mixed with glaze for the top coat, or use alkyd paint if you're using a tinted oil glaze (see step 1, facing page). Let it dry, then brush the color coat evenly over the base coat.

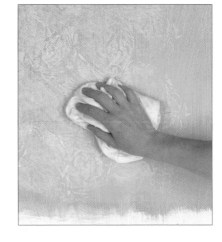

2 Crumple up a square of clean, lint-free fabric and gently press it against the wet color to lift some of it off. Move to the next section of wall, carefully blending the two areas together.

3 Keep dabbing until the fabric is covered with glaze; refold it to expose clean material. When the fabric is saturated with glaze, replace it with a new piece. If using oil-base mixes, to avoid spontaneous combustion, lay out the used fabric until it dries before discarding.

4 Continue to brush on the paint and dab it off until you reach the end of the wall. At a corner, apply the glaze by pulling the brush away from the edge to prevent a buildup of the glaze.

PAINT EFFECTS: RAG-ROLLING

YOU WILL NEED

Paint bucket for glaze
4-inch- (100-mm-) wide
paint brush
Small paint brush
Paint roller
Rags **or** paper towels
Clean, lint-free fabric

MATERIALS

Flat latex paint **or** alkyd
paint for the base coat
Flat latex paint for the color
coat and water-base glaze
or flat alkyd paint,
proprietary oil glaze, and
universal oil pigments such
as artist's oil colors

SEE ALSO

Painting basics pp.114–115
Using paint rollers
pp.118–119

A variation on ragging, rag-rolling uses additional—but still easy—techniques to create subtle differences in the final look. The glaze is stippled before the fabric is used to lift off the top color and the crumpled fabric is rolled over the surface instead of simply being dabbed against it.

Because the glaze usually dries quickly, there is a case for assembling a team—one person to apply the glaze and one to do the rag-rolling. When buying the materials make sure you purchase compatible products. You should never mix oil-base and water-base paints and glazes.

Create a random pattern by rolling the fabric across the surface in various directions or a blurry striped look by rolling the fabric down the wall.

1 Apply the base coat (see step 1, facing page). For a top coat, mix together the products using a small brush. Use four parts of latex paint for every one part of glaze. For an oil-base glaze, add the artist's oil colors a little at a time until the glaze is the desired color.

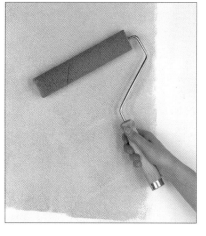

2 Stipple the surface using a paint roller with a short-pile mohair cover. Work in an area of no more than 10 square feet (1 sq m) at a time. Remove paint buildup from the cover by wiping it on clean, absorbent rags or paper towels.

3 Crumple the fabric into a cylindrical shape. If you want to make vertical stripes, roll the fabric up the wall as if you were using a rolling pin. Try to keep the stripes parallel and slightly overlapping each other.

4 For a random effect, roll the rag in different directions, refolding it from time to time. When the fabric is saturated, replace it with fresh material. If you are using oil-base mixes, to avoid spontaneous combustion, lay out the used fabric until it dries before discarding.

PAINT EFFECTS: STENCILING

YOU WILL NEED

Stenciling

Stencils (bought or
home-made)
Low-tack masking tape **or**
aerosol spray adhesive
Spirit level
Tape measure
Pencil
Stencil brush
Throwaway plastic **or**
paper palettes
Paper towels

Using a stamp

Stamp **or** artificial sponge
Small paint roller
Scrap paper

MATERIALS

Artist's acrylic tube paint
Water

SEE ALSO

Painting basics pp.114–115
Painting and stenciling
floorboards pp.184–185

*Stenciling brings both color
and pattern to walls. An
overall decorative effect can
be created by making a
border around a room at
ceiling level. You can also
use stencils in a grid pattern
or randomly.*

Atemplate, or stencil, can be used to transfer a pattern to your walls. Simply place the stencil onto the surface, apply paint through it to create the first section of the pattern, then reposition it and repeat the operation. More complex patterns may require the use of two or more colors or separate stencil sheets. Take care to keep the colors in register. To help reposition them, most stencils have registration marks on them or parts of the pattern are repeated.

The best paint to use for stenciling is artist's acrylic paint, which is quick-drying and available in a huge range of colors. Satin-gloss alkyd is the best surface for stenciling on because it allows you to easily wipe off any mistakes. You can also stencil over paint effects such as colorwashing (see p.122) or ragging (see p.126).

1 For a horizontal design, such as a frieze or border, use a spirit level to find a horizontal guide line, and make light pencil marks along the wall. If there is a chair or picture rail in place, you can use that as the guide. If the ceiling is uneven, lower the pattern so that the fault is less obvious.

2 Measure the length of your pattern and plan its spacing from wall to wall. Start over a focal point of the room and work toward the corners. Some stencils can be turned around corners. Others are best planned to end at the corner by slightly adjusting the spacing between each repeat. Make light registration marks with a pencil.

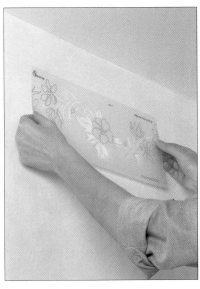

3 Position the stencil on the wall, carefully aligning it with the guide lines. To hold it in place, use low-tack masking tape or an aerosol adhesive sprayed on the back. When pressed in place with the spray, there is less chance of paint seeping under the stencil, and the stencil will easily peel off so you can reposition it.

4 Take a small amount of paint from your palette onto your stencilling brush, and dab the bristles onto clean paper until you get a smooth, even color; a little paint will go a long way. Start filling in each area of the stencil with a gentle, stabbing motion. To create highlights, add a lighter color.

5 Peel the stencil away from the wall and reposition it, carefully aligning it with the guidelines and any registration marks. Paint through it again to create the next pattern repeat. Wipe the stencil clean with paper towels whenever the paint builds up.

6 If you are using two or more colors, complete one color application and allow it to dry before going back and repositioning the stencil to apply the second color. To avoid getting one color of paint into an area planned as another color, you can use low-tack masking tape on the stencil to block out the area.

USING A STAMP

Instead of a stencil you can use a stamp to apply a random or regular pattern onto a wall. You can use a store-bought rubber stamp, or make your own to match patterns already in the room.

Use an artificial sponge to make a stamp with a simple pattern; cut out the shapes with a craft knife, leaving the area to be colored raised. To make a more intricate pattern, you can purchase linoleum from an arts and crafts shop, along with a carving tool to cut out the pattern.

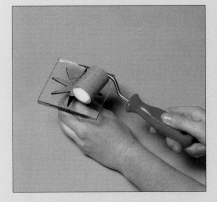

Use a small roller to spread the paint as evenly as possible, completely covering the raised area of the stamp.

Before applying the stamp to the wall, use it on scrap paper to get used to the amount of paint and pressure needed.

WALLCOVERING OPTIONS

POSSIBLE MATERIALS

VINYL
WALLPAPERS

LINCRUSTA
EMBOSSED
WALLPAPER

FLOCKED
WALLCOVERING

TEXTURED
WALLPAPER

JUTE
WALLCOVERING

SILK FABRIC
WALLCOVERING

BLOWN EMBOSSED
VINYL COVERING

LINING PAPER

WOODCHIP
PAPER

BORDERS AND FRIEZES

Wallpapers, or more accurately wallcoverings—they are not all paper-based—have two advantages that paint can't provide: they can cover walls and ceilings in a regular pattern or design, and they can provide a surface texture. The finished effect may be purely decorative, but it can offer practical benefits, too; for example, it may be hard-wearing and easy to clean. Decorating with wallpaper is not difficult once you have mastered the basic techniques, and it is a relatively quick decorating option. If you are a beginner, you should buy a prepasted wallpaper, and remember that some patterns are difficult to match and inexpensive paper has a tendency to tear.

▶ Floral wallpaper has a rustic and old-fashioned charm, which is completely in keeping with the style of this room. When restoring an old house, such wallpapers will help you recreate the look instantly.

▼ Borders and friezes are usually hung at chair rail or picture rail level, but they can also be used elsewhere to great effect. Here, a border makes a feature of an otherwise simple baseboard.

▶ In high-traffic areas, such as a kitchen or hallway, use a hard-wearing, washable vinyl paper.

▲ Narrow areas are better in plain wallpapers, perhaps with a simple, small pattern—a strong pattern can be tiring on the eyes. You can limit the use of the paper to below a chair rail.

▶ You can use wallpaper to create an illusion of space. Stripes can provide a feeling of height and spaciousness in a small room.

▶ Wallpaper designs come in a range of patterns and textures, including paint effects. Paste up an instant rag-rolled effect or, as used here, a striped colorwash effect.

▶ Wallpaper will cover any multitude of cracks in poorly finished walls and ceilings, making it an invaluable resource for decorating older houses. Alternatively, you can hang lining paper and paint over it.

◀ There is a wide variety of wallpaper designs available, including plain colors (white is popular) with embossed patterns.

WALLPAPER BASICS

YOU WILL NEED

Tape measure
Bucket
Wooden stick (for mixing)
Dust cloth
Wallpaper brush
Pencil

MATERIALS

Trisodium phosphate (TSP)
or strong detergent
Primer/sealer
Size (if required)
Roll of wallpaper

SEE ALSO

Stripping old wallpaper
pp.26–27
Washing down and
preparing surfaces pp.30–31
Interior design tricks
pp.110–111
Painting basics pp.114–115
Wallcovering options
pp.130–131
Cutting, pasting, and folding
wallpaper pp.134–135

There are preliminary stages you have to go through before you can start to paper a room. The first is to choose your wallpaper—a process that will be influenced by personal taste, but also by practical factors such as the need for a stain-resistant surface or a textured finish to disguise imperfections in the walls.

WALLPAPER PATTERNS

As well as looking for a pattern you like in the wallpaper you want, you should also consider how the pattern will line up between lengths; this may be important in estimating quantities. Unless the paper has a plain striped or randomly colored design, there will be a motif that is printed over and over again across and down the roll. The vertical distance between successive motifs is called the pattern repeat. It may be as small as 2 inches (50 mm) or as large as 12 inches (300 mm), or even more if the motif is really big.

The horizontal distance between motifs affects the way edge-to-edge pattern matches between lengths of paper are made. Some patterns will line up straight across, but others will require the lowering, or dropping, of one of the lengths to line up the pattern. If the pattern repeat is large, this can waste paper—you may have to trim off more than a narrow strip.

PLANNING AHEAD

Measure your floor-to-ceiling height, and check that you'll get four lengths out of each standard 33 foot (10 m) roll of paper (see box). If in doubt to the amount, order an extra roll.

Hang wallpaper on bare or painted plaster or plasterboard, never over old wallcovering. Unless there is a major feature in the room, start papering in the least obtrusive corner or next to the door; this will help to hide any problems with the pattern match when the last length hung meets the first.

PATTERN REPEATS
If a number of motifs repeats across a single width of wallpaper, there will be matching halves of the motif at opposite edges—these wallpapers have a straight pattern match. If a number of motifs repeats over two widths of the paper, the matching halves of the motif at opposite edges of each length will be offset by half the pattern repeat—such papers have an offset or drop pattern match.

ESTIMATING QUANTITIES

Measure the perimeter of the room and multiply it by the height to get the square feet of the room. Divide the measurement by the square feet on the label of the wallpaper to determine how many rolls you need. Subtract half a roll for each standard-size door or window. If the paper has a large pattern repeat, you'll need additional rolls. Add an extra roll for wastage to your final estimate. For ceilings, measure the length of one strip and count how many strips you need. Calculate how many strips you can cut from a 33 feet (10 m) roll to work out how many rolls you need.

Measurements around the room

Wall height	feet / meters	30 / 9	33 / 10	36 / 11	39 / 12	43 / 13	46 / 14	49 / 15	52 / 16	56 / 17	59 / 18	62 / 19	66 / 20
6 ft 6½ in to 7 ft 2 in (2.0 m to 2.2 m)		4	4	5	5	5	6	6	6	6	7	7	8
7 ft 2 in to 7 ft 10½ in (2.2 m to 2.4 m)		4	4	5	5	6	6	6	7	7	8	8	9
7 ft 10½ in to 8 ft 6 in (2.4 m to 2.6 m)		4	5	5	6	6	7	7	8	8	9	9	10
8 ft 6 in to 9 ft 2 in (2.6 m to 2.8 m)		5	5	6	6	7	7	8	8	9	9	10	11
9 ft 2 in to 9 ft 10 in (2.8 m to 3.0 m)		5	5	6	7	7	8	8	9	9	10	11	12

The table above is a guide to the number of rolls required for wallpaper that has a straight pattern match. For widths other than 20½ inches, see the pattern book.

1 Painted surfaces need no special preparation apart from washing down with a strong detergent or, preferably, trisodium phosphate (TSP). The porous surface of a bare plaster wall must be sealed and/or coated with size; mix the size according to the manufacturer's directions.

2 Apply a coat of size to the walls with a wallpaper brush. Without sizing, it will be difficult to slip the lengths of paper across the surface and match up the pattern as you hang them. Let the size dry before you start papering.

3 Mark where to start hanging the paper. If the room has a chimney breast or other prominent feature and the paper has a large motif, center the first length on the feature, then work outward around the room in both directions. Otherwise, start in a corner or inconspicuous area.

4 After deciding where to begin hanging, use a roll of wallpaper as a gauge to mark successive widths on the walls around the room. This will reveal any seams that will fall in odd places—for example, near outside corners. If necessary, alter your starting point slightly to avoid any problems.

CUTTING, PASTING, AND FOLDING WALLPAPER

YOU WILL NEED

Cutting, pasting, and folding wallpaper
Paste bucket and brush (for mixing)
Tape measure
Pencil
Pasting table
Paperhanging scissors
Pasting brush
Cloth

Prepasted wallpaper
Water tray
Tape measure
Pencil
Paperhanging scissors

MATERIALS

Cutting, pasting, and folding wallpaper
Wallpaper
Paste (powder **or** premixed)

Prepasted wallpaper
Wallpaper

SEE ALSO

Wallpaper basics pp.132–133
Hanging and trimming wallpaper pp.136–137

The type of wallpaper you choose and the shape of your room will determine how easy—or difficult—it will be to hang wallpaper. If you have not hung wallpaper before, choose a wallpaper with a random pattern match (or no match at all) so you can concentrate on perfecting your hanging technique without the added complication of coping with matching a pattern (see pp.132–133). Prepasted papers are also easier to hang.

Before beginning the job, decide which way up the pattern should hang (manufacturers usually place the TOP at the end of the roll), then mark the paper to keep the pattern the right way up. Placing pasted paper on a wall only to find that it is upside down can be frustrating and messy.

Make sure you buy enough rolls for the job (see pp.132–133) and that the labels all have the same batch number. This will ensure that there are no slight color variations between rolls.

SELECTING THE PASTE

An important point to check before buying a paste is whether you need one containing a fungicide. It is essential for impervious materials, such as washable and vinyl wallpapers, to prevent mold growing in the paste as it dries out. You should also use a paste with fungicide where you've had a problem with mold (see pp.12–13).

Read the instructions on the wallpaper label to find out what type of paste it needs. Powder pastes state on the container how many rolls they will hang. If you are using a premixed tub paste, expect ¾ quart (a liter) to hang about three rolls.

Helpful hints

After establishing the standard length to which you should cut your paper, subtract the length of your pasting table; then mark the leftover measurement on the table. You can now use the table as a gauge for marking standard lengths on the paper; for a pattern repeat, first match the pattern and mark it on the top.

1 If you are using powder paste, add it slowly to the required volume of water in your paste bucket, stirring continuously to prevent lumps from forming. Then let it stand and thicken for the time suggested on the package. The paste should be usable for about a week. (Liquid pastes are lump-free.)

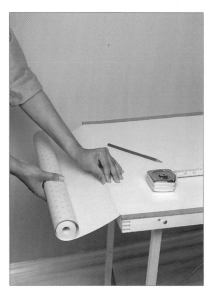

2 Measure the wall height and add 4 inches (100 mm) to allow for trimming at the top and bottom. Unroll the wallpaper and mark the length. Fold the paper at the mark, using the edge of the table to make a crease. Write TOP on the back of the length as a reminder, then cut along the fold line.

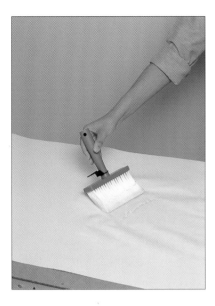

3 Position the paper so that one end and edge slightly overlap the end and near side of the table. Start applying paste to the center of the length, then brush it out toward the end and edge of the paper.

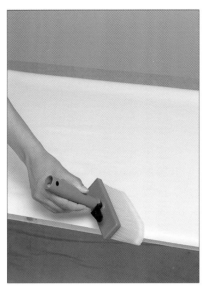

4 Move the paper over so its other edge is aligned with the far side of the table, and brush the paste out to that edge. This technique ensures that the edges are completely pasted without getting paste on the table and, in turn, onto the face of the wallpaper. If you do get paste on the table, remove it with a damp cloth.

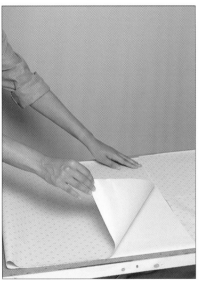

5 Fold in the pasted end of the length so that the pasted areas are against each other, and slide the length along the table so you can paste the rest of the length as described in steps 3 and 4. When you have finished pasting the length, fold in this end, too.

6 You're now ready to pick up the length and drape it over your arm to carry it to the wall where you intend to hang it. However, if it is a heavy paper, it will need time to soak; in this case, put it aside and paste another length.

PREPASTED WALLPAPER

If you have selected a washable or vinyl wallpaper that is prepasted, you can dispense with the traditional pasting equipment. All you need is a polystyrene tray, which you fill with cold water and place at the base of the wall where the length is to be hung.

Prepasted papers may begin to dry out at edges and seams if the length being hung needs detailed cutting and fitting. Mix up a small quantity of ordinary paste so you can paste down these edges.

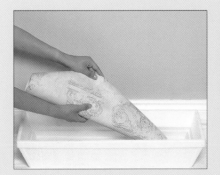

Cut the paper to length, plus a trimming allowance, and roll it up with the pattern side and the top end outermost. Immerse it in the tray and let it soak for the time suggested on the label.

Grip the top edge of the roll, and draw it up the wall toward the ceiling. Excess water will run into the tray as the roll unwinds. Position, hang, and trim the paper in the same way as other types.

HANGING AND TRIMMING WALLPAPER

The most important factor in getting a professional-looking result is the hanging technique. Wherever you have decided to hang the first length of wallpaper in a room, it is essential that you align it with a plumbed vertical line. Room corners are never perfectly vertical, and relying on one as a positioning guide can result in serious problems with your wallpaper pattern as you hang successive lengths. Stripes will not be truly vertical, and horizontal pattern motifs will begin to travel uphill, with very disconcerting effects at the ceiling and baseboards.

BEFORE YOU START

Speed is of the essence for the best results, because the paste can dry out quickly and cause adhesion problems along the seams and cuts. On painted walls, there will be excess paste that will need wiping away. Make sure you have at hand all the tools you need—

ideally, in a decorator's apron tied around your waist.

Because you will have to be able to reach the ceiling, make sure you have a stepladder readily at hand. Clear the area around the walls of any obstructions to make moving the stepladder a less cumbersome task, and remember the rules of ladder safety (see pp.114–115).

It is usually easier to work clockwise around the room if you are right-handed, and counterclockwise if you are left-handed, so select your starting point accordingly.

Helpful hints

If the first length bubbles, increase the soaking time of additional lengths. If you find a bubble after the paste has dried, make an X-shape incision, using a craft knife. Brush paste onto the underside of the paper and the wall surface, then press the paper in place and hold it for a few minutes. Wipe away any squeezed-out paste with a damp sponge, and smooth the area with a seam roller.

1 If you are starting work in a corner, draw your first plumb line on the wall about 1 inch (25 mm) less than the width of the wallpaper from the corner. This allows a small amount of paper to be turned into the inside angle. Hold the line and make two or three pencil marks down the wall to indicate the vertical.

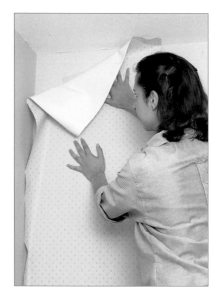

2 Carry the folded length of paper to the wall, climb onto your stool or ladder, and unfold the top end of the length so you can position it against the wall. First slide it upward and allow about 2 inches (50 mm) of wallpaper to overlap onto the ceiling, then move it sideways so the edge of the paper lines up with the plumbed line.

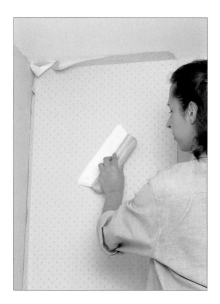

3 Use a paperhanging brush to smooth the top half of the length onto the wall surface, working from the top downward and from the center toward the edges to brush out any bubbles. Then allow the rest of the length to unfold down the wall and continue brushing it into place. Press the paper well into the corner.

4 Press the back of the blade of your paperhanging scissors between the wall and ceiling, and draw the tool along to mark the paper. Peel the paper away from the wall and cut along the marked line. Discard the waste and brush the trimmed end back into place. Repeat the process to trim the wallpaper at the baseboard.

5 Paste and fold the next length of paper, and bring it to the wall. Open the top fold as before, press it against the wall surface, and align the pattern with that on the first length. Then brush the length into place and trim at the top and bottom as in steps 3 and 4. Wipe away any stray paste while it is still wet, using a damp cloth.

6 Unless you are hanging an embossed wallpaper, use a seam roller to ensure good adhesion of the edges to the wall. If a seam has dried out and is lifting, raise the seam and brush a little fresh paste behind the wallpaper with an artist's paintbrush. Then roll the seam flat again and wipe off any excess adhesive.

HANGING LINING PAPER

Lining paper provides a smooth surface of even porosity when hanging wallpaper onto less-than-perfect wall surfaces. It can also be used on ceilings, and it can be covered with paint instead of wallpaper.

Hang the lining paper horizontally, with neat seams butting between lengths, using the same type of paste as for decorative wallpaper. Cut the lengths long enough to reach from one room corner to the next, and start hanging at the top edge of the walls.

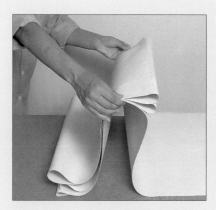

After cutting a length of lining paper and pasting it, fold it accordian fashion to make carrying and hanging it easier.

Brush the length out across the wall surface fold by fold. Repeat for each subsequent strip.

PAPERING AROUND CORNERS

YOU WILL NEED

Papering around corners
Plumb bob and string line, pencil, and straightedge **or** chalk line
Step stool **or** low stepladder
Paperhanging brush
Paperhanging scissors
Seam roller

Double corners
See above

MATERIALS

Papering around corners
Wallpaper
Paste (powder **or** premixed)
Vinyl overlap adhesive (if required)

Double corners
See above

SEE ALSO

Wallpaper basics
pp.132–133
Cutting, pasting, and folding wallpaper pp.134–135
Hanging and trimming wallpaper pp.136–137
Papering around doors and windows pp.140–141
Papering around obstacles pp.142–143
Papering a ceiling pp.144–145

A hallway is an ideal location for a washable wallpaper. It brings color and pattern to a confined area, and it is easy to clean off smudgy fingerprints.

the wallpaper around inside corners, as well as around outside corners in rooms containing chimney breasts or other projecting features.

Room corners are seldom truly square, so if you turn a length of paper from one wall onto the adjacent wall, the edge of the turned section will no longer be truly vertical. If this edge is used as a guide for hanging subsequent lengths of wallpaper, none of them will be true across the next wall. The solution is to draw a fresh plumbed line on each wall.

Helpful hints

If you're planning to hang a paper with vertical stripes or any other strong vertical design, hold a plumb bob and line to the wall at each inside and outside angle to see if the wall corners are true. If any are not within ¼ inch (6 mm) of being true, change your choice to a design without a vertical element.

I f you are hanging a wallcovering as a decorative feature on just one wall of a room, you won't have to tackle any corners. But most people paper an entire room, and so will have to take

1 After hanging the last full length before an inside corner, measure the distance from the edge of the paper to the angle at the top, center, and bottom of the wall. Add 1 inch (25 mm) to the largest of the measurements; cut a strip of paper to this width, making sure its machine-cut edge will butt the piece on the wall.

2 Paste the cut-to-size strip and hang it, butting its machine-cut edges of the two lengths snugly together. Use a paperhanging brush to tuck the hand-cut edge of the strip well into the inside angle. (Save the leftover part of the length.)

3 If the turned section of paper creases because the corner is not true, make release cuts in a vinyl paper or release tears in a standard wallpaper to allow the paper to lie flat.

4 Measure the width of the leftover length that was put aside, and mark a plumbed line on the next wall that distance from the inside angle. Paste and hang the strip with its machine-cut edge aligned with the plumbed line, and brush its hand-cut edge into the angle so it overlaps the turned section.

5 At an outside corner, use a similar technique to steps 1 and 2 to turn about 1 inch (25 mm) of paper around the angle and onto the adjacent wall. Again, make release cuts or tears, if necessary, to allow the turned section to lie flat.

6 Mark a plumbed line on the second wall, and hang the saved leftover length to the line so that its hand-cut edge overlaps the turned section, as in step 4. If you are hanging a vinyl paper, you'll need a special vinyl overlap adhesive to adhere the overlapping layers together at outside and inside corners.

DOUBLE CORNERS

If you have a boxed-in pipe or a projection where a dividing wall was removed, you may have to turn the same length of wallpaper around both inside and outside corners. This is best avoided; even if one corner is true, the next one is unlikely to be. Approach the first inside angle as for a room corner, and treat the last one in the same way. "Feathering" (see far right) the edge of the bottom-layer paper makes it less noticeable through the top paper.

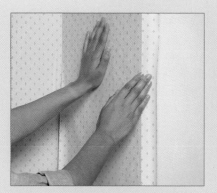

Cut a strip wide enough to cover the section of wall leading to the first out-side corner, plus 1 inch (25 mm) extra. Align the pattern at the outside angle.

Let 1 inch (25 mm) of the strip turn onto the next wall, and tear it along the edge. Hang additional strips in this way until you paper the whole projection.

PAPERING AROUND DOORS AND WINDOWS

Careful planning is the key to successful papering around doors and windows. It is difficult to match short lengths of paper both above and below a window to the next full length of paper. First paper above the window, where any misalignments would be more noticeable, then hang the full-length strip next to it and, finally, hand the short lengths below the window.

Papering around a doorway poses new problems, and papering the recess around a window (known as the reveal) can be awkward. Adjust the starting point to avoid narrow strips alongside the door and to avoid edges falling at the corners of the window.

You'll be trimming your wallpaper to fit against the window frame or the casing around a doorway, but gaps often open up along these angles. To get the best possible finish for your redecorating, take time to fill and paint these gaps before papering. Rake out any loose material and fill the joints with paintable, flexible acrylic caulk, using a cartridge gun. Then paint the casing or window frame, taking the paint over the caulk and onto the wall.

1 If the door is in a corner, you can have a pattern misalignment in that corner without it being noticed. If it is away from a corner, the pattern should continue over and past it. Regardless of the arrangement, hang the last full length before the door opening, then hang the next so it overlaps the casing.

2 Press the paper against the casing until you can see the corner of the molding through it. Using wallpaper scissors, make a diagonal cut from the edge of the length to the corner of the molding.

3 Use the wallpaper scissors to press the paper into the angles between the wall and the casing, and crease the cutting lines. Peel back the wallpaper and trim off the waste, then brush the paper back into the angles.

4 Cut and hang a short piece of paper above the door, and fit the subsequent length as you did in steps 1 to 3. If it will go into a corner, cut the length to fit between the door and corner, with an additional 1 inch (25 mm) so that you can turn it onto the adjacent wall.

5 At a window reveal, hang a length so it overlaps the window reveal, and make horizontal cuts into the edge of the length to allow the flap of paper to be turned onto the side wall of the reveal. Trim its edge if it reaches the frame. Wait until you've fitted the underside of the reveal before fitting an infill strip on the side wall.

6 Cut and fit a patch for the underside of the reveal. Turn its front edge onto the above face wall by 1 inch (25 mm), tucking it beneath the paper on the face wall and the side of the reveal.

7 Trim the back of the patch, then cut and fit an infill strip, if needed, at the side section of the reveal. Continue to hang short sections above the window, folding them onto the underside of the reveal, until you reach the next full-length strip. You may find small scissors easier to use for trimming.

8 Plumb a line to hang the full-length strip at the far side of the window, and hang the length to that line. Trim the full-length piece as in step 5, and add the infill strip if needed. Complete the job by hanging short lengths below the window, adjusting them to match the full lengths on either side as best you can.

PAPERING AROUND OBSTACLES

YOU WILL NEED

Papering an arch
See *Hanging and trimming wallpaper* pp.136–137
Tape measure

Papering at a face plate
See *Hanging and trimming wallpaper* pp.136–137
Small screwdriver

Papering around fixed objects
See *Hanging and trimming wallpaper* pp.136–137
Small scissors (if required)
Sharp knife (if required)

MATERIALS

Papering an arch
Wallpaper
Paste (powder **or** premixed)

Papering at a face plate
See above

Papering around fixed objects
See above

SEE ALSO

Wallpaper basics pp.132–133
Cutting, pasting, and folding wallpaper pp.134–135
Hanging and trimming wallpaper pp.136–137
Papering around corners pp.138–139

Apart from such major features as doors and windows, every room contains its fair share of paperhanging problems—light switches, wall outlets, mantelpieces, stair newel posts, even arches in alcoves and between rooms. These can all be awkward to cope with, but there is a solution in each case. The main thing that can go wrong is the paste drying out as you take the time necessary to trim and fit the wallpaper around the obstacle concerned. However, you can get around this problem by having some paste and a small brush handy for touch ups as you work.

Arches pose particular problems as far as pattern matching is concerned. It is impossible to get a direct match between the flat and curved surfaces. The best solution is to either use a plain or randomly patterned wallpaper or to paper the curve with a plain paper that complements what you are using on the walls.

BEFORE YOU START

Always remove as many wall-mounted obstacles as possible before papering. Shelves, display cabinets and the like will be attached with screws driven into wall anchors (see pp.18–19).

If you have any wall lights, turn off their power supply at the service panel. Then unscrew them from the wall, disconnect their supply cables, and set aside. Cover the bare cable wires individually with electrician's tape before restoring the power supply. Whenever you work near a light switch, outlet, or light, always turn off the power first (see pp.18–19).

Helpful hints

If you want to paper behind a radiator, simply tuck about 6 inches (150 mm) of wallpaper down behind the top edge of the radiator, and slide the paper behind the side edges as far as you can. A slim paint roller designed to fit behind radiators is ideal for pressing the paper into position. If there is a visible gap between the radiator and the baseboard, paper that, too.

PAPERING AN ARCH

1 If you intend to paper an arch between two rooms, first tackle the walls on either side of the opening. Trim lengths so that you can turn 1 inch (25 mm) of paper onto the arch surface. Make small V-shape cuts into the overlapping paper on the curved section so the tongues lie flat.

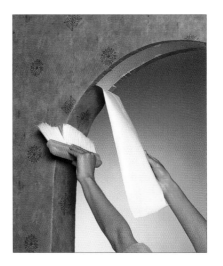

2 Cut two strips of paper to ⅛ inch (3 mm) less than the thickness of the arch. Hang each one from the bottom upward, adjusting it to match the pattern on the vertical sections. Let the two lengths overlap at the head of the arch; cut through both pieces and discard the offcuts.

PAPERING AT A FACE PLATE

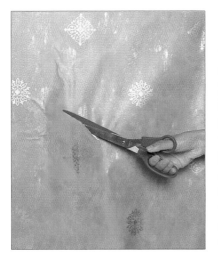

1 After turning off the power, loosen the screws holding the switch or outlet face plate to its backing box before you start papering. Paper over the face plate, then press the paper against it to mark the corners. Push scissors through the paper over the center of the face plate.

2 Make a cut to each corner of the plate, creating four triangular tongues. Trim off all but ¼ inch (6 mm) of each of the tongues. You may find small scissors easier to manipulate here.

3 Tuck the four tongues carefully behind the loosened face plate, and use a paperhanging brush to ensure that the paper lies flat and bonds well to the wall. Then tighten the mounting screws to trap the tongues in place. Once the paper has been fitted around all the switches and sockets, you can turn the power back on.

PAPERING AROUND FIXED OBJECTS

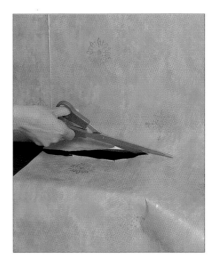

1 To paper around a fixed obstacle, such as a mantelpiece or stair newel post, start by allowing the paper to hang over the object and roughly cut it to shape.

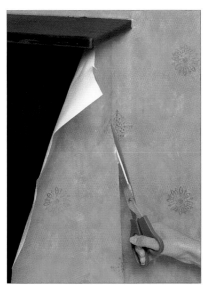

2 At intricate corners, such as at the top corner of a mantlepiece or at tight curves, use small scissors to make a succession of small release cuts into the edge of the wallpaper; this allows it to lie flat against the wall. Trim off any protruding pieces to about ¼ inch (6 mm) and continue to cut around the object.

3 You can now cut off each of the ¼ inch (6 mm) strips, using a sharp knife for vinyl or small scissors for paper; then use a wallpaper brush to press the paper snugly into place. Remember to wipe away surplus paste as you go. It is much harder to remove when dry.

PAPERING A CEILING

People paper ceilings for one of two reasons. The first is that they prefer looking up to a pattern or texture instead of the flat effect that a coat of paint creates. The second is that they want to conceal a less-than-perfect ceiling surface that may be suffering from unevenness and, on plaster, numerous hairline cracks.

You can, in theory, decorate a ceiling with any style of wallpaper; however, in practice, few people use wallpapers with patterns (especially strong ones) because they would need stripping and replacing at regular intervals to reflect changes in style or taste—and stripping old wallpaper off a ceiling is not an enjoyable job.

Papering a ceiling is not as difficult a task as it might at first appear. In fact, because ceilings have very few obstructions compared with walls, they are actually easier to decorate once you have mastered the knack of working above your head.

BEFORE YOU START

The most important consideration is to set up a proper work platform so you can reach the ceiling comfortably and move across the room on it as you work. Rental stores can offer a variety of options; staging on trestles is probably the best. Whatever you choose must be easy to reposition to allow you to hang successive lengths across the room.

Take down hanging lamps and light fixtures, making sure you first turn off the power at the service panel (see pp.18–19). Finally, treat the ceiling with a coat of sealer and/or wallpaper size if it has not been painted.

Helpful hints

Holding wallpaper while you position it on the ceiling can be a clumsy task. You have two options: either enlist a helper to support the folds of paper as you position it on the ceiling or use a roll of wallpaper still protected by its wrapper to balance the pasted folds of paper above you as you work.

1 It is easier to hang paper across the width of the room instead of along the length. Use a pencil and tape measure or a chalked line to mark a guideline across the ceiling parallel with the wall and just less than the width of the roll away from it.

2 Paste your paper (see pp.134–135) and fold it accordian fashion, then carry it to your starting point. Support the folds (or enlist a helper to do so) while you position the end of the length between the wall and ceiling and align it with the guideline. Push the paper into the corner, using your paperhanging brush.

3 Brush the rest of the length into place. Then peel back and trim the two ends and the long edge as you would with paper on the wall, and brush the trimmed edges back into place. Wipe away any surplus paste while it is wet, using a damp cloth.

4 Hang subsequent strips in the same way, butting them together at the seams and carefully matching any pattern or relief design. Except when hanging embossed papers, run a seam roller along the seams to ensure a good bond with the ceiling.

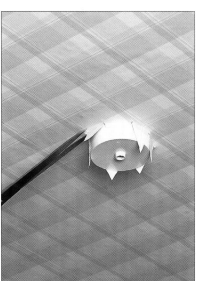

5 At a light fixture, with the power off, make a hole in the paper with the tip of your scissors, then make radial cuts out to the edge of the fixture (small scissors may be easier to use). Crease the tongues around the fixture; trim them off so they fit flush against the edge. Wipe away any squeezed out paste with a damp rag.

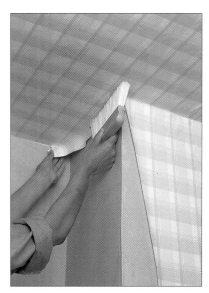

6 At a projection, let the paper hang down the wall and cut up to the ceiling. Cut off the excess, then brush and trim the paper into the angles between the ceiling and walls. To finish the ceiling, trim the final length in width before hanging it, but add 2 inches (50 mm) extra to the width to allow for trimming at the wall.

PAPERING SLOPING CEILINGS

If you want to paper a room with a sloping ceiling, you have two choices. The first is to create an artificial break at waist or head level by putting up a decorative frieze, and to paper below it and paint above it. The second is to choose a paper with an unobtrusive, random pattern, and to paper the entire room with it. Draw a guideline along the center of the ceiling and hang separate lengths from there down each roof slope.

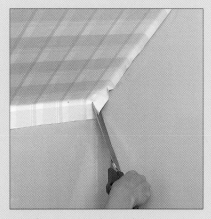

Start by papering the roof slope; make release cuts where it meets a corner.

After the ceiling is papered, hang the paper on the wall and trim it to fit.

USING FRIEZES

YOU WILL NEED

Torpedo level **or** carpenter's level
Metal straightedge rule
Pencil
Pasting brush (unless product is self-adhesive)
Paperhanging brush
Paperhanging scissors
Utility knife
Seam roller

MATERIALS

Frieze
Paste (unless product is self-adhesive)

SEE ALSO

Wallpaper basics pp.132–133
Cutting, pasting, and folding wallpaper pp.134–135

You can hang a frieze at ceiling level or in line with a horizontal feature such as a picture rail or chair rail (make sure it's the right way up). Apply it to a painted wall, or hang it over a complementary wallpaper. It comes in a range of widths in standard rolls 5 yards (15 ft) long.

You can hang a frieze (and a border, see opposite page) using ordinary wallpaper paste if you're putting it on a painted wall or over a standard printed wallpaper. However, ordinary wallpaper paste will not bond to a vinyl or washable wallpaper. If you want to apply a frieze on top of either

A band of pattern can be created by hanging a frieze around the perimeter of a room.

of these materials, you can use a suitable premixed tub adhesive or select a self-adhesive product.

1 Unless you are aligning your frieze with a feature of the room, such as the ceiling line or a picture rail, use a torpedo level balanced on a metal straight-edge (or use a carpenter's level) to draw a horizontal guideline around the room with a pencil.

2 Cut a section of frieze 4 inches (100 mm) longer than the wall on which it will be placed, paste it, fold it accordian fashion, and take it to the wall. Position it so that 2 inches (50 mm) turns around a corner, and brush it into place. Wipe away any squeezed-out paste.

3 Prepare the piece for the next wall as before, and hang it so it overlaps the turned end of the previous length. Match the pattern carefully and brush the length into place.

4 Using a utility knife and metal straightedge, cut through both lengths of frieze about 1 inch (25 mm) from the corner. Peel back the strips and remove the offcuts, then brush the ends back into position to form a neat seam.

FRAMING WITH BORDERS

YOU WILL NEED

Torpedo level **or**
carpenter's level
Metal straightedge rule
Pencil
Pasting brush (unless
product is self-adhesive)
Paperhanging brush
Paperhanging scissors
Utility knife
Seam roller

MATERIALS

Border
Paste (unless product is
self-adhesive)

SEE ALSO

Wallpaper basics
pp.132–133
Cutting, pasting, and folding
wallpaper pp.134–135

Narrower than friezes, borders are ideal for framing door and window openings, and for creating decorative display panels on a wall or ceiling surface within which a mirror or pictures can be displayed. As in the case of friezes (see opposite page), borders come in standard-size rolls.

It is a good idea to experiment with the positioning of borders (and friezes) before they are permanently in place. You can do this by attaching short lengths to the wall, using low-tack masking tape.

Decorative borders can enliven otherwise plain walls in a room—they are ideal for a nursery.

1 If you're using a border to frame a feature, draw pencil guidelines around it, using a metal straight-edge. To create a decorative panel away from a room feature, use a level to ensure true vertical and horizontal guidelines.

2 Position the first strip, letting its end overlap the adjacent guideline by about 1 inch (25 mm). Brush the strip into place and wipe away any squeezed-out paste. Position an intersecting length, using a piece of paper to avoid paste getting on the bottom piece.

3 To create a neatly mitered corner, cut through both strips, using a sharp knife and a metal straightedge. (You can use the straightedge to align the miter with a miter in the door or window frame.)

4 Peel away and discard the waste pieces, and remove the piece of paper. Roll the mitred joint flat with a seam roller. For a self-adhesive product, peel off the appropriate amount of the backing paper and position the strips as indicated for paste.

PUTTING UP CROWN MOLDING

Crown molding is fitted around a room between the walls and ceiling. It may be a plain, concave coving or an elaborately detailed cornice. Milled lumber and molded fibrous plaster are the traditional materials. Molded foam plastic is an excellent substitute for plaster—it is much lighter and easier to install.

Some types of plastic coving are put up with prefabricated corner joints, while others require cutting the corner joints during installation. To install wood molding, attach it to wall studs and ceiling joists or furring strips (see pp.164–165) with finishing nails.

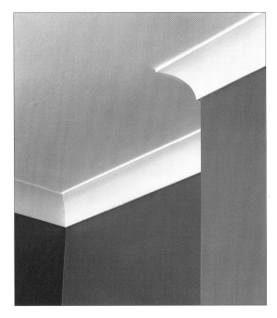

Coving frames the ceiling neatly, and it also conceals any gaps between the ceiling and the walls.

1 Pencil guidelines around the room on the walls and ceiling. Scratch the areas between the guidelines with a shavehook or pointed can opener to provide a key for the adhesive to grip. For a plaster-type coving, you must remove any wallpaper in the area.

2 Start at the left-hand end of the longest wall in the room. Cut the correct miter: the one here is for the lefthand end of an inside corner (or righthand end of an outside corner). Use the opposite angle for a righthand, inside corner (or lefthand, outside corner).

3 Apply adhesive to the rear of the molding, set it in place, and fasten it with screws or use small nails to support it temporarily. Miter and fit a length at the other end of this wall. Then fit lengths as required between the two end sections, the last one cut to size.

4 Start the next wall, butting the mitered ends together and filling the joint with adhesive. For a fireplace, cut miters on both ends and fit the coving for the back walls of the alcoves; then fit the coving along the sides of the fireplace and, finally, the front.

INSTALLING PICTURE AND CHAIR RAILS

YOU WILL NEED

Carpenter's level and pencil
Tape measure
Tenon saw
Electric drill plus twist, countersink, and masonry drill bits
Screwdriver
Coping saw
Miter box
Putty knife

MATERIALS

Picture **or** chair rail
Flathead wood screws or
Wall anchors (if required)
Finishing nails
PVA adhesive
Wood filler

SEE ALSO

Putting up coving p.148

Picture and chair, or dado rails, are wooden moldings attached to walls, the former above head height and the latter at waist height. Picture rails allow pictures to be hung without marking the walls with hooks, and they provide a visual break in rooms with high ceilings; to take the weight of the pictures, they must be installed with screws. Chair rails protect the wall from damage by furniture; install them on wallboard with finishing nails sunk below the surface with a nail set, and fill with wood putty.

Fashionable in Victorian times, picture and chair rails add authenticity to restored interiors.

1 To install picture or chair rails with screws, use wall anchors on plaster walls (see p.227) or screws driven into wall studs for wallboard. Start by drawing a horizontal pencil guideline around the room at the level you want to fit the rail.

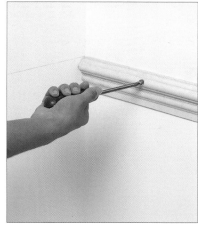

2 Drill countersink pilot holes in rails 16 inches (for studs) or 24 inches (600 mm) apart. Hold a rail with one end at an inside corner, mark the screw positions on the wall, and drill and insert the anchors, if needed. Screw the rail to the wall, with the screw heads recessed.

3 Butt joint the other lengths together until you reach the next inside corner. Trace the rail profile onto the end of the next length; cut it to shape with a coping saw. Repeat the stages in step 2 to fit it, and continue fitting the rail around the room.

4 At an outside corner, cut miters at a 45° angle on the rails, using a tenon saw and miter box. Glue and nail the joint once the lengths have been fastened to the wall; this prevents them from opening up in the future. Finally, cover the screw heads with a wood filler.

TILING OPTIONS

POSSIBLE MATERIALS

HAND-MADE TILE

TERRA-COTTA TILE

RELIEF BORDER TILE

RELIEF PATTERN TILE

STANDARD FIELD TILE

CAP RAIL BORDER TILE

ROPE TWIST BORDER TILE

BORDER TILE

PICTORIAL TILE

ROUND-EDGE TILE

MOSAIC TILES

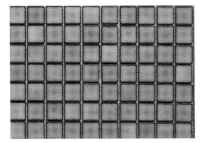

Ceramic tiles are used as a wall covering in two main areas of the home—the kitchen and the bathroom. In each case they are chosen mainly because they offer a hard-wearing and completely waterproof surface that is easy to clean. They are fastened in place with a special tile adhesive, and they can be attached to plaster, wallboard, waterproof plywood, and even old tiles. Tiles come in a wide range of plain colors and decorative patterns and are made in several standard sizes. Tiling a wall is an easy task (but perhaps a little time-consuming) once the tile layout has been properly planned. However, as a wall decorating option, it is relatively expensive.

▶ Small mosaic tiles are perfect for tiling over large areas— the lines of grout help break up the color. Avoid using dark tiles for a shower recess if you live in a hard water area; otherwise, the tiles will always appear to be covered in a white film of limescale.

◀ Half tiling—up to a height of 4 feet (1220 mm)—is an economical and stylish option for the bathroom. White tiles are usually the most economical. Finish off the upper edge of the tiled area with a row of border or edge tiles (you can use these to add some color); plastic edge trims or wood molding are other alternatives.

◀ The variety of designs and patterns available on ceramic tiles is extensive, enabling you to create your own decorative effects. Some tiles fit together to create a larger motif.

▲ Patterned tiles can be used as borders or friezes. Here, the lower, narrow border breaks up the strong color of the tiles. At the top edge, the cap rail border tiles complement the patterned border tiles between them.

▲ The total area of a kitchen backsplash is relatively small, so you can use strong colors that could be overpowering on a larger scale.

▼ You can tile more than just the walls in a bathroom—for a more unified look, tile the floor and bathtub enclosure.

◀ In kitchens, tiles are used to create a backsplash, providing a hard-wearing, easy-to-clean wall surface between the countertops and cabinets. You can combine colors to create a simple geometric pattern with the tiles. Alternatively, you can scatter patterned tiles at random across a field of plain tiles.

TILING BASICS

LAYING OUT THE TILES
*A plain wall without any
obstructions should have
cut tiles—shown below in
orange—of equal width
(left). When planning a
partially tiled wall, use
whole tiles at the top edge,
perhaps finished with a
row of dado-style profile
tiles (center). If you tile
around a window, it is best
to center the tiles around
it—this may mean that you
have to cut tiles of uneven
sizes at the ends of the
rows and columns (right).*

Tiling a wall may appear to be a straightforward job. Wall tiles are relatively small and easy to handle, and modern tile adhesives are strong enough to stick them to almost any surface. You can even buy small plastic spacers to ensure that the tiles line up accurately with each other. However, in practice, things can be a little more difficult.

PLANNING THE LAYOUT

Because ceramic tiles are a fixed size, you'll have to cut a number of tiles to complete the job. To achieve a professional look, center the whole tiles across the wall. Cut tiles of equal size to fit at each end of any horizontal row of tiles, as well as at the top and bottom of the wall-to-ceiling columns. These pieces should be between one-quarter and three-quarters of the width of the tile; anything narrower or wider is difficult to cut accurately. Because rooms are not truly square, you'll have to place all the whole tiles before you can

measure and fit each of the cut pieces. This makes planning the tile layout the most important part of the job.

Centering tiles is relatively easy on a wall with no major obstacles such as door or window openings. Introduce these obstacles, however, and things get more complex, especially at windows. Because a window is such a major feature on a wall, you'll have to center the tiles on this instead.

PREPARING THE WALLS

To allow the tile adhesive to adhere to the wall, remove any wallpaper or sand down any paint (see p.30), using coarse paper and a sanding block. You may need to strip the paint (see *Helpful hints*). Wash down the prepared wall with trisodium phosphate (TSP) or detergent. Fill any large cracks and holes; the adhesive will fill minor ones. Seal new plaster or bare wallboard with a plaster primer or latex paint. If existing tiles are sound and flat, you can tile over them after washing down the surface to remove dirt and grease.

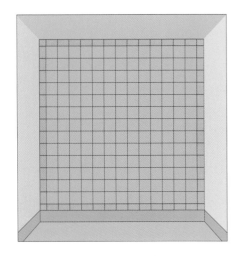

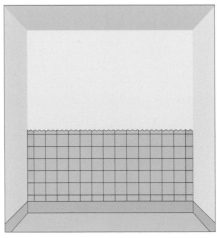

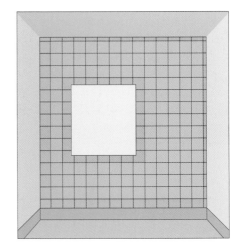

1 To plan the layout of the tiles, make a tile gauge, or story pole. Use a 3 feet (1 m) length of 1 inch x 2 inch (25 mm x 50 mm) lumber that has been planed to a true straight edge. Use several tiles—plus tile spacers to allow for the grout joints if the tiles do not have lugs (see step 4, p.155)— to mark their widths along the gauge.

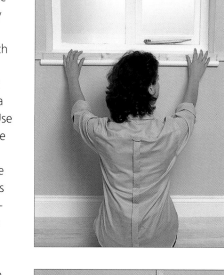

2 Hold the gauge horizontally against the bottom of the wall to work out where the whole tiles will fall. Adjust it so that the pieces at the ends will be of equal size. However, if there is a window, center the tile layout on the window opening, with cut pieces of equal size fitting at each side of the window.

3 If you center the gauge and find that you will be faced with cutting narrow pieces of tile (less than one-quarter of its width), move the gauge along by half a tile's width to increase the width of the cut tile.

4 Repeat the process in the vertical plane. This process will tell you how many tiles will be needed for each row (count cut tiles as whole tiles) and how many in each column.

ESTIMATING QUANTITIES

Once you have determined where the whole and cut tiles will be positioned on the wall, it is a simple matter to multiply the number of tiles in one column by the number of tiles in one row to find the quantity of tiles required. This total counts cut pieces as whole tiles, and you should add some extra tiles to allow for breakages. How many depends on the general scale of the job and how good you are at cutting tiles, but 5–10 percent of the total is a reasonable number. Finally, find out how many tiles come in a unit and then calculate how many units you will require for the job.

You will also need some tile adhesive (check the tubs for the wall area each will cover), plus grout to fill the gaps between the tiles.

Helpful hints

It is always wise to save a dozen or so extra tiles after the job is completed. They will be useful for replacing tiles that may have to be removed to make repairs, such as to pipes or wiring hidden in the wall behind them, or for replacing any tiles that have been drilled to install fixtures or have become damaged. (To remove a damaged tile, see p.28.)

Not all painted walls can be tiled. The best way to test the surface is to stick masking tape on an area and leave it overnight. Pull off the tape. If the paint comes off with it, the paint must be stripped (see pp.28–29)—otherwise the tiles will fall off the wall.

TILING A WALL

When you are tiling a whole wall or room, the most important thing to remember is that walls are seldom square to each other. Even apparent horizontals, such as baseboards, may not be true, so do not use them as tile guides. Instead, fix horizontal and vertical guide strips to each wall, positioned in accordance with the starting points you planned earlier with your tile gauge. However, if you are tiling above a bathtub or kitchen countertop that you know to be level, there is no need for guide strips. The first row of tiles can be fastened so they rest directly on top of the tub or counter.

For more details on tiling at corners and around doors and windows, see pp.156–157. Tiling in bathrooms and kitchens may demand using a special adhesive (see pp.158–159).

MOSAIC TILES

Sheets of small tiles stuck to a net backing or paper facing are available—these are known as mosaic tiles. The sheets allow you to apply a number of tiles at a time, without spacing each individual tile.

Mosaic tiles use the same adhesive and grout as their larger cousins. Press the sheet into the bed of adhesive, allowing grouting space between sheets. Tap the tiles in place, using a wooden mallet against a carpet-covered board. Trim the facing or backing if you need to fill areas with strips or single tiles. If there is a paper facing, wait for the adhesive to dry before soaking off the paper with a wet sponge.

1 Pre-drill holes in your horizontal guide strip to take nails. Hold the strip in place, following the marks made previously with the tile gauge, and use a carpenter's level to get the strip truly horizontal. Drive the nails in partly, leaving the heads protruding so you can pry them out later. Use masonry nails for brick or concrete walls.

2 Fit a second strip at one edge of the area to be tiled, at right angles to the horizontal strip (use the carpenter's level), to act as a vertical guide to the edge column of tiles. Attach horizontal and vertical strips to other walls being tiled.

3 Scoop out some tile adhesive and spread a band of it on the wall, a little wider than the height of the first row of tiles, starting at the lower corner created by the strips. Press the teeth of the spreader firmly against the wall to leave ridges of adhesive that are of equal height.

4 Rest the edge of the first tile on the horizontal strip, align it with the vertical one, and press it into the adhesive. Working horizontally, press the next tile into place. Butt together tiles that have spacing lugs; use plastic tile spacers for square-edge tiles. Continue the process until all the whole tiles are in place.

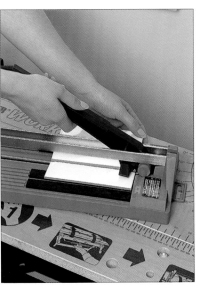

5 Let the adhesive harden for at least four hours, then pry off the vertical strips. Measure each edge tile individually for cutting, using a grease pencil to make your markings. You will get the best results (and the fewest breakages) if you use a platform-style tile cutter instead of a handheld pencil-point tile cutter.

6 After cutting a tile, set it into place by spreading the adhesive on the back of the tile instead of on the wall. Continue cutting and setting each edge tile, one at a time.

7 After completing the edge tiles up the sides of the wall, remove the horizontal strips and tile along the bottom edge. To fit a tile into a corner, you may have to cut it both horizontally and vertically. Once the adhesive on the edge tiles has set, you can finish off with grout and any sealant (see pp.160–161).

Helpful hints

Notched adhesive spreaders apply an even coat of adhesive. However, if a section of the wall is slightly undulating, the tiles may not lie flat. As you work, use a carpenter's level laid across the faces of several tiles to make sure they are flush with each other. If one is protruding, gently push against it until it is flush.

Wipe off any adhesive that gets onto the face of the tile while it is still wet—the adhesive will be difficult to remove once it has dried.

TILING AT CORNERS, WINDOWS, AND DOORS

If you are tiling adjacent walls or a whole room, you will have to tile at inside and, possibly, outside corners. Because corners are seldom straight or true, tile each wall by itself, working from the horizontal guide strips. Take particular care in setting the levels of the horizontal guide strips on adjacent walls so that they are level with each other. If they are fractionally out of alignment, the tile columns will run out of true as you work, and if you are tiling to ceiling level, the tile rows will not align where they meet above the door.

When tiling around a window recess, tile the face of the wall with whole tiles first, then the cut tiles, the sides of the recess, and the sill. If the door to the room is in the center of a wall and you are tiling to ceiling level, center the tile layout on the wall as best you can to avoid narrow cut pieces beside the door and at the room corners. If the door is in the corner of the room,

Finishing a window recess with tiles will help it blend in with a wall tiled from ceiling to floor.

set out the two walls as usual, then cut tiles in the area above the door to complete floor-to-ceiling tiling. A window is shown being tiled here, but the principles also apply to a door.

1 If you are tiling to ceiling level, place all the whole tiles up to the window, but not over the window. Fasten a strip to the wall, with its top edge aligned with the bottom edge of the lowest row of whole tiles above the height of the window. The strip supports the whole tiles applied above the window.

2 Position the cut tiles around the window. Start near the sill, where you may have to make an L-shape cut (see step 3) or use tile nippers (see step 5) to fit the tile around the sill. Make sure you plan the tile layout ahead of time to avoid making difficult cuts (see pp.152–153).

3 To cut an L shape, mark cutting lines on the tile face with a grease pencil. Clamp the tile between scrap wood (or the wooden jaws of a work station) to cut the first line with a tile saw or a carbide rod in a hack saw. (To stop a thin tile from breaking, clamp it horizontally.) Score and snap the second cut; smooth the edges with a tile file.

4 Wait for the adhesive to set before removing the strip at the top of the window and fitting the remaining tiles on the wall. You may have to cut L-shape tiles to fit at the corners. Make sure you plan ahead to avoid thin strips that can easily break as you make the cuts.

5 If you have to trim off only a thin strip, make a score mark with a tile cutter, then nibble away the waste area with tile nippers. Finish off by using a tile file to smooth the cut. (You can also use tile nippers to make a curved edge if you score the tile with a handheld pencil-point tile cutter.)

6 Place all the whole tiles inside the window recess. If the tiles do not have spacing lugs, make sure you use tile spacers between the bottom tiles and window sill to allow for a grouting gap.

7 Finally, measure and cut each individual tile to fill in the back of the window recess. Once the adhesive dries, after about 4 hours, you can finish off by grouting (see pp.160–161).

Helpful hints

For an inside corner, cut and fit each of the tiles in the last column on one wall so that they run to the corner. Then fit the last column of tiles for the second wall, using tile spacers to leave a grouting gap in the angle between the two columns.

At an outside corner, place whole tiles on each side of the angle. If the tiles you are using have fully glazed edges, let the tiles on the most prominent wall overlap the others; otherwise, use a plastic corner trim embedded in tile adhesive.

TILING IN BATHROOMS AND KITCHENS

YOU WILL NEED

Tape measure and grease pencil
Straightedge
Levels (topedo and carpenter's)
Furring strips and box **or** masonry nails
Hammer
Flexible putty knife
Notched adhesive spreader
Tile spacers (if required)
Tile cutter
Work surface plus clamps and scrap wood
Tile saw **or** hacksaw plus carbide rod
Tile file
Profile gauge

MATERIALS

Tiles
Waterproof tile adhesive
Tile edge trim **or** border tiles

SEE ALSO

Tiling basics pp.152–153
Tiling a wall pp.154–155
Tiling at corners, windows, and doors pp.156–157
Grouting and sealing pp.160–161

A small area of tiles makes an ideal waterproof backsplash around a washbasin, even if the rest of the room is decorated in another finish.

Ceramic tiles are perfect for areas in the bathroom and kitchen that require protection from water. You can use them to create a backsplash behind a washbasin, bathtub, or kitchen countertop. They provide a waterproof finish for the solid walls of a shower stall, but all corners and joints with other materials must be completely

waterproof. You can also tile the paneling around the bathtub.

Tiling a backsplash for a countertop or bathtub is simple. It should be at least 24 inches (600 mm) high to protect the wall from moisture. For a bathtub, place whole tiles at the outer edges of the backsplash, aligned with the edge of the tub, and fit cut tiles in the internal angles. To tile a shower stall, apply the adhesive to the walls and set the bottom row of tiles so they overlap the edges of the shower tray.

Treat a bathtub panel as you would any tiled area, centering tiles if you are fitting only the panel along the side of the tub. Fit the tiles so their top edges are beneath the rim of the tub. To fit both a side panel and end panel, place whole tiles on each side of the outside angle and fit cut tiles in the inside angles where the panels meet the walls.

1 A backsplash around a basin can be as narrow as the basin itself or can extend by one or two tiles at each side of the basin. Center the tiles behind the basin, using a tiling gauge to determine the layout of the tiles. Use a torpedo level to mark the center of the lay-out and a carpenter's level to find a true horizontal line.

2 If the tiles extend beyond the basin, attach a furring strip with its top edge flush with the top of the basin. If the tile will be close to the edges of the tiled area, put the adhesive on the back of the tile to avoid getting it onto untiled areas; then use the notched spreader to spread it evenly. In larger areas, apply the adhesive to the wall.

3 Begin by applying the first row of tiles above the basin, starting from the center and working toward the edges. Depending on the size of the tiles, you should have at least one or two rows to make a backsplash roughly 12 inches (300 mm) high.

4 To fit tiles around the curve of the basin, use a profile gauge to transfer the shape to the tiles. Clamp the tile flat on a work surface and use a tile saw to make the cut; then use a tile file to smooth the cut edge. Continue applying the tiles, using a furring strip to keep them vertically aligned at the edges.

5 To add border tiles around the backsplash, center them along the top. After applying the last whole tile, measure and mark a tile to make a miter corner— remember that the top of the miter should extend beyond the tiled area. Clamp the tile to a work surface; cut it with a tile saw or hacksaw fitted with a carbide rod.

6 Test-fit the second mitered tile before applying the adhesive to the back of the tile. You may have to use a tile file to help the fit of the joint. Finish applying the last of the border tiles, and wait for the adhesive to dry before adding the grout and sealant (see pp.160–161).

Helpful hints

To tile a bathtub panel, replace the plastic panel with exterior-grade plywood on a strong wood framework. Clamp a furring strip below the tub rim, then fasten a strip to the floor, directly below the top strip. Cut vertical posts to fit between the two strips, set them at intervals of 18 inches (460 mm) and drive screws through them into the horizontal strips. Cut plywood panels to size and nail in place, then tile them. To reach plumbing for a whirlpool, tile the panels before attaching them to the frame with round-head screws (to drill a hole in a tile for a screw, see right).

MAKING HOLES IN TILES

To tile around the water supply pipes for a bathtub or shower, turn off the water valves and remove the handles. Center the tiles at the pipes; use tile nippers to cut away semicircles to fit around them.

To drill a hole in a tile (for example, to install a towel rack), use a masonry bit. Mark the position for the hole with a grease pencil, then cover it with clear tape to prevent the bit from slipping.

GROUTING AND SEALING

YOU WILL NEED

Grout spreader
Grout finisher **or** dowel
Bucket
Sponge
Caulking gun (for cartridge-type silicone sealant)
Utility knife
Clean, lint-free cloth

MATERIALS

Grout
Silicone sealant

SEE ALSO

Tiling a wall pp.154–155

An area of ceramic tiles is not waterproof until the gaps between the tiles have been filled—a process known as grouting. You can buy grout in powder form or as a ready-mixed product. Most people choose white grout; however, colored grout is also available and you can create a striking look by using grout in a bright color against white or mainly white tiles.

SEALANTS

Where an area of tiles meets another surface, such as a bathtub, shower stall, or kitchen countertop, there is always a risk of water penetration should the two surfaces move apart, which can occur with typical house movement. To eliminate this hazard, seal the gap with silicone sealant—a waterproof compound that bonds to both surfaces, yet remains elastic enough to cope with any movement without cracking or splitting. This

A shower cubicle requires grouting between tiles, as well as sealant between the bottom row of the tiles and the shower tray, to become truly waterproof.

sealant is available in white, as well as in several popular colors. It comes in cartridges that fit into an ordinary caulking gun fitted with a trigger, and in a squeezable tube with a nozzle.

1 Use your grout spreader to press some grout into the gaps between the tiles, drawing the blade across the tiles at right angles to each grout line. Scrape away any excess grout from the face of the tiles as you work.

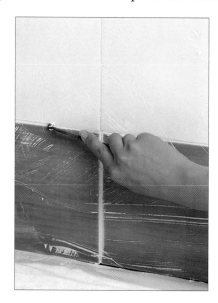

2 Draw a grout finisher along the grout lines to give them a neat concave finish. Alternatively, you can use a piece of dowel or other rounded object, such as a ballpoint pen top, to create the same effect, or use a sponge.

3 Let the grout harden, then wipe the surface of the tiles with a clean damp sponge to remove any excess grout.

4 Place the sealant cartridge into the caulking gun. Cut the cartridge nozzle at a 45° angle, at a point that will produce an extruded bead wide enough to bridge the gap between the two surfaces.

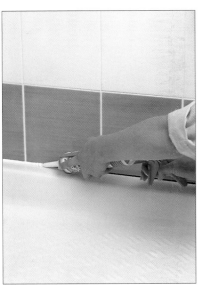

5 Following the manufacturer's directions, squeeze the trigger and push or pull the nozzle along the gap as you hold it at a 45° angle to both surfaces. On cartridges that are pushed, the edge of the nozzle helps to shape the sealant bead into a neat concave shape as it is extruded. If your cartridge doesn't state what to do, push it.

6 When you have finished applying the sealant, release the trigger and set the gun aside. If you want, dip a gloved finger or a cloth in mineral spirits and run it along the bead to smooth it.

7 Finally, finish off by using a dry cloth to wipe away any remaining traces of grout—there is often a fine white residue left over from the previous sponging.

Helpful hints

Getting a smooth straight bead of silicone sealant between a tiled area and another surface can be more difficult than it looks. To get a feel for using the gun, practice on a piece of scrap material such as cardboard or hardboard.

Before starting to seal the gap, you can place strips of masking tape on each surface, leaving a space a little wider than the gap you need to fill. Peel off the strips of masking tape once the sealant is touch dry.

PANELING OPTIONS

POSSIBLE MATERIALS

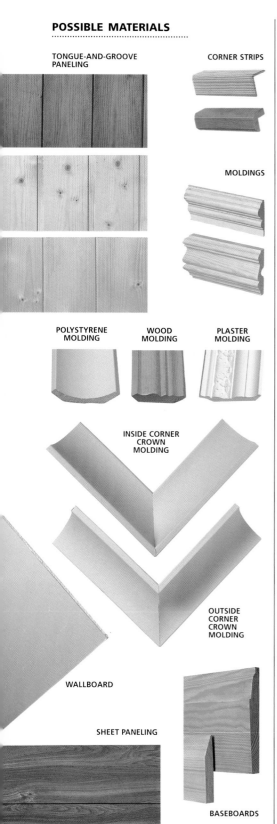

TONGUE-AND-GROOVE PANELING

CORNER STRIPS

MOLDINGS

POLYSTYRENE MOLDING

WOOD MOLDING

PLASTER MOLDING

INSIDE CORNER CROWN MOLDING

OUTSIDE CORNER CROWN MOLDING

WALLBOARD

SHEET PANELING

BASEBOARDS

Lining interior wall surfaces with wood in the form of paneling has been popular for centuries. The surface created is hard-wearing, warm to the touch, and an excellent cover-up for less-than-perfect masonry or plasterwork. It can be crafted and finished in a number of different ways, depending on how the paneling is used.

Paneling has practical applications, too. Fitting insulation behind paneling on exterior walls dramatically reduces heat loss—this is useful in homes with solid walls, which are otherwise difficult to insulate effectively. Paneling can also help reduce noise transmission between rooms when it is used on interior walls.

▲ A less expensive alternative to solid wood paneling is sheet paneling, a manmade product similar to plywood. It is available with a range of surface finishes (including wood veneer), which have a protective coating. Because of the cumbersome size of the panels, this type of paneling is best used on unobstructed walls.

◀ You can finish natural wood paneling with paint, varnish, or wood stain. If you're using varnish, you can choose either clear or colored varnish. The latter will give the wood a moderate depth of color; use a wood stain and clear varnish if you want a dark shade.

◀ You can install the paneling vertically, or horizontally. Conceal any joints, such as those at a window, with molding. You can use crown molding at the ceiling level and baseboards at the floor level.

▶ Boarded ceilings were popular in Victorian times as an alternative to lath and plaster. The wood boards were always painted.

◀ There is no need for a supporting framework when paneling a ceiling. The boards are fastened in place by driving nails through the existing ceiling surface and into the joists above. Light fixtures are the only obstructions that you'll have to work around.

▶ Prepare wood-paneled walls for painting like any other wood surface. The boards can look particularly attractive if treated with a paint effect such as stenciling, dragging, or colorwashing.

▲ Paneling up a wall to waist level and topping the area with a cap rail can be used to good effect in the bathroom or hallway. You can use paneling to surround the bathtub, too.

▶ To preserve the look of natural wood, protect the paneling with a clear matte varnish (see pp.182–183). For a paler finish, try liming wax.

PREPARING WALLS FOR PANELING

YOU WILL NEED

Fixing the battens
Tape measure and pencil
Carpenter's level
Tenon saw **or** jigsaw
Electric drill plus twist bit **or** hammer drill plus masonry bit (for plaster walls)

Insulating a wall
Work gloves
Dust mask
Staple gun (if attaching a vapor barrier)

MATERIALS

Mounting furring strips
1 inch x 2 inch (25 mm x 50 mm) furring strips
Masonry nails **or** screws and wall anchors

Insulating a wall
Insulation batts (for an exterior wall or sound-proofing) and 4 mil polythene vapor barrier (for an exterior wall) **or** rigid expanded polystyrene insulation board

SEE ALSO

Installing tongue-and-groove paneling pp.166–167
Installing sheet paneling pp.168–169

If you are installing floor-to-ceiling wood paneling or sheet paneling, you may be fitting it to just one wall as a decorative feature. Waist-high paneling, or wainscoting, finished with a chair (or dado) rail on top, often runs around the room.

You'll need horizontal furring strips running across the wall surface to which boards will be attached. For an exterior wall, use 1 inch × 4 inch (25 mm × 100 mm) studs at 3 feet (900 mm) intervals. Wall-to-ceiling paneling requires strips at floor and ceiling level and at 30 inch (760 mm) intervals in between. For wainscoting, three equally spaced strips are ideal. The top one should be at 34 inches (860 mm). To run tongue-and-groove paneling horizontally, mount the strips vertically. For more details on sheet paneling, including using an adhesive instead of strips, see pp.168–169.

You can use the existing baseboard as the lowest strip if it is thick enough.

Removing baseboards without damaging them is difficult (see pp.36–37), so leave them in place and finish the wall with new boards that match the existing ones (see pp.38–39).

Insulation is not necessary on an interior wall, unless you want to soundproof it. You should always insulate an exterior wall and use a vapor barrier before paneling it.

Helpful hints

When you are estimating the quantity of tongue-and-groove paneling you'll need for the job, remember that the actual face width of each board is noticeably less than the nominal width, thanks to the presence of the tongue and groove. For example, a board that is nominally 4 inches (100 mm) wide will have an exposed face width of 3½ inches (90 mm) once it is interlocked with its neighbors.

It is also important to find out in what lengths your lumber yard stocks paneling, so that you can minimize wastage. Buying lumber in 6 feet (1.8 m) lengths for use as wainscoting 34 inches (860 mm) high would waste far less than cutting pieces from wood that is 6 feet 6 inches (2 m) long.

MOUNTING FURRING STRIPS

1 For wainscoting, measure up from the floor 34 inches (860 mm) and mark the wall for the first furring strip, using a level. Draw a line for middle strip 17 inches (430 mm) up from the floor in the same way. For full-height paneling, start by fastening lengths of furring at ceiling level.

2 To install a strip, cut it to size. Drill equally spaced pilot holes along its length or to match the wall studs (see p.229) in a wallboard wall. For a plaster wall, position the strip on the wall and mark holes; drill holes into the wall and insert wall anchors. Screw the strip to either type of wall.

3 When paneling more than one wall, butt together the strips at outside corners. At inside corners, with one strip fastened, position the adjacent strip and hold a scrap piece of paneling between them to leave a gap for the paneling. Install the strip as in step 2. (Fasten the paneling running to the corner first.)

4 Use a small piece of cardboard, folded over to the required thickness, to fill any gaps between a furring strip and the wall before screwing the strip on.

INSULATING A WALL

1 Wearing gloves and a mask, cut off small lengths of insulation and push them between the strips. If you plan to install sheet paneling, first secure vertical strips between the horizontal ones, centered where the ends of the sheets will meet (see p.168).

2 A vapor barrier is only neccessary on external walls. Cut a length of polythene and staple one end to the top strip. Get a helper to pull the length down taut. Starting from the top, staple the taut polythene onto the other strips. Trim off the excess at the floor.

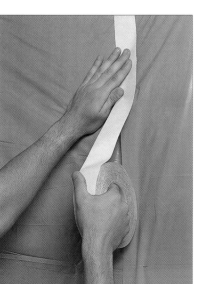

3 To ensure the vapor barrier is efficient, you must tape the vertical seams. Position the tape at the top of the seam. Unroll it and, while keeping it taut, press it onto the polythene until you reach the bottom of the seam. Always use a waterproof tape.

EXPANDED POLYSTYRENE BOARDS

You can use rigid expanded polystyrene boards instead of insulation batts. Cut pieces to size with a fine-tooth saw and wedge them between the battens. These boards are waterproof, so there is no need for a vapor barrier when installing them.

INSTALLING TONGUE-AND-GROOVE PANELING

YOU WILL NEED

Tape measure
Carpenter's level
Scribing block and pencil
Tenon saw **or** jigsaw
Work surface
Clamp
Hammer
Finishing nails **or**
mounting clips
Nail set
Electric drill plus twist bit
Keyhole saw
Plane
Putty knife

MATERIALS

Tongue-and-groove paneling
Dado cap
Baseboard
Wood filler

SEE ALSO

Replacing baseboards
pp.38–39
Preparing walls for paneling
pp.164–165
Installing sheet paneling
pp.168–169

*Tongue-and-groove
paneling that has been
finished with a dado cap
and baseboard is one
attractive way to break up
a large expanse of wall.*

With the furring strips installed (see pp.164–165), it is time to cut and install the paneling. Waist-high paneling, or waitscoting, is typically installed around a room. However, the steps below describe how to fit the end boards if you don't wish to do a whole room (especially when installing paneling at floor-to-ceiling height).

You can nail through the face of the boards, then punch in and fill over the nail heads. However, you will get a neater finish if you nail through the tongue of each board or use mounting clips that grip the grooved edge of the board. In each case the fastener is concealed by the adjacent board.

Stack the paneling in the room a few days before installation to allow it to acclimatize to the temperature and humidity of the room. This minimizes the risk of the wood shrinking or splitting after the paneling is installed.

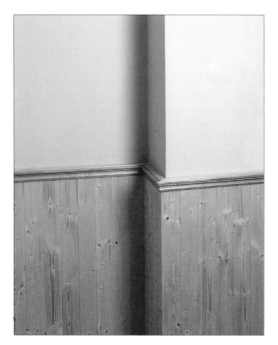

Helpful hints

A light switch or outlet on the wall that you are paneling may have to be repositioned if it is flush mounted. After turning the power off at the service panel, remove the cover plate and install an extender ring in the box so its edge will be flush with the finished surface. If it is surface mounted, fit the boards around the box to leave it flush mounted. In either case, fasten short strips around the wiring accessory to support the cut ends of the boards (see p.168).

1 If you are paneling just one wall, the first board (and the last one) needs to fit snugly against the adjacent wall. Cut the board to length. With its grooved edge against the adjacent wall, use a carpenter's level to check that it is vertical; then temporarily attach the board to the top and bottom furring strips, using small nails.

2 Position a scribing block (a small block of wood) and a pencil at the top of the board. With the block touching the adjacent wall, bring the block and pencil down the board, transferring the profile of the wall onto the board. Remove the nails; clamp the board to a work surface and cut along the line with a jigsaw.

3 Nail the first board onto the strips by driving nails through its tongue at a 45° angle. Use a nail set to punch the nails below the surface so the groove of the next board can fit over the tongue. Push the next board in place, with the tops level, and nail as before. Drill pilot holes for nails if the tongues are brittle and split.

4 Continue to the last board for the wall, which may need trimming with a saw or plane to fit—or you may have to scribe it if you are not paneling the next wall. When paneling inside corners between two walls, butt the last board of the first row to the adjacent wall, then butt the first board of the second row to the adjacent paneling.

5 Where paneling meets at an outside corner, temporarily attach the last board with its end protruding beyond the corner. Use the paneled wall as a guide to draw a pencil line on the protruding board. Remove and clamp the last board to a work surface, and plane or saw off the waste indicated by the pencil line.

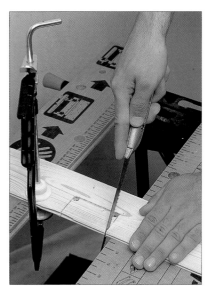

6 To cut out the profile of a switch plate or outlet, mark out its position on the board. Clamp the board to a work surface and drill a hole in each corner. Insert a keyhole saw into a hole and cut along the marks. (To fit strips around an electrical box that protrudes, see step 2, page 168.)

7 When fastening strips up to window or door reveals or to end at an outside corner, they should stop short by the thickness of a board. Finish the end of the paneling by cutting a piece of paneling lengthways the same width as the end of the run of paneling. Then nail it in place onto the ends of the strips.

8 To finish the top of the paneling, cut lengths of board to the width from the front of the paneling to the wall. At corners, cut miters at the ends (see p.148). Nail the lengths on top of the paneling. Cut the dado cap and nail it to the face of the paneling; use a nail set to sink the nails below the surface and cover with a wood filler.

INSTALLING SHEET PANELING

YOU WILL NEED

Tape measure and pencil
Panel saw and keyhole saw
or jigsaw
Hammer
Screwdriver (if required)
Utility knife
Scribing block
Work surface
Profile gauge
Caulking gun (if required)

MATERIALS

Furring strips **or**
1 inch x 4 inch (25 mm
x 100 mm) studs
Masonry nails **or** screws and
wall anchors
Panel nails **or** screws
or panel adhesive
Sheet paneling
Baseboard (if required)
Crown molding (if required)
Sealant

SEE ALSO

Replacing baseboard
pp.38–39
Putting up crown molding
p.148
Preparing walls for paneling
pp.164–165
Installing tongue-and-groove
paneling pp.166–167

Sheet paneling has either a natural wood veneer finish or a printed and laminated decorative surface layer. The core, or substrate, may be hardboard or thin plywood; standard size panels come in 4 feet × 8 feet (1220 mm × 2440 mm). Because of the large size of the individual sheets, it is important to plan how the joints will fall on the wall before you start the work. Door or window openings provide obvious sites for joints.

You can nail or screw the panels to a framework of furring strips, in much the same way as solid tongue-and-groove wood paneling is installed. Modern panel adhesives are capable of securing full-height sheets with ease, although nailing or screwing them in place does at least mean that they can be removed more easily if you wanted a change of decor in the future.

Smaller obstacles such as light switches and outlets may need repositioning (see pp.166–167) if the

If you want to give one or more of your walls the appearance of wood paneling or ceramic tiling, without the expense or the intricate fastening methods, then manmade sheet paneling could be the solution.

boards are being attached over furring strips. Once the wall has been paneled, seal the vertical seams between the sheets with a sealant the same color as the vertical grooves in the laminate.

1 To install sheets over furring strips, fasten horizontal and vertical strips to support all the sheet edges, with intermediate strips at 2 feet (60 cm) intervals. On exterior walls, use 1 inch x 4 inch (25 mm x 100 mm) studs at 3 feet (90 cm) intervals. Install the strips (or studs) in the same way as for those on pp.164–165.

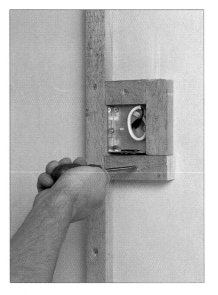

2 Fasten furring strips around light switches and outlet boxes. Cut the strips to fit snugly against the box. For wallboard walls, use panel adhesive. For masonry or plaster walls, drill equally spaced pilot holes in the strips, mark the positions of the holes on the wall, drill and insert wall anchors, then screw the strips in place.

3 To cut the sheet to the height of the wall, it must be well supported. Measure and mark the required length with a pencil line; then score along this line with a utility knife to prevent the laminate from splitting while sawing. Have a helper hold the sheet steady while you saw along the waste side of the scored line.

4 You may have to scribe and cut the first sheet to fit tightly against the adjacent wall (see p.166). Once cut, hold the sheet firmly against the furring strips. Starting at the top, drive nails or screws through the sheet into the vertical and horizontal strips until you reach the bottom. Butt the next sheet against this and continue the process.

5 To make a cut-out around a light switch or outlet, lay the sheet on a work surface. Mark the position of the light switch on the sheet and drill a hole into the waste area at each corner. Insert a keyhole saw into the holes and cut along the drawn lines.

6 When a sheet is butted up to an inside corner, the profile of the base-board must be cut out. You can use a profile gauge to transfer the shape of the baseboard to the bottom of the sheet. Cut along the pencil line with a jigsaw. Once the paneling is installed, add base-board and crown molding if you want.

USING ADHESIVES

Instead of nails or screws, you can use a panel adhesive on the strips to secure the sheets to the walls. If the walls are smooth and without any imperfections, you can dispense with the strips and glue the sheets directly onto the walls.

To fit around a flush switch or outlet, with the power off at the service panel, remove the faceplate. Make a cut-out for the box (see step 5). Install an extender ring in the electrical box (see p.166), then refit the faceplate using longer screws.

Apply glue to the back of the sheet in a zig-zag line around the edges, across the middle, and diagonally from corners.

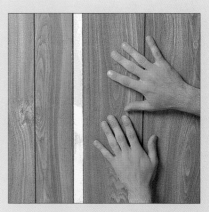

Position one end against the bottom of the wall. Slide it up to the adjacent sheet, then press it firmly into place.

BUILDING A PARTITION WALL

YOU WILL NEED

Tape measure and pencil
Chalk line
Panel saw **or** jigsaw
Carpenter's level
Electric drill plus twist bit
and masonry drill bit (for
masonry walls)
Claw hammer
Screwdriver
Wide putty knife

MATERIALS

2 inch x 4 inch (50 mm x
100 mm framing lumber
8d, 10d, and 16d common
nails for assembling
framework
Screws and wall anchors
Wallboard
Wallboard nails
Joint tape
Joint filler

SEE ALSO

Replacing baseboard
pp.38–39
Repairing door casing
pp.78–79
A new door: measuring up
and fitting hinges pp.82–83
A new door: hanging it and
fitting handles pp.84–85
Painting basics pp.114–115
Putting up crown molding
p.148

Few homes make the best use of the room space available, and family needs often change as time goes by. One way of altering the way you use the space you have is to subdivide existing rooms—for example, to create two separate bedrooms out of one larger room, to form an en suite bathroom, or to partition off a dining area in a large living room.

The actual construction and sheathing of the wall framework is a straightforward, two-person job. However, the job requires careful planning to get optimum results. If the wall runs parallel with the existing floor joists, you should position it directly over a joist if possible. Make sure new doors will have room to open without any obstruction. Lastly, plan to run any extension to the house wiring, plumbing, or heating within the framework of the new wall. You will also have to alter the existing room lighting arrangement.

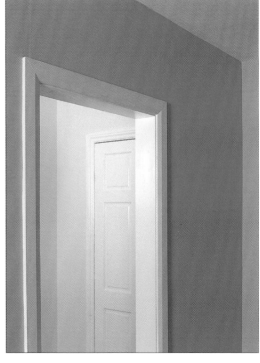

A partition wall can allow you to reorganize the space in your home to suit your own needs.

Helpful hints

Seek advice from your local building inspector to ensure your partition wall meets the building code regulations. For example, a bedroom must have a window and a bathroom must have some ventilation such as an exhaust fan.

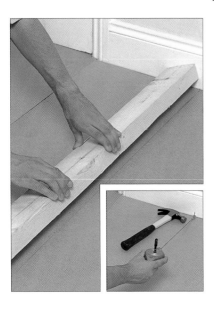

1 Mark the position of the wall on the floor with a chalk line. Position the sole plate along the chalk line, leaving a gap for a door, if needed; secure it to joists below with 16d (3½-inch) nails (or screws if upstairs). Mark positions for the stud on the sole plate at 24 inch (600 mm) centers; use intervals of 16 inches (400 mm) for extra support.

2 Measure and cut vertical end studs to fit between the head and sole plates, making notches to fit over baseboards. Prop the head plate in place; tap the studs into position, using a level to keep them vertically aligned above the sole plate. Drill clearance holes in them and the walls, tap in wall anchors and drive in screws.

3 Measure, cut, and fit the remaining studs. Cut a piece of wood to a length that matches the stud separation, and use it between the studs as a nailing support. Check that the stud is vertical by using a level, then fasten it to the sole and top plates by toe-nailing, with nails at a 45° angle. Use 8d (2½-inch) nails.

4 After you fasten a stud, make sure that the frame is truly vertical, using a level. If it starts to wander out of alignment, use a hammer to tap the top plate into the correct position. Drive a screw through the top plate, between attached studs. (Nailing can crack the ceiling.)

5 After you have fastened in place all the studs (leaving space for a door, if necessary) add horizontal braces, known as blockings, halfway up the wall. Stagger them as shown so that you can nail through the studs into the ends of the blocks. Toe-nail the blocks at the end studs, using 10d (3-inch) nails.

6 To frame a door opening, measure and cut a stud, or header, to fit horizontally between the two studs that form door sides. Nail through the studs into the ends of the header, using 10d (3-inch) nails. Fasten a short vertical stud between the header and top plate, toe-nailing it at the head plate with 8d (2½-inch) nails.

7 If you have no plumbing or wiring experience, hire someone to run any necessary additions in the wall frame. Use a utility knife to trim the wallboard to fit horizontally or vertically, and nail it to both sides of the wall frame. Use notches above each side of the door frame to accept a piece of wallboard above the door.

8 Run joint tape down each joint. Cover with two coats of joint compound. Use the compound to cover any nail heads. Sand joints smooth, then add crown molding, baseboard, and casing, and hang the door. You'll also want to paint your walls—use a primer to seal the wallboard before applying one or two coats of paint.

4

FLOORS

FLOORS DIRECTORY

WOOD FLOOR OPTIONS

SEE PAGES 178–179

For the subfloor beneath any finished floor, you should use either softwood floorboards or sheets of plywood or particleboard. As a decorative wood floor covering, you can choose from solid hardwood strip flooring laid as a "floating" floor, thicker "laminate" flooring (hardwood veneer on a softwood base) nailed on top of or to replace an existing floor, parquet floor coverings (small strips laid in a pattern such as "basketweave") or solid woodblock flooring (which is appropriate for solid concrete floors).

Wood floorboards should be sealed with varnish; you may want to stain or paint the wood first, or create a special decorative effect with the paint by using liming wax or stenciling.

SANDING FLOORBOARDS

SKILL LEVEL High
TIME FRAME 1 day
SPECIAL TOOLS Floor sander

(rented), edging sander (rented) or belt sander, dust mask, safety glasses, protective ear muffs, floor scraper
SEE PAGES 180–181

Sanding can revive the appearance of old floorboards that have become grimy with years of use. Don't worry if you have a newer board that seems to be a lighter hue—sanding will restore all the boards to their original color. They should then be protected with a varnish (see below).

Another reason for sanding floorboards is to provide a flat surface before laying a decorative floor covering on top of them. Never sand laminated floorboards.

You'll have to learn how to use an industrial floor sander, which is readily available for rent—ask for a demonstration from the shop.

STAINING AND VARNISHING FLOORBOARDS

SKILL LEVEL Low
TIME FRAME 1 to 2 days
SPECIAL TOOLS Paint brushes, rubber gloves, wire brush

SEE PAGES 182–183
Instructions on how to enhance new floorboards or existing older ones that have been sanded and otherwise repaired. Stains give the wood a deeper color; varnishes protect it from future damage. The time necessary depends on the number of coats applied and on the types of products that are used.

Also included are details for liming floorboards, which enhances the natural grain of open-grain woods such as oak and ash.

PAINTING AND STENCILING FLOORBOARDS

SKILL LEVEL Low to medium
TIME FRAME 1 to 2 days
SPECIAL TOOLS Paint brushes, stencil brush
SEE PAGES 184–185

Methods for achieving a decorative paint effect on either new floorboards or existing older ones that have been sanded. Details are given on how to stencil in a diamond- or square-shape

overall repeat (to stencil a border around the perimeter of a room, follow instructions on pp.128–129), as well as on how to "age" paint, where small areas of floorboard (or a base coat) are exposed through a top coat.

The time necessary depends on the number of coats applied and on the type of products used.

LAYING NEW FLOORBOARDS

SKILL LEVEL High
TIME FRAME 2 days
SPECIAL TOOLS Floorboard nailer (rented), panel saw or jigsaw, crowbar, plane
SEE PAGES 186–187

If the old floorboards in a room are beyond repair, or you want exposed floorboards but the existing ones include mismatched replacement boards, the solution is to replace them with new softwood floorboards. This means cutting them to length and making sure they are laid with no gaps. For "blind nailing" tongue-and-groove floorboards, see pp.194–195.

BELT SANDER

DUST MASKS

CIRCULAR SAW

BLACK&DECKER
KS 855N   1200W

SAFETY GLASSES

LAYING A SUBFLOOR

SKILL LEVEL High
TIME FRAME 2 days
SPECIAL TOOLS Electric drill plus screw-driving bits, circular saw, jigsaw
SEE PAGES 188–189

A less expensive—and easier—method of replacing old subfloor boards is to use sheets of particleboard. The same techniques can also be used for laying a new floor in an addition or attic conversion. (You may want to cut sheets to make them easier to get into an attic.)

Particleboard is not a material that you would want to leave exposed as finished floor covering; however, it provides an ideal surface for covering with decorative floor coverings such as carpet, sheet vinyl flooring, or vinyl tiles.

LAYING A FLOATING FLOOR

SKILL LEVEL High
TIME FRAME 2 days or more
SPECIAL TOOLS Panel saw, circular saw or plane, crowbar, tenon saw
SEE PAGES 190–191
By laying woodstrip flooring over an existing wood floor with mismatched boards or a solid concrete floor, you can provide an atractive decorative finish. With the exception of the two end rows, the floorboards are attached to each other with adhesive or special clips that are provided by the manufacturer—not to the floor below—hence the term "floating."

Time must be allowed for the flooring to acclimatize before it is laid and for preparing the existing floor surface. The total time depends on the size and complexity of the room.

PARQUET FLOORING

SKILL LEVEL Medium to high
TIME FRAME 2 days or more
SPECIAL TOOLS Notched adhesive spreader, tenon saw
SEE PAGES 192–193

An alternative to woodstrip flooring, this material, which is usually hardwood, comes as "tiles" in which strips of wood, known as fingers, are held together on a backing. The fingers are set in a variety of patterns, including basket-weave and herringbone.

Parquat flooring is fixed to the floor with an adhesive. The total time necessary depends on the size and complexity of the room.

NAILING LAMINATE-STRIP FLOORING

SKILL LEVEL High
TIME FRAME 2 days or more
SPECIAL TOOLS Tenon saw, nail set, circular saw or plane, profile gauge
SEE PAGES 194–195

These thicker strips of wood can either be laid in place of existing floorboards or laid on top of them. However, unlike solid woodstrip flooring, the surface hardwood veneer cannot be sanded down if it becomes damaged.

The technique described is known as blind nailing, in which nails are driven through the tongue of one strip before being covered with the groove of the next. It isn't difficult if you have a hammer and a nail set. The total time necessary depends on the size and complexity of the room.

ROLL FLOOR COVERINGS OPTIONS

SEE PAGES 196–197
The choices available in sheets of "soft," or resilient, floor coverings—which come in rolls—include carpet, natural floor coverings (such as sisal and jute), vinyl, and linoleum. All are quiet and soft underfoot and are good choices for bedrooms and living rooms. They come in a variety of colors and patterns, and some of the coverings, such as carpets, have different textures. Some types, such as vinyl and linoleum, are easy to clean, making them a good choice in bathrooms, kitchens, and children's rooms. Linoleum is best laid by a professional.

LAYING SHEET VINYL FLOORING

SKILL LEVEL Low
TIME FRAME 1 day
SPECIAL TOOLS Adhesive spreader
SEE PAGES 198–199

Probably the most popular of all resilient floor coverings, vinyl sheet has the combined advantages of being soft and quiet underfoot and of being easy to clean—as well as being inexpensive and relatively easy to lay.

This section describes how to lay a slightly oversized sheet of vinyl in one go,

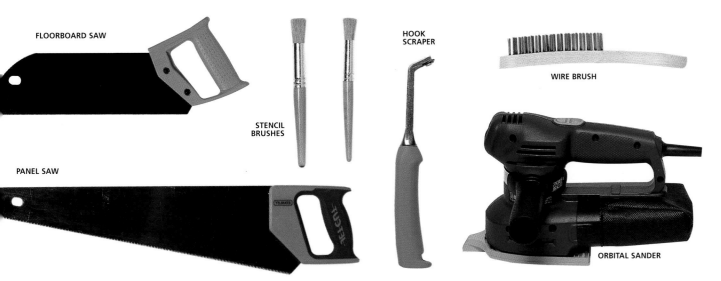

FLOORBOARD SAW

PANEL SAW

STENCIL BRUSHES

HOOK SCRAPER

WIRE BRUSH

ORBITAL SANDER

cutting it to fit within a room that has no obstacles such as a toilet or kitchen island.

If you have a large room that requires two sheets of vinyl, details are given for joining them—make sure the seam is placed where there will be the least amount of foot traffic.

USING A TEMPLATE FOR VINYL FLOORING

SKILL LEVEL Low to medium
TIME FRAME 1 day
SPECIAL TOOLS Adhesive spreader, weights, wax pencil
SEE PAGES 200–201

The best way to lay vinyl flooring in a room with permanently attached obstacles—particularly a bathroom with basin and toilet pedestals or a kitchen with an island—involves making a paper pattern, or template, of the shape of the room. This allows you to cut the sheet vinyl roughly to shape in a larger room before laying it as described on pp.198–199.

To make the template so it follows the contours of the room precisely, you must use a wood block and pencil in a procedure known as scribing.

The only difficult part of the job is to take care that you always hold the pencil at the same angle.

LAYING CUSHION-BACKED CARPET

SKILL LEVEL Low to medium
TIME FRAME ½ to 1 day
SPECIAL TOOLS Staple gun, carpet tool or bolster chisel, hacksaw, utility knife plus carpet trimming blades
SEE PAGES 202–203

This type of carpet is the easiest to lay, even for the inexperienced do-it-yourselfer, and it can be laid virtually anywhere within the house—apart from stairs. Basic floor preparation is likely to be the main part of the job.

The actual laying of the carpet is not difficult: it simply requires stapling a paper underlay in place, applying double-sided tape around the perimeter of the room, and trimming the carpet after you position it. To stop the carpet from fraying and to prevent people from tripping on the edges, you'll have to fit a threshold strip at any doorways in the room, using screws or masonry nails.

LAYING STANDARD CARPET

SKILL LEVEL Medium to high
TIME FRAME 1 to 2 days
SPECIAL TOOLS Staple gun, tenon saw, utility knife plus carpet trimming blades, kneekicker (rented), carpet tool or bolster chisel, hacksaw
SEE PAGES 204–205

While this type of carpet is much more luxurious than cushion-backed carpet—both visually and to the touch—standard carpet is also more difficult to lay. It requires laying down a separate rubber or felt padding, as well as attaching tackless strips around the perimeter of the room, and the carpet itself must be stretched to the walls with a kneekicker in order to prevent it from eventually rippling after use.

The total time necessary depends on the size and complexity of the room and how quickly you adapt to using a kneekicker.

LAYING STAIR CARPET

SKILL LEVEL Medium to high
TIME FRAME ½ to 1 day
SPECIAL TOOLS Tenon saw or hacksaw, utility knife with carpet

trimming blades, staple gun, carpet tool or bolster chisel, rubber mallet
SEE PAGES 206–207

Standard carpet can be used for staircases, either as "fitted" carpet, with the material running to the two edges of the stairs, or as a stair "runner," with a 2-inch (50 mm) gap on either side. Before laying the carpet, tackless strips must be mounted on each step at the angle between the riser and tread, and rubber or felt padding must be attached to the treads. If you have a lot of steps, you may find pounding the carpet into the angles a tiring job.

The complexity of the job depends on the type of staircase—straight flights are much easier to carpet than stairs with landings, and carpeting a curved staircase will require a high skill level and much more time.

FLOOR TILE OPTIONS

SEE PAGES 208–209

The choice of tiles falls into two categories: "hard" materials, such as ceramic, terracotta, and quarry, and

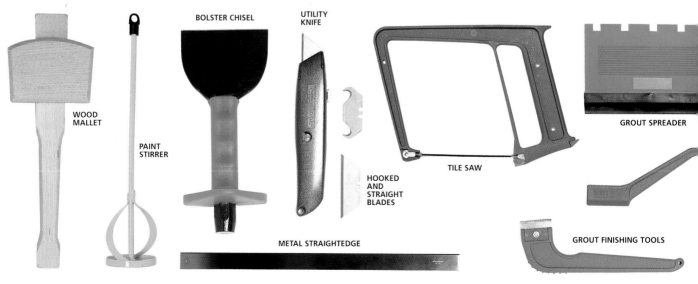

WOOD MALLET

PAINT STIRRER

BOLSTER CHISEL

UTILITY KNIFE

HOOKED AND STRAIGHT BLADES

METAL STRAIGHTEDGE

TILE SAW

GROUT SPREADER

GROUT FINISHING TOOLS

"soft" resilient materials, including cork, vinyl, carpet, linoleum, and rubber. Hard tiles are more durable, but they can be cold to walk on with bare feet and noisy if wearing shoes. Soft tiles are not only quiet and warm, but they are generally much easier to lay. Another advantage is that it is easier to replace a damaged tile than a section of a larger flooring material.

Tiles are available in a huge range of colors and patterns. Ceramic tiles also come in a range of sizes. Tiles allow you to create your own patterns by mixing ones of different colors, using soft tiles cut on a diagonal or by adding "inset" tiles at the corners.

LAYING VINYL AND OTHER SOFT FLOOR TILES

SKILL LEVEL Medium
TIME FRAME 1 day
SPECIAL TOOLS Notched adhesive spreader
SEE PAGES 210–211

One of the easiest of all flooring jobs is laying soft tiles—they are lightweight, small, and easy to cut, using only a utility knife and metal straightedge. The instructions given are for vinyl tiles, but follow them for laying other types of soft tiles, including carpet, cork, and rubber.

Most of the work will be in preparing a flat smooth surface on which to lay the tiles, planning how to lay them from the center of the room, and cutting the tiles to fit around the edges and any obstacles within the room. Each edge tile should be measured and cut individually, following the three-tile cutting method. The tiles may be laid using an adhesive, but they may be self-adhesive (such as some vinyl tiles)—you simply peel off a paper backing before pressing them in place.

LAYING CERAMIC FLOOR TILES

SKILL LEVEL Medium to high
TIME FRAME 2 days
SPECIAL TOOLS Tile cutter, tile file, notched adhesive spreader, electric grinder, rubber grout squeegee
SEE PAGES 212–213

Although similar to ceramic wall tiles, ceramic floor tiles stand up to more abuse, so they are thicker, stronger, and generally bigger—which makes them harder to cut.

As with all floor coverings, the basic floor must be smooth and dry. Tiling starts by laying whole tiles from the middle of a room, working outward to the edges. You should let them set before fitting the edge tiles, and you'll need to wait again before filling the gaps between tiles with grout.

Border tiles for framing the perimeter of the room are available. These require more complicated planning before starting the job.

LAYING QUARRY TILES

SKILL LEVEL High
TIME FRAME 3 days
SPECIAL TOOLS Notched adhesive spreader, carpenter's level, mallet, tile cutter, tile-cutting saw, grout spreader
SEE PAGES 214–215

Quarry tiles are more durable than ceramic tiles, have a non-glazed surface, and are more porous. Because they are not glazed, they are less slippery, making them a suitable flooring material for an entryway. Handmade tiles will be more difficult to lay than machinemade tiles, which are more readily available. Terracotta tiles are similar to quarry tiles, but they are warmer and quieter; you can lay them in the same way as quarry tiles.

Quarry tiles are laid in a cement-base adhesive, and a cement-base grout is used to fill the gaps, which are larger than those left between ceramic tiles. These tiles are difficult to cut successfully, and are best restricted to areas that won't require a large amount of cutting.

PAINTING A CONCRETE FLOOR

SKILL LEVEL Low
TIME FRAME 1 day
SPECIAL TOOLS Flexible putty knife, paint brush, paint roller with extension pole
SEE PAGES 216–217

One of the best methods for treating a solid concrete floor is to paint it. Paint makes it look more attractive and easier to clean, and it prevents dust from collecting. This treatment is appropriate for workshops, garages, and utility rooms.

The job itself is not difficult once you have removed all the furniture and equipment in the room and prepared the floor surface.

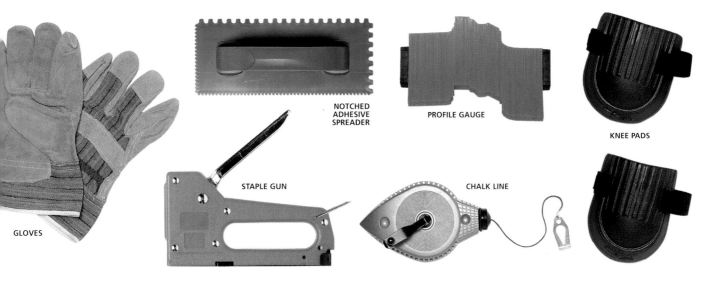

GLOVES

NOTCHED ADHESIVE SPREADER

PROFILE GAUGE

KNEE PADS

STAPLE GUN

CHALK LINE

WOOD FLOOR OPTIONS

POSSIBLE MATERIALS

FLOOR VARNISH

WOOD STAIN

GLOSS FLOOR PAINT

LIMING WAX

FLOOR WAX

FLOOR STAIN COLORS

WOOD PARQUET PANELS

LAMINATED BOARD

TONGUE-AND-GROOVE-SOFTWOOD BOARD

SQUARE-EDGE PINE BOARD

The natural beauty of wood has made it a popular choice as a flooring material. The main structure of the floor, consisting of planks of wood—the floorboards—nailed down to floor joists, may be left uncovered (but protected with a varnish) if the floorboards are in good shape. A wood floor covering is a decorative feature and may be laid over existing floorboards, particleboard subflooring, or concrete floors. There are many options to choose from, depending on whether you are replacing or renovating an existing floor or putting in a wood floor covering over an existing floor.

▶ The clean simple lines of a warm and practical wood floor make it one of the few flooring materials that look great in any room of the house. Wood ages gracefully, increasing in character as the years go by.

◀ Footsteps and chairs being moved across a wood floor may create noise in a room below it—a problem experienced by many apartment dwellers. Laying an underlayment of a sound-insulating material, such as cork or a special sound-proofing foam, increases the sound insulation between floors.

▲ Larger widths of natural wood flooring are usually more expensive than narrow widths because they require higher-quality wood.

▶ All wood floorboards (except laminated veneer strips) can be stained with a colorwash or tinted varnish.

▶ Wood floors can be treated with a number of special painted finishes, including liming and stenciling.

▲ Laminated wood floors are relatively inexpensive because only the top layer of each panel is expensive hardwood. Unlike solid wood floors, laminate flooring cannot be rejuvenated by sanding it down at a later date.

◀ Parquet floor tiles consist of small strips of wood arranged in a basketweave, herringbone, or similar pattern.

▶ Paint can be applied to the floorboards in a variety of ways—for example, as a solid color or in a checkerboard pattern. You should apply top coats of varnish to protect it.

SANDING FLOORBOARDS

YOU WILL NEED

Electric floor sander (rented)
Edging sander (rented) **or** belt sander
Face mask, safety goggles, and protective ear muffs
Hammer and nail set
Hook-blade scraper (if required)
Cork sanding block
Tack cloth **or** rag

MATERIALS

Coarse-, medium-, and fine-grade sanding belts
Medium- and fine-grade sandpaper

SEE ALSO

Removing floor coverings pp.40–41
Making minor repairs to a wood floor pp.42–43
Replacing a damaged floorboard pp.44–45
Staining and varnishing floorboards pp.182–183
Painting and stenciling floorboards pp.184–185

Over time, solid wooden floor-boards begin to show signs of age as the wood warps, splits, and builds up a residue of wax and other finishes. Sanding the floor down to bare wood is the first step in restoring them to original condition.

Sanding floorboards is a three-stage process: sanding the main floor area with a coarse or medium-grade sanding belt; repeating with a fine-grade belt; then finishing off the edges. You have to rent an electric floor sander, as well as an edging sander (unless you own a belt sander), for finishing off the edges.

BEFORE YOU START

You must first of all strip the floor of any covering if there is one (see pp.40–41) and repair any damage to the floorboards (see pp.42–45). The one thing that is especially important to do before you sand is to make sure there are no nails or staples (which are widely used for anchoring underlayment) protruding above the floor surface—these will rip the sanding belt and possibly damage the sander. Nail heads may appear during the sanding process and will need driving down with a nail set.

You must remove all the furniture from the room to give a clear area to work. The sanding process creates a lot of dust, so you should also remove items such as pictures hanging on the wall; completely seal other items, such as built-in bookcases, with plastic sheets and tape. It is also a good idea to tape over the door edges to prevent dust getting into the rest of the house and to open all the windows in the room to let the dust escape.

Before using the sander, make sure you clearly understand the instructions for operating it and for fitting the sanding belts securely. Once the floorboards are sanded, stain them, if you want, and protect them with varnish (see pp.182–183).

1 Before starting a floor sander, tilt it backward. Make sure the power cord is well out of the way (preferably over your shoulder). Turn the power on and lower the sander as you move it forward; you'll have to hold on firmly to stop it running away from you.

2 If you are dealing with warped floorboards, fit a coarse belt to the machine and sand diagonally across the room, starting in one corner. Go over each area several times, then sand across the other diagonal. A dustbag will collect most, but not all, of the dust produced.

3 Give the room a quick vacuum to remove dust, and fit a medium-grade belt to the machine. (With floorboards that are not warped, you can start with this belt.) Re-sand the floor, this time working along the line of the floorboards; if you're sanding a herringbone parquet floor, follow the diagonal lines.

4 As you work, keep an eye open for any nailheads that may be exposed by the sanding. If you come across one, use a nail set to drive it below the surface of the wood. Switch to a fine-grade belt on the machine, and, once more, sand along the line of the floorboards.

5 Go around the edges of the room, using an edging sander or belt sander. Turn the power on before you lower the sander to the floor. Move the sander in a circular motion and allow it to overlap the area sanded by the large floor sander. Start with a medium-grade paper, then finish with a fine-grade paper.

6 Most power sanders won't reach into corners or under obstructions such as radiators. Use a hook-blade scraper or sandpaper wrapped around a sanding block (but don't use the block at the baseboards) to reach into these areas. To blend in scraped areas with those sanded by machine, use the sandpaper.

7 Sweep up all the dust and go over the whole floor with a vacuum cleaner, then use a tack cloth or damp rag to remove any leftover dust particles, which could ruin any finish you then apply.

Helpful hints

There are a few points that an inexperienced user of an electric floor sander should know before operating one. Sanding is a noisy process—make sure you wear ear muffs to protect your hearing. To avoid upsetting your neighbors, do the sanding when it will be least likely to disturb them. Once the sanding belt makes contact with the floor—you'll know it has from the increased noise—never let it sit in one place or try to hold it back even for an instant; otherwise, it will gouge the floor.

One of the best methods for removing fine dust is to use a tack cloth—a cloth impregnated with a resin that will pick up dust.

STAINING AND VARNISHING FLOORBOARDS

YOU WILL NEED

Staining and varnishing
Steel wool
Lint-free clean cloth
4-inch- (100-mm-) wide
paint brush
Fine abrasive paper
Sanding block
Paint bucket (if required)
Drop cloth **or** newspapers
Small brush (if required)
Rubber gloves

Liming floorboards
Wire brush
Small brush
Steel wool
Rubber gloves
(See above for varnishing)

MATERIALS

Staining and varnishing
Water-base stain **or** oil-
base stain
Water-base varnish **or** oil-
base varnish
Mineral spirits (if required)

Liming floorboards
Liming wax **or** liming paste
Water-base varnish **or** oil-
base varnish

SEE ALSO

Removing floor coverings
pp.40–41
Sanding floorboards
pp.180–181

The natural grain and texture of a wood floor are highlighted by a stain and protective varnish finish.

N atural wood floors can be transformed and protected by using stains and varnishes. The best effects will be achieved on new floorboards, but you can stain and varnish existing ones that are in good condition. You'll have to remove any old floor covering to inspect the boards, and they will require sanding before you can apply a new finish.

THE STAINS AND VARNISHES

A stain penetrates into the wood itself, giving it a new color; a varnish treats the surface of the wood, enhancing and protecting it. Varnishes are available in matte, semi-gloss, and gloss finishes. You can use the varnish alone or after you apply a stain, or you can use a colored varnish (which may simulate various types of wood).

Stains and varnishes are available in environmentally friendly, water-base versions, as well as the traditional oil-base products. These should never be used together. Stains can be mixed to create a new color. A water-base stain raises the wood grain, which requires a light sanding after it dries.

1 Before applying a stain, first clean the floorboards with steel wool and mineral spirits to make sure that there is no wax or grease on the floorboard surface—otherwise, the stain may not be absorbed evenly, which can cause patches.

2 Unless you are happy with one particular stain color, mix together different stains to achieve the color you want. Use a folded drop cloth or newspaper to prevent spills on the floor. A small brush is the best mixing tool. You can also mix colored varnishes. In both cases, use compatible products from the same manufacturer.

3 Apply the stain using a clean, lint-free cloth, such as cheesecloth or a section of an old sheet, or use a paint brush. Work quickly along the length of a few boards at a time so that the stain does not dry out in the middle of the floor. If the color is not deep enough after one application, apply a second coat.

4 After the stain dries, apply the varnish. Thin the first coat—which acts as a primer—by 10 percent with mineral spirits for an oil-base varnish or polyurethane or water for a water-base varnish. (Never shake a can of varnish; this creates bubbles, which disfigure the finish.) Use a clean, lint-free cloth to rub the coat into the wood.

5 After the varnish dries, lightly rub the surface with fine abrasive paper wrapped around a sanding block; work with the grain to avoid scratches. This creates a "key" for the next coat and smooths the surface. Before applying a new coat of varnish, use a clean, dry cloth to remove the dust created by the sanding.

6 Apply up to three coats of varnish to achieve the necessary protection, sanding between coats. Use a 4-inch- (100-mm-) wide brush to apply the varnish quickly. If using a colored varnish, use a clear varnish for the final coat—or coats if the color is dark enough. Each new coat of colored varnish will make the floor darker.

LIMING FLOORBOARDS

Wood can be limed with a wax or paste before being varnished. The wax is easier to apply, but it will eventually wear away. The wood should be unvarnished and clean, although it can be stained. Before applying the wax or paste, use a wire brush in the direction of the grain; this opens the grain, helping it to take the wax or paste. Apply the paste with a burlap cloth or extra-fine steel wool, first in one direction, then the other; remove the dried paste with a rag or burlap cloth.

Rub liming wax into the wood with extra-fine steel wool. Allow it to dry before removing the excess with a cloth.

Liming enhances the natural grain of open-grain wood, such as oak and ash, either of which can be stained first.

PAINTING AND STENCILING FLOORBOARDS

YOU WILL NEED

Stenciling floorboards
String, nails, and pencil
Straightedge metal rule
Stencil
Spray mount adhesive **or**
painter's masking tape
Stencil brushes
Large paint brush

Aging paint
Small paint brush
Large paint brush
Paint roller and tray
Lint-free cloth
Fine abrasive paper
Scraper (if required)

MATERIALS

Stenciling floorboards
Water- or oil-base paint
Floor-grade varnish

Aging paint
Paste wax **or** petroleum jelly
Water-base paint
Floor-grade varnish

SEE ALSO

Making minor repairs to
a wood floor pp.42–43
Replacing a damaged
floorboard pp.44–45
Sanding floorboards
pp.180–181
Staining and varnishing
floorboards pp.182–183

The most straightforward way of painting new or refurbished floorboards is to paint the whole floor the same color, using a paint brush around the perimeter of the room and a roller for the center. You can use any type of paint (water- or oil-base), as long as it is covered with three coats of floor-grade varnish. You can also cover the floor with a special paint effect, perhaps "aging" the paint to evoke an old-fashioned kitchen or decorating with a repeat pattern, using a stencil. Before painting floorboards, repair any surface damage, sand them down, and use steel wool with mineral spirits to remove any wax or grease.

MAKING A STENCIL

You can buy ready-made stencils or make your own. A transparent acetate sheet is the best material to use: lay it over a pattern for tracing, then cut out the design, leaving "bridges" so parts of the design don't fall out of the

Stencils are traditionally used to form a border (see pp.128–129), but you can use them to create your own design, including a diamond pattern.

stencil. The best tool for cutting the stencil is a craft knife with a sharp blade. A continuous pattern requires a registration mark to align the stencil: use an element in the design or draw a line on the stencil.

1 Plan out your pattern on a scale drawing of the floor, starting at the center of the room and using small squares to indicate how often the pattern is repeated. On the floor itself, find the center (see p.192 and p.210), but instead of using chalk lines, use two lengths of string tied to small nails tapped partway into the floorboards.

2 Measure and mark the positions for several of the surrounding patterns. By marking the patterns as you go, you can make slight adjustments if you start to go off course. With each new group of marks, double check for overall appearance before you commit yourself by applying the paint.

3 The easiest way to secure the stencil to the floor is to spray the back with a spray mount adhesive. This will hold the stencil in place while you paint, but allow you to peel it off and reposition it afterward. Or you can use painter's masking tape.

4 Load a stencil brush with some of the paint and dab it on a sheet of white paper to find the right amount to use (a little stencil paint goes a long way). Apply the paint to the floor, using a short dabbing motion to prevent the paint from going under the edges of the stencil.

5 If you want to use a second color, allow the first one to dry completely (water-base paints will dry quickly). If using more than one stencil sheet (some ready-made stencil kits have a separate sheet for each color), make sure the stencil is correctly aligned over the previous image before applying the new color.

6 Remove and reposition the stencil, continuing until you finish the room. When the paint has completely dried, cover the final result with three coats of floor-grade varnish, painting the full length of a few planks at a time.

AGING PAINT

It is easy to make painted floorboards look older than their true age. Before painting, apply a barrier in random patches onto clean floorboards to prevent paint from seeping into the wood. Once the paint is dry, simply remove the barrier (use a scraper on difficult lumps) and blend in the painted and unpainted areas. Seal the work with a few coats of protective varnish. For a unique look, give the floorboards a coat of a contrasting base color before applying the barrier.

Randomly apply lumps of a barrier, such as paste wax or petroleum jelly, to the floorboards before painting them.

After the paint dries, use a cloth to remove the wax and lightly sand the edges to blend in with the painted areas.

LAYING NEW FLOORBOARDS

When you replace individual damaged floorboards, the new ones won't blend in completely—they often are a slightly different size, look flatter and smoother, and they will be a different color whatever you do to the floor. If your old floorboards are damaged in several places, consider replacing all of them with new ones.

In some older homes, you will not find subflooring under floorboards on the top floors. As shown here, the floorboards are secured directly to the joists. However, you can follow the same steps to install floorboards over subflooring.

New floorboards may have either square edges or tongues and grooves; the laying technique varies only slightly. If tongue-and-groove floorboards will be left exposed, you can "secret" nail them to the joists in the same way as laminated woodstrip flooring (see pp.194–195), and they won't need clamping.

Floorboards come in different widths and thicknesses. The correct thickness depends on the joist spacing; the width affects the appearance. Use the size of the old boards as a guide. The starting point, after you remove all the old floorboards (and the baseboards), will be the bare joists or subflooring—carefully check for damage. Have any damaged joists replaced and weakened ones strengthened before you start. Remove and replace damaged subflooring. To strengthen an old floor without a subflooring, install one before replacing the floorboards.

Helpful hints

To create an old-fashion pegged look, you can install "pegs." Use a spade bit to drill a pair of holes partway through at each end of a floorboard. (You can make a template to space the holes evenly apart by drilling a pair of holes all the way through an offcut of floorboard.) Squeeze a little white glue into the holes; insert caps cut from hardwood dowels.

1 Start by removing the first floorboard (see pp.44–45). Once it is up, use a crowbar to lever up the other boards where they are nailed to the joists below. Inspect the joists; if they are weak or damaged, seek professional help. Save a few boards to use as a work platform; lay them at a right angle to the joists where you plan to work.

2 Fit the first board along a wall at a right angle to the joists; leave a ⅜ inch (10 mm) gap between the board and the wall (fit tongue-and-groove boards with the groove facing the wall). Bang two nails in at each joist (use the nail pattern on subflooring panels to find the joists); drive the nail heads just below the surface.

3 Ideally, a board should fit the whole length of the room, less ¾ inch (20 mm) for expansion gaps. Where the boards are less than the length of the room, cut them so that the joints between boards will be exactly centered on a joist, but stagger the joints across the room.

4 Lay the next five or six rows of boards without nails for the moment (unless you're secret nailing), leaving the same ⅜ inch (10 mm) gap at each end of the rows and making sure that any joints are centered on joists and are staggered from one board to the next.

5 Push the boards tightly together as you go. For tongue-and-groove boards, make sure the groove fits snugly over the tongue of the previous board by using an offcut with a groove (to protect the tongue) and hammering the boards together. (If you're secret nailing tongue-and-groove boards, proceed to step 8.)

6 Wedge the group of floorboards together. If you can find them, use special floorboard clamps spced 6 feet (180 cm) apart. (Or wedge the floorboards as shown in step 7.) Starting in the center and working toward the ends, nail down each of the floorboards.

7 Instead of floor-board clamps, use wood wedges (offcuts of the flooring material) and a wood strip temporarily nailed to the joists a short distance away to force boards together for nailing. Again, use offcuts to protect the boards. Nail down each floorboard, starting in the center and working toward the ends.

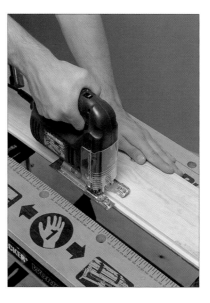

8 Continue until you have less than one floorboard's width left. Saw or plane the last row of boards down so that they will fit with a ⅜ inch (10 mm) gap to the wall; slot them into place. Remove the bottom of the groove from tongue-and-groove floorboards if they do not fit easily into place. Replace the baseboards.

LAYING A SUBFLOOR

YOU WILL NEED

Tape measure
Pencil
Hammer plus C clamps
(if required)
Try square
Chalkline **or** 4-foot-
(1200-mm-) long
straightedge (such as
a wood batten)
Caulking gun
Hammer **or** power
screw gun
Circular saw

MATERIALS

Plywood subflooring
(C-D or CDX grade) **or**
oriented strand board
(OSB) panels
8d ring-shank **or** spiral-
shank flooring nails **or**
bugle-head screws
Subflooring adhesive

SEE ALSO

Removing baseboards
and moldings pp.36–37
Replacing baseboards
pp.38–39
Replacing a damaged
floorboard pp.44–45
Laying new floorboards
pp.186–187

Subflooring strengthens a floor's framing—the joists—by tying it together. It also provides a fastening surface for finish flooring, such as hardwood, tile, or carpet, and allows using a thinner finish flooring, which is less expensive than thicker material. Plywood, ⅝ inch (15 mm) or ¾ inch (20 mm) thick, is the strongest subflooring material, but you can use ¾-inch- (20-mm-) thick oriented strand board (OSB), which is less expensive and nearly as strong. On floors to be covered with vinyl or resilient tile or carpet, subflooring is covered by thin sheets of plywood, hardboard or particleboard as underlayment to create a smooth surface. Subflooring by itself may be sufficient where looks don't count such as in an attic.

Standard subflooring panels measure 4 × 8 feet (1200 mm × 2400 mm). Longer sizes are sometimes available for house construction, but they are heavy and awkward to move. Estimate the amount of subflooring needed by determining the square footage of floor space and dividing the figure by 32 (the square footage of a standard-size panel). On large or irregular jobs, add an extra 15 percent for waste.

When installing the panels, make sure their edges meet over joist centers so there will be support for nails. Stagger the edges of panels by starting every other row, or course, with a half-size panel so that support for panel edges is distributed over different joists. As with laying new floorboards (see pp.186–187), start by checking and repairing the floor joists.

Helpful hints

Choose ring-shank or spiral flooring nails about three times longer than the thickness of the subflooring; 2-inch- (50-mm-) long 8d nails are good for ¾-inch- (20-mm-) thick plywood or OSB. All-purpose, bugle-head screws grip better than nails, so the floor will less likely squeak, but their drawback are the expense and the difficulty of driving them flush with the surface.

1 Measure across the joists; their centerlines should be 4 feet (1200 mm) apart to support panel edges. To correct a misaligned joist, nail a 2 x 4 (1200 mm x 2400 mm) alongside it, with their top edges flush—this creates a wider supporting surface. Or cut panels so their edges will lie along joist centerlines.

2 Place the first panel in position at a corner and align it so that the panel's long edges are perpendicular to the joists. If aligning the panel creates a gap along the wall, measure its length and width at both ends, then cut a filler strip of subflooring to fit the space. Lift the panel and prop it out of the way.

3 To reduce floor squeaks, spread subflooring adhesive over the joists and any other framing that the first panel will cover. Include the area of the filler strip if there is one. Use a caulking gun to spread a ¼-inch (5-mm-) wide bead of adhesive along the top of each joist.

4 Set the panel, smooth side up, over the joists (with the filler strip if there is one). If the panel has tongue-and-groove edges, the tongued edge should face the wall. (If a filler strip is used, first trim off the panel's tongued edge with a circular saw.) Use a straightedge to mark joist centerlines or strike chalklines.

5 Fasten the panel with nails or screws at 12-inch (300 mm) intervals along the joists and at 6-inch (150 mm) intervals along any framing next to the walls. If using screws or nailing into OSB, first drill pilot holes.

6 To allow for expansion and contraction during wet and dry months, leave ⅛ inch (3 mm) gaps between panel sides and ¹⁄₁₆ inch (2 mm) gaps between ends. Use large nails or a pair of screwdrivers as spacers to position adjacent panels that are not tongue-and-groove. (Tongue-and-groove panels usually have built-in gaps.)

7 Apply subflooring adhesive to the joists as in Step 3 and position the next panel, smooth side up, end-to-end against the first. Fasten as in steps 4 and 5. If the panel is tongue and groove, ensure adjacent ends mate, then pound the new panel gently into place with a mallet or large hammer (protect the panel's edge with a wood block).

8 After completing the first course, or row, of panels, start the next one with a half-sheet panel (cut it to size with a circular saw) placed side-to-side against the first panel—the ends of the panels should not fall on the same joists. Alternate full and half-size panels for the start of each course.

LAYING A FLOATING FLOOR

YOU WILL NEED

Tape measure and pencil
Low-tack tape
Hammer
Panel saw
Circular saw **or** plane
Small crowbar
Utility knife

MATERIALS

Foam/foil underlay plus
moisture barrier (if required)
and waterproof tape **or**
lightweight building felt
Cork expansion strips
Laminated strip flooring
Clips (if required)
PVA adhesive
Quarter-round **or**
shoe molding (if required)
Floor sealer

SEE ALSO

Removing baseboards
and moldings pp.36–37
Replacing baseboards
pp.38–39
Making minor repairs to a
wood floor pp.42–43
Replacing a damaged
floorboard pp.44–45
Laying a hardboard underlay
pp.46–47
Leveling a concrete floor
pp.50–51
Staining and varnishing
floorboards pp.182–183

Laminated strip flooring is not attached to the floor below; instead, the individual wood strips are secured together. Because this flooring is relatively thin, it must be laid on a flat, smooth surface. Before laying the boards, make sure existing wood floor surfaces are in good condition, and level a solid floor with floor-leveling compound if necessary. Cover wood floorboards with sheets of hardboard, or, if the floorboards are uneven, with sheets of plywood to provide a flat, level surface. Some strip flooring manufacturers recommend a felt underlay to reduce noise heard in rooms below; on solid floors, a moisture barrier must be used.

Decide on the direction in which to lay the flooring—normally with the length of the boards running the length of the room—and check how many widths are required. To avoid cutting a narrow width for the last strip to be laid, you may need to cut

"Floating" floorboards are not connected to the floor, so they can expand and contract as the temperature in the room changes.

the first length down; use a circular saw or plane on the tongue side of the strip. The floorboards may require sealing after being laid; follow the manufacturer's recommendations.

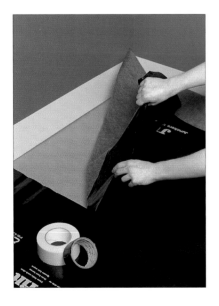

1 If needed, remove the baseboards (see pp.36–37). Lay down building felt or the foam/aluminum underlay, following the manufacturer's instructions. If you are using a moisture barrier, lay it down before the foam/ aluminum underlay. Depending on the material used, you may have to overlap or tape the edges.

2 Place cork expansion strips along the side walls. To allow an expansion gap, use spacer blocks between the strip and wall and set the first length of floorboard with its grooved edge ⅜ inch (10 mm) from the wall. Cut the next length to reach the other side wall (the leftover piece can start the next row), allowing for the cork strip.

3 Where clips are used to secure strips together, these are fitted before each strip is laid. For all methods, apply PVA adhesive to the groove end of the board before pushing the tongue at the end of the other board into it. Wipe off any squeezed out adhesive, using a damp cloth.

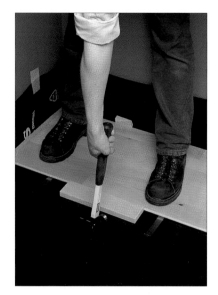

4 To fit an adjacent row, align each strip (with the joints staggered) and install the clips with a hammer. If you're not using clips, apply adhesive to the long grooves, then push them over the tongues of the first row. For either method, force the strips together by tapping with a hammer against a protective block.

5 When you come to the end of each row, force together the strips using a small crowbar or a special tool that comes with the boards. Continue across the room until you reach the opposite wall, where the last strip will have to be sawn or planed to fit, leaving room for a ⅜ inch (10 mm) expansion gap.

6 To fit a board around a pipe, mark its position on the relevant piece of flooring. Drill a hole to fit the pipe, using a hole saw bit, then cut a wedge from the hole to the wall edge of the strip, which can be glued in place after the floorboard has been laid.

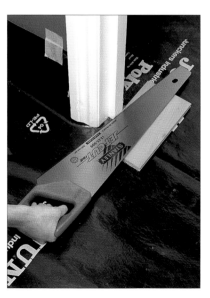

7 To fit the flooring around the door casing, use a saw resting on an offcut of floorboard (it gives the correct height for the cut). Trim it halfway if the flooring will end in the room—install a reduction or threshold strip—or trim all the way around if the flooring will continue into the next room. To trim the door to fit, see pp.76–77.

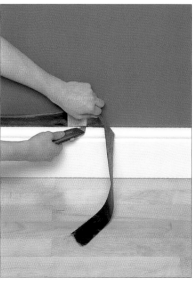

8 Replace the baseboards if necessary. If the baseboards were not removed, cover the expansion gaps by nailing quarter-round or shoe molding onto the baseboards—not the floor. Trim off the overlay, if necessary, using a utility knife. Finish off by applying a sealer to the boards.

PARQUET FLOORING

YOU WILL NEED

Square
Chalk line
Tape measure
Pencil
Notched adhesive spreader
Clean rag
Felt-tip pen **or** wax pencil
Backsaw
Utility knife
Hammer
Nail set

MATERIALS

Parquet flooring
Adhesive (unless flooring is
self-adhesive)
Cork expansion strips
Finishing sealant
Quarter-round **or**
shoe molding (if required)
Panel nails (if required)

SEE ALSO

Removing baseboards
and moldings pp.36–37
Replacing baseboards
pp.38–39
Making minor repairs to
a wood floor pp.55–45
Replacing a damaged
floorboard pp.46–47
Laying a hardboard
underlayment pp.46–47
Leveling a concrete floor
pp.50–51

The advantages of parquet flooring include it being easy to lay and its ability to cope with a slightly uneven surface. In fact, parquets have a degree of flexibility unmatched in any other type of wood floor. Parquet flooring should be laid on as flat and smooth a surface as you can manage, which means laying hardboard sheeting, rough side up, over repaired, existing wood floors or leveling a solid floor with floor leveling compound.

Before you start, check each of the tiles. They should be exactly square and all the same size; an irregular panel in the middle of the floor leaves unsightly gaps. However, you can put aside any tiles that are a different size and cut them down as edge pieces for the perimeter of the room.

Leave the tiles for a few days in the room where they will be laid to allow their moisture content to adjust to the humidity. When laying the tiles, leave a gap around the room to allow them

Wood flooring gives a warm feeling to any room. It also provides an unsuitable environment for house dust mites (which trigger asthma in some people).

to expand. Parquet tiles are held in place with adhesive; use the type recommended by the manufacturer. Some tiles are self-adhesive and require only the removal of a backing paper.

1 This type of wood flooring is laid starting at the center of the room, so start by "snapping" a chalk line from the midpoints of opposite walls to find the center point. Use this as a reference point for setting out the tiles. For a room without square walls, see p.210.

2 Starting at the center, lay a dry run of tiles along the length of the room and across the width to work out any gaps at the walls (but allow for the expansion gaps). Divide the gaps equally between the edge tiles, adjusting the center tile as necessary to avoid making cuts along the length of a "finger," or strip.

3 The center tiles are laid first. Draw lines on the floor parallel to the center marking lines and extend them well beyond the position of the first tiles. Spread the adhesive (use one suggested by the manufacturer of the tiles) on the floor, using a notched adhesive spreader.

4 Lay the central tiles in place, firmly pressing them into the adhesive. Working outward from the center in one quarter of the room at a time, position the remaining whole tiles. While it is still wet, use a clean rag to wipe off any excess adhesive that squeezes through the joints.

5 To cut the edge tiles to size, lay a whole tile over the last full tile to be laid and lay a third tile on top of this, with its edge the correct distance from the wall (use pieces of cork strip to allow for the expansion gap). Draw a cutting line onto the middle tile.

6 To trim tiles to fit around the edge, you can break off a whole "finger" by cutting through the backing with a utility knife. Use a backsaw to cut across a "finger." For easier handling of the tile, remove a section at a time. Fit the edge tiles in place.

7 Fill gaps between the tiles and walls with cork strips. Refit the baseboards, or nail hardwood quarter-round or shoe molding to the baseboards, using finishing nails and a small hammer (protect the parquets with a piece of paper). Sink the nails with a nail set (see p.38) and fill the nail holes (see p.195). Apply any recommended finish.

Helpful hints

Parquet flooring comes in a variety of styles, with the fingers arranged in a number of different geometric patterns. You can create your own look by mixing tiles of different patterns or stain finishes. For example, use darker tiles to create a border around the primeter of the room. Alternatively, short wood slats are available, which you can lay in your own geometric pattern—however, this will be a time-consuming task.

Before you lay down the tiles, do a dry run without the adhesive to make sure you will appreciate the overall effect— once you lay them down with adhesive, you'll be committed to the pattern or the direction they run in (see p.212).

Take tiles randomly from different boxes, even if you're using tiles of only one pattern and color. This will give a more uniform look, because tiles from different boxes are slightly different.

NAILING LAMINATE-STRIP FLOORING

This flooring simulates traditional floorboards and is available in a wide choice of attractive woods.

While thinner laminate-strip flooring usually is "floated" by joining the pieces (see pp.190–191), most thicker wood flooring is nailed down to the existing floorboards. A technique called "blind nailing" is used, where each strip is secured to the surface below with nails passing through the inside corner of the tongue before being covered by the groove of the adjacent board. It is vital that the nail doesn't interfere with the fit between the tongue and the groove, and that finishing nails, which can be punched below the surface, are used.

Make any repairs to the floor before laying the new strips. Measure the room, allowing for the expansion gaps, to see how many strips you will need; normally, the strips are laid with their length parallel with the longest walls of the room. If the last strip will be too narrow, cut both the first and the last strips to equal size with a circular saw, cutting the groove off the first piece and the tongue off the last.

The flooring usually comes with a sealed finish, but it may require further coats of sealer once it is laid. For the type of sealer to use, follow the manufacturer's recommendation.

1 Lay the first strip parallel with the wall (the long grooved side facing the wall), allowing for an expansion gap (follow the manufacturer's recommendations). Place nails through the face close to the wall edge, 16 inches (400 mm) apart, and force them below the surface with a nail set. Then "blind nail" the tongue (see step 3).

2 Continue the row, applying PVA adhesive to the short grooved ends to join adjacent strips. Using a tenon saw, cut the last length for the first row to size, allowing for the expansion gap. Place the cut edge near the wall.

3 Use the offcut from the previous row to start the next one, making sure the joints are staggered. Use a hammer against a block of wood to fit the groove tightly into the tongue. Blind nail by driving the nail just above the tongue, at a 45° angle to the board, and sink it below the surface. Continue to apply glue to the short ends.

4 Continue in the same way across the room until you reach the opposite side. For the last row, use a small crowbar against a small piece of offcut to force the boards together. This last row cannot be blind nailed, but will have to be nailed through the face. Sink the nails below the surface with a nail set and fill the holes.

5 To trim around a door casing, use a profile gauge to transfer the shape to the strip. This device is simply pressed against the casing to capture its shape. You can also use a compass: with the strip placed near the casing, use the steel leg to follow the casing's contour—the pencil will trace it onto the strip.

6 With the strip securely clamped in place, use a jigsaw to cut out the contour. Alternatively, you can trim the door casing and slide the flooring underneath it (see step 7, p.191). To fit a strip around a pipe, see pp.190–191.

7 Replace the baseboards if you've removed them. Or fit quarter-round or shoe molding to cover the gaps, nailing them to baseboards or using an adhesive. Fill the nail holes in the flooring with a wood filler, as well as any holes in the molding. Apply the recommended finish to the flooring; paint the molding.

Helpful hints

Laminate-strip flooring, other floorboards, and parquet tiles laid on top of existing floorboards can raise the floor level considerably. You can leave the baseboards in place and trim the boards around the door casing, as shown here. Alternatively, you can remove the baseboards and replace them once the flooring has been laid, and cut through the bottom of the casing so that the flooring fits underneath, as shown in *Laying a floating floor* (see pp.190–191).

Whichever method you decide to choose, the door itself will have to be trimmed so that you can open it over the new floor covering (see pp.76–77).

ROLL FLOOR COVERING OPTIONS

POSSIBLE MATERIALS

SEA GRASS

JUTE

SISAL

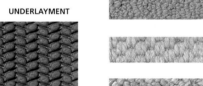

UNDERLAYMENT

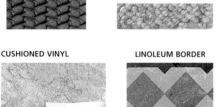

CUSHIONED VINYL

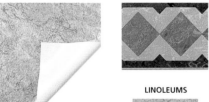

SHEET VINYL

CORD PILE CARPETS

VELVET PILE CARPETS

LOOPED PILE CARPETS

LINOLEUM BORDER

LINOLEUMS

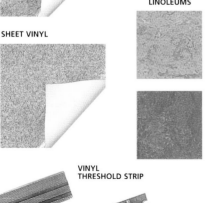

VINYL THRESHOLD STRIP

CARPET THRESHOLD STRIP

The two main types of flooring that come in a roll are carpet, (including natural floor coverings) and "sheet" flooring—mainly vinyl and linoleum. Carpets are generally described by the type of backing they have (foam or jute) and the way in which the fibers are connected to it, known as the pile. The fibers may be natural wool, manmade, or a combination of the two.

Natural floor coverings are becoming increasingly popular; these include coir (coconut fiber), sisal, and sea grass. Of these, sisal is the most hardwearing. Sheet vinyl and linoleum are also hardwearing. Laying sheet vinyl is an easy job; however, putting down linoleum is best left to a professional.

▲ Sheet vinyl is available in a huge range of colors and patterns, including this checkerboard pattern (which imitates a common tile pattern). There are two main types of vinyl: plain vinyl and backed vinyl (also known as cushioned vinyl), which has an additional resilient underlayer, making it softer, warmer, and quieter to walk on.

◄ Sheet vinyl and linoleum are particularly useful in the kitchen because food and grime cannot become trapped as they can do between tiles, and cleaning the floor is much easier. However, some vinyls can become slippery when wet.

◀ Based on the carpet's durability, it may be rated for light-, medium-, or heavy-duty use. Use light-duty carpet for an occasionally used guest room, medium-duty carpet for a regularly used bedroom, and heavy-duty carpet for stairs and other high-traffic areas.

◀ The fibers in natural floor coverings are derived from plants and woven together to form a mat. Sometimes the fibers are woven with wool to create a softer texture without losing the character of the natural fibers.

▶ Carpet in a neutral color provides a suitable backdrop for many decorating schemes. Protect pale carpet from spills by treating the carpet with a stain inhibitor.

▲ Striped or patterned carpet, or carpet with borders, can bring life to an otherwise plain flight of stairs. Carpet also helps deaden noise—an ideal choice for a wood staircase.

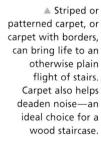

◀ The price of carpet increases in relation to the amount of wool used, which is the most expensive fiber in roll-floor coverings. Within each price range there will be different piles to choose from. Here, the velvet pile is very short, giving the feel and look of velvet.

◀ For areas where dirt is likely to be brought in from outside, particularly in a hallway, the best choice is a carpet in a dark color.

LAYING SHEET-VINYL FLOORING

YOU WILL NEED

Rented floor roller **or** push broom
Utility knife
Scissors (if required)
Metal straightedge
Protective material such as a sheet of hardboard
Notched adhesive spreader
Screwdriver

MATERIALS

Sheet vinyl
Adhesive **or** double-sided carpet tape (the tape is necessary for joining two sheets)
Threshold strips and screws
Electric drill plus masonry drill bit (if required)

SEE ALSO

Making minor repairs to a wood floor pp.42–43
Replacing a damaged floorboard pp.44–45
Laying a hardboard underlayment pp.46–47
Leveling a concrete floor pp.50–51
Using a template for vinyl flooring pp.200–201

Where a room is not too large—13 feet (4 m) wide or less—you can lay a single sheet of vinyl flooring. This has the advantage that there will be no seam, but the laying is slightly more difficult. Shorter widths are lighter and easier to move about.

Before you start, repair any damage to wood floorboards and lay down hardboard sheets; if necessary, level a concrete floor. Measure the room carefully: include features, such as alcoves and bay windows, and add on half the depth of any door thresholds. A pattern should lead away from the main entrance into the room. If more than one sheet is needed, allow extra to match up any pattern repeats.

To allow it to acclimatize, leave the roll unwrapped and loosely unrolled for two days in the room where it is to be used. Some vinyl flooring will not require all-over adhesive—follow the manufacturer's instructions. To fit it around odd shapes, see pp.200–201.

Vinyl flooring offers an extensive choice of patterns, colors, and textures for dressing up an otherwise drab room or utilitarian hallway.

Helpful hints

Instead of adhesive, use double-sided carpet tape around the perimeter of a room if it isn't subjected to heavy foot traffic. The flooring will be easier to remove at a later stage.

1 Unroll the vinyl sheet onto the floor with the pattern in the right direction. To remove air bubbles, smooth it down from the center of the room toward the edges with a rented floor roller if the floor is smooth or a push broom . Use a utility knife or scissors to cut the vinyl roughly to size; allow 2 inches (5 cm) extra at each edge for trimming.

2 At an external corner, roll back the vinyl and insert a protective material, such as hardboard, between the layers. Using a utility knife, make a cut to the end of the sheet, starting 2 inches (5 cm) from the corner. Slightly angle the cut toward the waste side (to the left in the situation shown here).

3 At an internal corner, fold the "V" and make a cut down the center with the utility knife. Overlap the two flaps (see inset), then cut up along the corner. Remove the offcuts and push the ends into place.

4 To apply adhesive, fold back half of the sheet (start away from the door). Spread the adhesive with a notched tool; follow the manufacturer's instructions. In some cases the adhesive may be applied only around the edges of the room. Reposition the vinyl and, once again, smooth it down flat. Repeat for the other half of the floor.

5 To trim the sheet to size, use a metal straightedge to push the vinyl firmly into the corner made by the floor and the baseboard. Cut the vinyl by running a sharp utility knife at a 45° angle along the straightedge.

6 At a doorway, make a series of vertical cuts, following the shape of the casing, then cut out the shape carefully. Trim the end of the sheet so that it lies under the middle of the door.

7 Finish off by fitting a threshold strip at the doorway. These strips are available in various styles, depending on the type of floor covering in the next room, and they are screwed down to the floor. On a concrete floor, drill holes (using a masonry drill bit) to take plastic plugs for the screws.

TRIMMING TWO SHEETS

If using two sheets of vinyl, work from each side of the room. Before cutting the edges to fit, overlap the sheets and match the pattern where the seam will be (avoid high foot-traffic areas such as by a door). Cut through the overlap so the two sheets join exactly. Unless you are using adhesive, secure the seam with double-sided tape.

USING A TEMPLATE FOR VINYL FLOORING

YOU WILL NEED

Weights
Scissors (if required)
Utility knife
Small wood block
Pencil
Grease pencil (for vinyl with a shiny surface)
Compass (if required)
Rented floor roller **or** push broom
Notched adhesive spreader (if required)
Caulking gun

MATERIALS

Paper underlay
Masking tape
Sheet vinyl
Adhesive (if required)
Threshold strips and screws
Silicone sealant

SEE ALSO

Making minor repairs to a wood floor pp.42–43
Replacing a damaged floorboard pp.44–45
Laying a hardboard underlayment pp.46–47
Leveling a concrete floor pp.50–51
Laying sheet-vinyl flooring pp.198–199

A paper pattern, or template, of a room with an unusual shape or several obstructions can be used as a guide to cut a sheet of vinyl flooring. The technique to create the paper template is known as "scribing," a process in which you transfer the exact profile of the room walls and other shapes onto the paper. You can use the paper normally sold for laying under carpets; alternatively, tape together several lengths of brown paper.

Measure from the longest points of the room, and consider that any pattern should run from the door. Before you start, repair any damage to wood floorboards and lay hardboard sheets to provide a smooth surface; level a concrete floor if necessary.

It is generally best to use adhesive to secure the vinyl in a bathroom (or other rooms where water gets splashed about such as a kitchen) because this will prevent any possibility of water getting under the edge of the sheet.

Trimming sheet vinyl for a room containing a number of obstacles, such as a toilet and basin in a bathroom, is made easier by using a template.

Helpful hints

While cutting the template to fit the room, you may accidentally move the paper. One way to avoid this is to weigh down the paper, using books or other heavy items, until you have trimmed it and taped it in place for scribing.

1 Cut the paper roughly to the shape of the room, allowing 2 inches (50 mm) on each edge for trimming. If you need to use two pieces of paper, tape them together using strong masking tape on both sides. Make pencil marks across the seams to use as a guide in case the sheets are separated.

2 Use scissors or a utility knife to cut the paper to about ½ inch (12 mm) less than the size of the room, and make a cut the same distance around any shapes. The exact distance is not crucial, but it must be less than the thickness of the wood "scribing" block (see step 3). Tape the paper to the floor to keep it from moving.

3 Starting in a corner, hold a wood block 1–2 inches (25–50 mm) wide firmly against the wall, with a pencil placed against the other end. Draw a line on the paper, sliding the block along the wall. Use it around any shapes, taking care that the block doesn't tilt. Keep the block the same way around all the time.

4 At a water pipe, use the block as a guide to draw a box the width of the pipe. Draw the lines perpedicular to the wall, then mark the distance away from the wall, using the short side of the block to measure from the front and back of the pipe. Use a compass to draw a circle in the box.

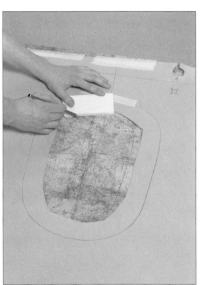

5 In another (larger) room, lay the vinyl flat on the floor, right side face up, and secure the paper template to it, using masking tape. Now use the wood block (positioned the same way around) to draw a line onto the vinyl, working outward from the line on the paper. Copy any shapes, including those for water pipes.

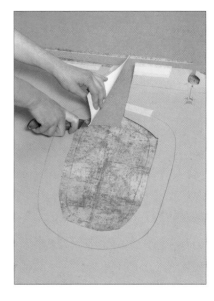

6 Trim the vinyl with a utility knife. To cut the hole for the pipe, use a short length of pipe of the same size (use a file to sharpen the inside of the end of the pipe, but do not reduce the diameter). Cut slits from any holes to the edge of the vinyl so that the sheet can be slipped around the obstacles.

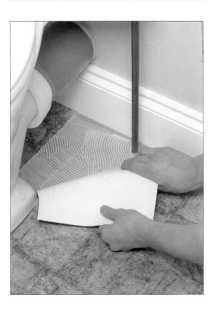

7 Position the vinyl in the room. Fold back half of the vinyl and, following the manufacturer's directions, spread the adhesive. Reposition the vinyl and use a roller or broom to remove any bubbles (see pp.198–199). Repeat on the other half. If you're not using adhesive, use double-sided carpet tape at any slits.

8 Finish off at the pedestals by squeezing a bead of waterproof silicone sealant around them, holding the gun at about a 45° angle. As well as sealing the edges, the sealant will hide any rough cuts. To install a threshold strip, see pp.198–199.

LAYING CUSHION-BACKED CARPET

YOU WILL NEED

Utility knife plus carpet trimming blades
Staple gun
Tape measure
Metal straightedge
Carpet-layer's stair tool
Screwdriver
Hacksaw
Electric drill plus masonry bit

MATERIALS

Paper felt padding
(if required)
Foam-backed carpet
Double-sided adhesive tape
Threshold strips
Latex adhesive

SEE ALSO

Removing floor coverings
pp.40–41
Making minor repairs to
a wood floor pp.42–43
Replacing a damaged
floorboard pp.44–45
Minor concrete floor defects
pp.48–49
Leveling a concrete floor
pp.50–51
Laying standard carpet
pp.204–205

One of the advantages of cushion-backed carpet is that it's easy to lay: it doesn't require padding or stretching. It comes in rolls of different widths and in different wear qualities.

The floor must be dry, dust-free, and level before the carpet is laid. Repair the floorboards (see pp.42–45) and fit sheets of hardboard underlayment, unless the existing flooring is flat; level a concrete floor and damp-proof it, if necessary (see pp.48–49). You should

Cushion-backed carpet can be laid almost anywhere in the house, except for on stairs.

carry out all decorating (especially painting) before laying a new carpet.

A paper felt padding on wood floors prevents staining of the carpet from dust below the floorboards—it may be all you need on particleboard subfloors or smooth floorboards. Before you start, remove all furniture and take the door off its hinges (it may need trimming later on, see pp.76–77).

1 After clearing the room of furniture and preparing the floor, put down paper felt padding. Cut it to fit around the room, then use a staple gun to hold it in place; make sure that the staple heads do not tear the paper. If in a little used room, lay the padding to the walls; where there will be heavy use, leave a border for the tape.

2 Stick double-sided tape around the perimeter of the room, leaving the backing paper in place. In large rooms, put down additional double-sided adhesive tape across the width of the room to secure the carpet. If the room will be heavily used, make sure the tape is laid directly onto the floor—and not the paper underlay.

3 Measure the room; in a larger room (or outside) cut the carpet roughly to shape, adding 2 inches (50 mm) to each edge for trimming. If using more than one length, check that the piles are going the same way (facing away from the main window). With the carpet laid in the room, trim it to 1 inch (25 mm).

5 Smooth the carpet down all over the room; then, working along one wall at a time, remove the backing from the double-sided adhesive tape and firmly press the carpet into place.

7 To join two pieces of carpet, overlap the edges; then cut through both of them with a trimming knife guided along a metal straightedge. Remove the offcuts and butt the edges together. Lift them up, lay down a strip of double-sided tape, then apply latex adhesive to the edges to stop them from fraying. Push the edges down in place.

4 For an inside corner, make a diagonal cut across the corner of the carpet so that it can be pushed into its final position. For an outside corner, make a cut parallel with (but slightly outside) the sides of the alcove, using a piece of wood underneath the folded carpet to avoid cutting through the carpet underneath.

6 Use the back of the knife to push the carpet into the floor-wall angle; then cut it to size with the trimming knife held at a 45° angle and guided along the baseboard. Replace the blades on the knife often; they dull quickly. Use a carpet-layer's stair tool to push any loose fibers down at the edges.

Helpful hints

Use a hacksaw to cut threshold strips for any doors to length, then screw these down to the floor after cutting the carpet neatly to fit underneath. On concrete floors you will need an electric drill with a masonry bit to drill holes for anchors to take the screws. Alternatively, use an epoxy-base adhesive.

To fit carpet around plumbing or heating pipes, make a cut from the edge of the room to the position of the pipe, then use your trimming knife to carefully cut neatly around the pipe until the carpet lies flat.

Use a vacuum cleaner to remove loose bits of carpet fibers before replacing the furniture.

LAYING STANDARD CARPET

YOU WILL NEED

Staple gun
Tape measure
Backsaw
Utility knife plus carpet
trimming blades
Hammer
Kneekicker (rented)
Carpet-layers stair tool
Screwdriver
Hacksaw
Electric drill plus masonry
bit (if required)

MATERIALS

Paper felt underlay
(if required)
Tackless strips
Epoxy-based adhesive
(if required)
Rubber **or** felt underlay
Jute-backed carpet
Double-sided adhesive tape
Carpet seaming tape and
latex adhesive (if required)
Threshold strip

SEE ALSO

Making minor repairs to
a wood floor pp.42–43
Replacing a damaged
floorboard pp.44–45
Laying a hardboard
underlayment pp.46–47
Laying cushion-backed
carpet pp.202–203

A carpet stretched from wall to wall creates a luxurious floor covering that is comfortable for relaxing on and against bare feet.

Standard carpet must be stretched as it is laid to prevent it from creasing later on. Given the right tools (such as a kneekicker) and the proper laying technique, you should achieve a reasonable result.

You must first prepare the floor (see pp.42–47 for a wood floor, pp.48–51 for a concrete floor); you'll also need to put down felt or foam rubber padding before laying the carpet.

TACKLESS STRIPS OR TACKS

Professionals use "tackless strips," thin strips of wood with angled, upward-pointing tacks to hold carpet in place (the name refers to the fact that individual tacks are not needed). They are nailed down around the edges of the room (or glued down on concrete floors); the carpet is forced down over them. The tack points are sharp, so handle them with care. The strips give the best finished result.

You can use carpet tacks on wood floors, with carpet folded under itself and the tacks driven through both thicknesses. The only benefit is cost-savings; tacks don't give as good a grip and the final result is not smooth.

1 To fit prenailed tackless strips around the room, use a backsaw to cut the strips to length (use short lengths around door casings and French windows); then nail them down to the floor, with the teeth facing toward the wall. To attach strips to a concrete floor, use an epoxy-base adhesive instead of nails.

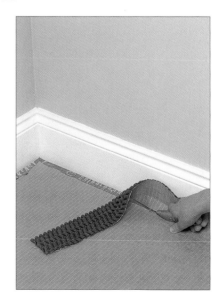

2 On a wood floor, staple down a paper underlay to prevent dirt blowing through floorboards. Lay down felt or rubber padding, cut it to fit inside the tackless strips, and staple it in place; use double-sided adhesive carpet tape between lengths. On a concrete floor, use the double-sided tape for the whole pad.

3 In a larger room (or outside if a nice day), cut carpet roughly to size; allow 4 inches (100 mm) for trimming at each edge. Lay it out in the room, adjusting it, if necessary, to square up any pattern. Walk out any large wrinkles in the carpet, moving from the center of the room toward the walls.

4 Make diagonal cuts at both inside and outside corners (see step 4, p.203). Before you make the cut at an inside corner, trim off some of the excess to help the carpet lay in place.

5 Use the knife to trim the carpet along the baseboard, holding it at a 45° angle. If you're not confident with the knife, leave a ⅜ inch (10 mm) allowance and finish off after stretching the carpet in step 6. Hook the carpet to the tackless strips at one corner, then along the two adjoining walls to the far corners.

6 Stretch the carpet with a kneekicker first across, then along the room, hooking it onto the tackless strips at the two remaining walls. As you secure the carpet to the strips, push the carpet down behind them, using a carpet-layer's stair tool. (Or finish the trimming after stretching the carpet, then push the carpet down with the tool.)

7 At a door, use a special tackless threshold strip. Screw it down on a wood floor; for a concrete floor, glue it down or screw it to anchors set in holes made with an electric drill fitted with a masonry drill bit. Fit the carpet over the teeth, then bang down the top of the strip, protecting it with a piece of carpet.

Helpful hints

You may have to join two lengths of carpet in a large room. The traditional method is to sew them together, but because this is not easy, use carpet seaming tape instead. Place it below the joint between the two pieces of carpet and give it a generous coating of latex adhesive; use more adhesive on the back of the two pieces of carpet and on the edges up to the bottom of the pile (to prevent fraying). Allow the adhesive to become touch dry before pressing the two pieces of carpet together along the tape—a wallpaper seam roller is ideal for pressing down the joint. You can use the adhesive and carpet tape to repair any cuts.

LAYING STAIR CARPET

Laying carpet on stairs requires working on each step in turn while in a confined space— however, the final result will make the effort well worthwhile.

There are two methods of carpeting a staircase: fitting the carpet to cover the stairs completely or laying a "runner" with a gap along each side. A stair runner is easier to lay, and you can easily move it to distribute wear evenly at the front edge, or nosing, of the steps. A fitted carpet will always look better, but is more difficult to lay.

To find the length needed for straight stairs, add together the depth of one tread (front to back) and the height of one riser; multiply by the number of steps. If the stairs turn a corner, measure from the deepest part of the tread. Carpets are sold by the yard (or meter); order the next highest yard (or meter) above your measurement.

1 After doing repairs and painting, nail down tackless strips at the angles between the treads and risers. Use L-shape stair strips, with tacks pointing toward the angles (use a spacer between the strip and the wall). Or use normal strips: nail a strip on the riser, then a strip on the tread, both of them ½ inch (12 mm) from the angle.

2 At a landing, cut the tackless strips to length with a tenon saw, and fit them as you would fit tackless strips around a room (see pp.204–205). Fit all the tackless strips for the complete staircase before going on to the next step.

3 Cut the padding to the width of the carpet and into short lengths the width of a tread plus 1 inch (25 mm). Position a length on the top tread, letting it overhang the nosing. Use carpet tacks or staples to secure the padding in place, fastening it along the back and side edges. Continue until all the treads are covered.

4 Take the carpet from the landing above and cut it so that it covers the top riser, using a utility knife fitted with a carpet trimming blade. Push the carpet firmly into the tackless strip (see step 6), then trim off the excess.

5 While balancing the runner on the step below, position the top of the runner so that it's centered on the tread. Push the end down into the tackless strip and secure it in place with a stair tool and mallet (see step 6). Allow the roll to move down, one step at a time, as you secure the carpet to the tackless strips.

6 For each step, check that the carpet is properly aligned, and reposition the roll if necessary. Use a carpet-layer's stair tool to push the carpet onto tackless strips, working along the angle from end to end; then secure the carpet by hitting the stair tool with a rubber mallet as you, once again, working along the angle.

7 At the end of each flight, trim off the excess carpet, using the utility knife; then return to the top of the steps to trim off any excess at the top of the run. Fit the carpet at the landing in the same way that you would fit standard carpet in a room (see pp.204–205).

Helpful hints

To move the carpet when it wears at the nosing, don't fit a tackless strip on the top tread. Instead, fold a wearing allowance (the depth of the tread) underneath, and use carpet tacks through both layers of carpet. Lay the carpet as described. Whenever the carpet begins to wear, pull it up and reposition it, with the allowance gradually shifting to the last riser.

To cope with fitting carpet on winding stairs, cut a fitted carpet for each step (tread and riser below) just slightly over size; then fit it to the tackless strips before cutting it to size. Where a stair runner is being used on a curved staircase, instead of cutting the carpet, make angled folds on each riser, then use carpet tacks through the layers of carpet.

FLOOR TILE OPTIONS

POSSIBLE MATERIALS

QUARRY TILE

CERAMIC TILE

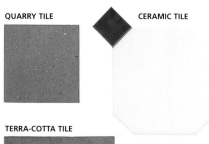

TERRA-COTTA TILE

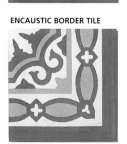

QUARRY TILES

ENCAUSTIC BORDER TILE

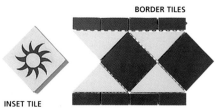

BORDER TILES

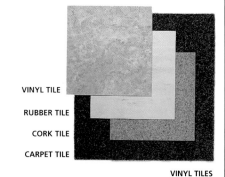

INSET TILE

VINYL TILE

RUBBER TILE

CORK TILE

CARPET TILE

VINYL TILES

The advantage of using floor tiles is that you can mix and match colors and use patterns in a greater diversity than other floor coverings. Tiles can be easier to lay, especially in awkwardly shaped rooms, because you don't have to handle large sheets of material. However, they can take more time to lay because a lot of cutting may be needed, and the planning of where to start laying the tiles is vital.

Tiles for floors break down neatly into two groups: soft, resilient tiles, which include carpet, cork, linoleum, rubber, and vinyl, and hard tiles, including ceramic, quarry, and terra-cotta. Each is used in a different situation for a different purpose, and laying methods vary.

▶ A large room can handle the strong effect created by mixing black and white ceramic tiles in a checkerboard pattern. These and other hard tiles are characterized by their durability and natural beauty—and also by the fact that they are cold and noisy underfoot.

◀ Quarry and terra-cotta tiles are very durable, and they come in a range of earth colors and a variety of shapes and sizes, with a smooth or textured surface. If they are machine made (they'll be a regular size), they can be as easy to lay as standard ceramic tiles—but cutting them is considerably more difficult.

▶ Vinyl tiles are the most popular of the soft, resilient floor tiles and come in a variety of patterns, including simulated brick, marble, and stone.

▼ Plain white ceramic tiles are made more interesting by using ones octagonal in shape and adding colored inset tiles.

▲ Carpet tiles have the appearance of carpet, but have the advantage that if a single tile is damaged, it can be easily replaced (always buy spare tiles). You can use them in bedrooms, kitchens, bathrooms, and home offices.

▶ Carpet tiles are often set in a checkerboard pattern, but you can achieve interesting effects by cutting tiles diagonally in half or into even smaller sections.

◀ Pattern has been created when laying these vinyl tiles by combining tiles of a variety of colors. Like all resilient floor tiles, vinyl tiles are soft and warm underfoot, quiet, and easy to keep clean. However, remember they can be slippery when wet.

▶ Ceramic floor tiles are one of the easiest surfaces to keep clean, making them ideal for bathrooms and kitchens. The dark color of these tiles is less likely to show dirt and footprints.

LAYING VINYL AND OTHER SOFT FLOOR TILES

YOU WILL NEED

Chalk line
Straightedge
Hammer
Wooden strip and nails
(if required)
Pencil
Utility knife
Scissors (if required)
Paper template **or** profile
gauge (if required)
Notched adhesive spreader

MATERIALS

Vinyl tiles **or** other soft
floor tiles
Adhesive

SEE ALSO

Making minor repairs to
a wood floor pp.42–43
Replacing a damaged
floorboard pp.44–457
Laying a hardboard
underlayment pp.46–47
Leveling a concrete floor
pp.50–51
Laying sheet-vinyl flooring
pp.198–199
Using a template for vinyl
flooring pp.200–201

One of the most effortless of all flooring jobs is laying soft floor tiles, which are easy to cut and handle. All types—vinyl, linoleum, carpet, rubber, and cork—are laid in the same way, except the adhesive used may be different. The manufacturer will recommend the correct adhesive. Some carpet tiles can be laid with adhesive at only the perimeter of the room, and some vinyl and cork tiles are self-adhesive: simply remove the backing paper before positioning them.

The tiles are thin and the adhesive layer is not thick enough to cover any irregularities, so a smooth and flat, dry floor surface is the necessary starting point. Hardboard sheeting is the ideal way of preparing existing wood floors; concrete floors should also be in good condition and level.

Solvent-base adhesives dry more quickly than water-base ones but may be flammable—always follow the manufacturer's safety precautions.

You can create a dramatic effect by mixing plain colored tiles to form a checkerboard pattern and using complementary tile insets.

Helpful hints

To lay tiles on a diagonal, use chalk lines snapped from the corners of the room as guidelines. If you use lines snapped from the midpoints of the walls, establish the diagonals by using the procedures in steps 1 and 2.

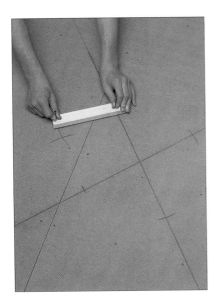

1 To find a room's center, snap chalk lines from the mid-points of the walls (see p.192). If the room isn't square, snap the lines from the corners of the room. Hammer a nail through the ends of a wooden strip. With one nail at the center of the chalk lines, scribe arcs on the lines; scribe bisecting arcs from the first arcs.

2 The bisecting arcs should be centered between the chalk lines. Draw a line through the center of two opposing bisecting arcs, using a metal straightedge as a guide. Repeat with the other two bisecting arcs. Extend these lines to the edge of the room—these are the center lines.

3 Dry-lay tiles from the center point along the center lines to establish how the tiles should be laid. Try to minimize cutting at the edges. Ideally, no edge tile should be cut less than half a tile's width, but you might want to have whole (or nearly whole) tiles where they are more visible, with thinner strips against a less visible wall.

4 Mark any changes in the position of the center, extending beyond the position of the central tiles. If required, spread adhesive on the floor, covering 10 square feet (1 sq m) at a time, starting in one quarter. With rubber tiles, spread adhesive on tiles too; for carpet tiles, hold the first one down with double-sided adhesive tape.

5 Start positioning the tiles on the adhesive (or, one at a time, remove the backing paper, then position the tile). Some tiles have arrows on the back, indicating the pattern (or pile) direction. Make sure adjacent tiles butt together. Continue laying the tiles to the edges of the room, adding any inset tiles as you go.

6 To trim a tile to fit the edge, lay a whole tile exactly on top of the last whole tile laid. Lay a third tile on top of that, with an edge against the wall, and run a utility knife along its opposite edge to cut the central tile. (To mark a carpet tile, nick the edges with a utility knife and draw a cutting line on the back of the tile.)

7 To cut a corner tile to fit, follow step 6 for one width, then repeat against the adjacent wall for the other. If you're not confident about your cutting abilities, use a pencil to draw cutting lines on the central tile; then remove it to do the cutting on a work surface, using a metal straightedge as a guide for the knife.

8 To mark gentle curves, you can use a template (see pp.200–201), but for intricate shapes (such as a door casing) use a profile gauge (see p.195) to transfer the shape to the tile. Trim the tile with a utility knife. To cut a hole for a water pipe, see p.201. To install a threshold strip at a door, see p.199. Cork tiles may need sealing.

LAYING CERAMIC FLOOR TILES

YOU WILL NEED

Chalk line
Floor tile spacers
Long wooden straightedge
Notched adhesive spreader
Carpenter's level
Hammer and wood block
Felt-tip pen **or** wax pencil
Tile cutter
Portable electric grinder
with ceramic tile-cutting
blade (if required), plus
protective goggles and
heavy-duty work gloves
Rubber spreader
Damp sponge **or** cloth

MATERIALS

Ceramic floor tiles
Nails
Adhesive
Plastic tile spacers
Grout

SEE ALSO

Making minor repairs to
a wood floor pp.42–43
Laying a hardboard
underlayment pp.46–47
Leveling a concrete floor
pp.50–51

*Ceramic floor tiles are ideal
in a bathroom, but they can
also be used in a kitchen,
utility room, or hallway.*

Although a floor laid with ceramic tiles can be cold and noisy, it will be durable and easy to keep clean. The technique for laying ceramic floor tiles is similar to that required for putting ceramic tiles on a wall (see pp.152–155); the differences are that the tiles are thicker—making them more difficult to cut—and that you start in the middle of the tiled area instead of in one corner.

A normal (waterproof) ceramic tile adhesive will allow the necessary degree of flexibility if you're tiling onto a wood floor; on a concrete floor, use a cement-based adhesive. In either case, the underlying floor surface must be both smooth and level; lay thick hardboard or plywood sheets on a wood floor or use floor-leveling compound on a concrete floor.

CHOOSING THE CENTER

Once you have found the center of the room (by snapping chalk lines; see p.192 and p.210), choose one of these starting points for the central tiles: a single tile centered on the center point; two tiles meeting at the center; or four tiles meeting at the center. You may want to adjust the center point to align the tiles with a room feature, such as a fireplace, or to set the tiles on a diagonal (see p.210).

1 Working from the center, dry-lay a row of tiles (allowing for the recommended grouting gap) along and across the room. You may need to adjust the center lines so that the edge tiles are equal in size and no less than one half a tile's width.

2 Divide the room in two and nail a wooden straightedge to the floor along the chalk line (or the adjusted chalk line). Sink the nails only enough to hold the straightedge in place, because it will have to be removed later. On concrete floors, use masonry nails.

3 Starting in the half of the room farthest from the door, spread adhesive on an area 3 feet (1 m) long and just wider than the tiles. Lay the tiles against the strip (starting at center), using tile spacers to create a grouting gap between the tiles. Some manufacturers recommend applying adhesive to the tile as well as to the floor.

4 Use a level to ensure that the tiles are flush. If not, tap a tile in place with a hammer against a wood block. Lay all the full tiles for one half of the room; after the adhesive sets, carefully remove the wooden straightedge and repeat for the other half, finishing at the door. Allow the adhesive to set before fitting edge tiles.

5 Mark the edge tiles by using the three-tile technique: that is, lay a whole tile exactly on top of the last full tile laid, lay a third tile on top of that (using spacers at the wall to allow for grouting gaps); then draw a line on the middle tile of the sandwich, using the top one as a guide.

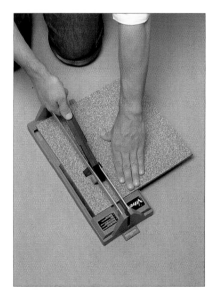

6 Use a tile cutter for cutting ceramic floor tiles. Make a single, deliberate score on the tile, then use the handle to snap the tile along the score by pressing it down at the end of the tile. Apply adhesive to the back of the edge tiles before inserting them in place.

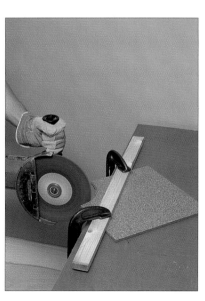

7 If you have to make a curved cut (see p.211 for marking it), securely clamp the tile to a work surface with the section to be cut extending from the end. Wearing protective goggles and work gloves, use an electric grinder with a ceramic tile-cutting blade (which can be hired) to cut the curve. You can smooth the cut with a tile file.

8 After allowing 24 hours for the adhesive to dry, use the recommended grouting medium for the tiles (this must be a flexible type if used on wood sub-floors). Work the grout into the spaces between the tiles with a rubber spreader, then wipe off any grout from the surface of the tiles with a damp sponge or cloth.

LAYING QUARRY TILES

YOU WILL NEED

Chalk line
Wooden straightedge
Notched adhesive spreader
Carpenter's level
Wooden **or** rubber mallet
Wood block
Tile cutter **or** tile-cutting saw with diamond cutting wheel plus protective goggles and heavy-duty work gloves
Grout spreader
Garden hose (if required)

MATERIALS

Quarry tiles
¼ inch (6 mm) dowels
Cement-base adhesive
Cement-base grout
Top-coat sealer (if required)
Silicone-rubber compound **or** caulking

SEE ALSO

Making minor repairs to a wood floor pp.42–43
Laying a hardboard overlay pp.46–47
Leveling a concrete floor pp.50–51

A traditional flooring material, quarry tiles provide an earthy colored hard-wearing floor.

Although quarry tiles are less likely to crack than ceramic tiles, they are harder to cut, and handmade ones (machine-made tiles are more common) are more difficult to lay. Terracotta tiles are similar to quarry tiles, but are warmer and less noisy underfoot.

The floor surface must be smooth and level. A concrete floor is the best substrate. Wood floors must be covered with exterior-grade plywood (which is laid in the same way as hardboard, but screwed down). Doors may require trimming to accommodate the extra height (see pp.76–77). Quarry tiles are always laid with a cement-base adhesive, and a cement-base grout is used to fill the gaps.

You cannot cut quarry tiles with a handheld cutter. Some platform-style tile cutters can't cut quarry tiles, so use one that specifically claims to be able to cut them, or hire a tile-cutting saw with a diamond-cutting wheel. Before you start, soak the tiles in water to reduce their absorbency; otherwise, the adhesive may be weakened.

Helpful hints

To fit a tile around a pipe, mark the exact position of the pipe on the tile. Drill a hole the size of the pipe, using a hole saw with a ceramic-cutting blade; then cut the tile in two so that the halves fit on either side of the pipe.

1 If you have baseboard tiles, do a dry-run (with the dowels) to establish the grouting gap and corner tiles. Adjust the tiles to avoid cuts, keeping whole tiles in more visible areas. Use a tile-cutting saw (see step 6) if you must cut a tile, starting at the thick end. Apply adhesive to the back of the tiles and set them in place.

2 Snap chalk lines (see p.192 and p.210) to find the center of the room. Set a dry-run of two rows of tiles (with dowels to allow for the grouting gap) and reposition them to align with baseboard tiles and to avoid making cuts; re-snap the chalk line. If you must cut tiles, adjust the lines to avoid cutting narrow strips.

3 Nail a wooden straightedge down the center of the room (leave the nail heads raised for easy removal later on) and spread 10 square feet (1 sq m) of adhesive on the floor, using a notched adhesive spreader. The adhesive should be at least ¼ inch (6 mm) thick, especially if the tiles vary in thickness.

4 Lay the first whole tiles up against the strip, using short lengths of ¼ inch (6 mm) dowels to create the grouting gaps. Press the tiles down firmly into the adhesive, using a carpenter's level to check that they are flush, and sliding the tiles, if necessary, to ensure the gaps for the grout are straight and uniform.

5 If the tiles are not level, tap a wooden or rubber mallet against a piece of wood laid across them. Continue with all the whole tiles until half of the room is covered. Remove the straightedge and finish off the other half of the room. Leave for 24 hours before fitting the edge tiles. Measure and mark each of the edge tiles (see p.213).

6 Cut and set each edge tile, with the adhesive on the back of the tile. For a clean cut without cracking the tile, use a tile-cutting saw with a water-cooled diamond cutting wheel (it can be hired). It will only cut straight lines (and L-shapes). To make a convex cut, use an electric grinder fitted with a masonry cutting disc (see p.213).

7 After 24 hours, use a rubber spreader to apply a cement-base grout to fill the joints, leaving an expansion gap between the floor tiles and baseboard (or at the edge of the room). If you want, make a concave shape in the grout, using a piece of garden hose. If recommended, apply a top-coat sealer before you apply the grout.

8 Completely clean off all the grout before it sets, using a damp sponge or cloth. Even a fine film left after rinsing can leave a haze that is difficult to remove if left to dry. Fill the expansion gap (which allows the floor to move in a centrally heated home) with caulking or a silicone-rubber compound.

PAINTING A CONCRETE FLOOR

If left untreated, a concrete floor in a playroom, utility room, workshop, or garage can rapidly become dusty and dirty. The answer is a specially-formulated floor paint, which will prevent dust forming and make the floor much easier to keep clean.

Floor paints are available in solvent-base and water-base versions. The solvent-base type is for heavy-duty floors (such as a garage) and can also be used outside. The low-odor water-base type can be used inside and has the advantage of drying quickly; it is ready to walk on after three hours. Special paints are also sold specifically for garage floors (they are harder wearing than normal floor paints) and for use on doorsteps (these contain a nonslip additive).

Leave a newly laid concrete floor for at least a month before applying floor paint; if an existing floor is dusty, treat it with a concrete sealer before painting (see pp.48–49).

Floor paints are available in several colors such as blue, green, gray, black, and white. Dark colors are more appropriate in a workshop or garage.

Where it is impossible to remove all the furniture from a room (for example, in a garage that doubles as a workshop), it may be possible to paint the room in two halves.

1 Before you start painting, remove all loose and flaking material from the floor. If flaking paint is left on the floor, the new paint will flake off.

2 You must clean the floor of dirt and debris—an industrial vacuum cleaner is ideal for this. If the concrete has been prone to creating dust, apply a concrete sealer (see pp.48–49).

3 The floor does not need to be leveled, but you may have to repair any holes or cracks, using a sand-and-cement mortar mix; press it well into any depressions and smooth it level with the remaining floor surface (for more details, see pp.48–49).

4 The floor must be thoroughly clean and free of oil and grease if the paint is to adhere. If mineral spirits won't remove all the stains, you can use a proprietary degreasing agent to clean the floor.

5 You may need to dilute the first coat by 10 percent with mineral spirits. Make sure you mix it thoroughly—an attachment for an electric drill that is specially designed to mix paint is the best tool for the job. Always turn off the drill before lifting the paint stirrer from the bucket.

6 Use a 4-inch- (100-mm-) wide paint brush to apply a strip of floor paint around the perimeter of the room. If you don't have a steady hand, stick lengths of low-tack masking tape along the edges of the walls to protect them.

7 The best method for painting a floor is to use a shaggy nylon pile sleeve on a paint roller with an extension handle. Start in the corner farthest from the door to avoid painting yourself into a blind corner. After it dries, apply a second full-strength coat, starting at the other far corner and working your way toward the door.

PAINTING A BAND

The neatest way to finish the floor is to create a band along the walls at baseboard height. Measure up from the floor and use a carpenter's level to draw a guideline. Apply low-tack masking tape along the line, then paint up to it. Remove the tape before the paint is dry.

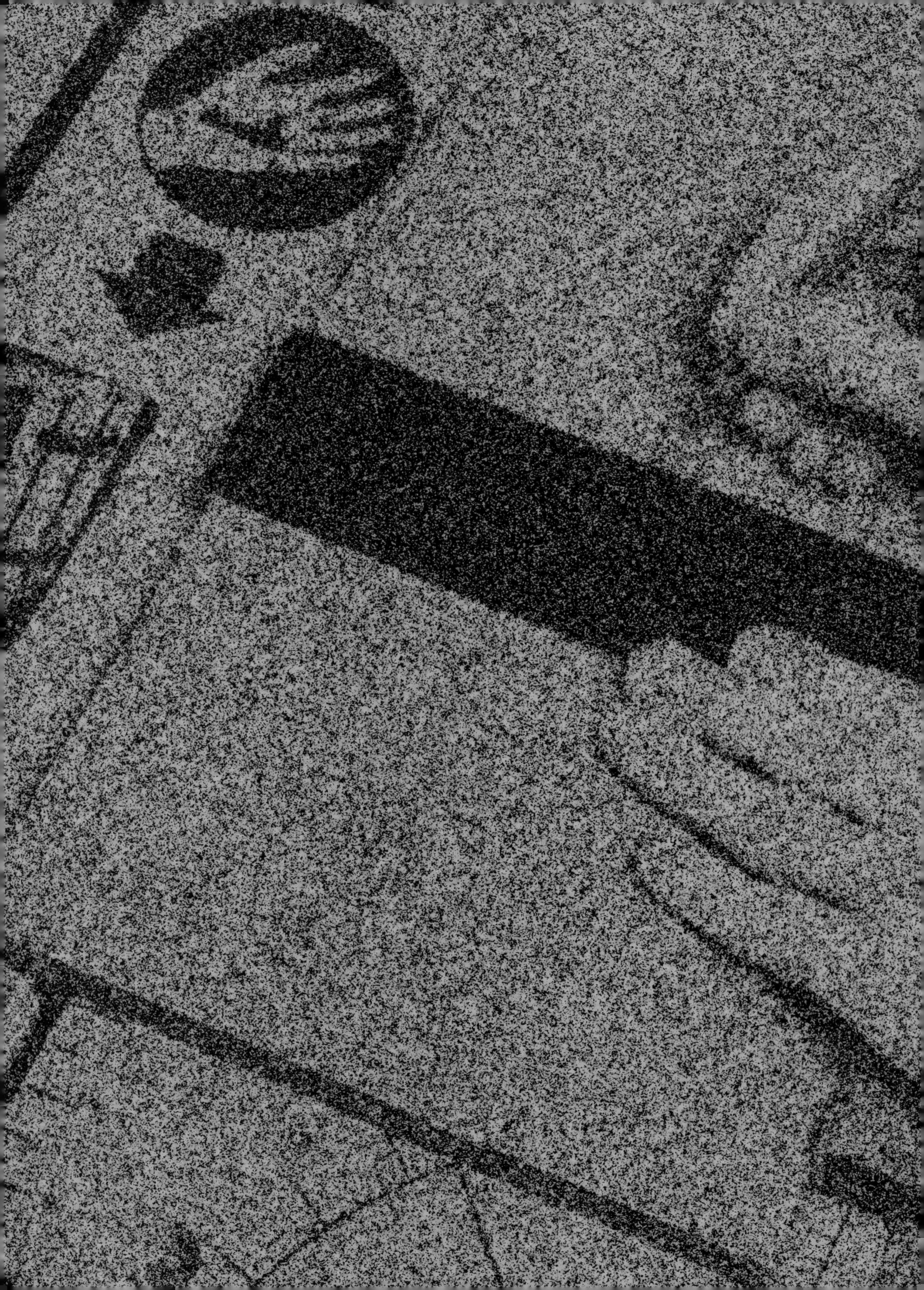

5

SHELVING AND STORAGE

SHELVING AND STORAGE DIRECTORY

SHELVING OPTIONS

PAGES 222–223

There are several methods for installing shelves, and a huge variety of materials available to meet any budget. You can plan shelves to suit your needs and tastes, using anything from one simple store-bought, fixed shelf to a homemade stack of individually fitted, built-in alcove shelves.

PUTTING UP FIXED SHELVES

SKILL LEVEL Low
TIME FRAME Under 2 hours
SPECIAL TOOLS Carpenter's level, electric drill, masonry bit
SEE PAGES 224–225

The simplest arrangement involves putting up a single shelf supported on two shelf brackets. Longer shelves require more brackets, and you can mount shelves one above the other. The most important part of the job is installing secure fasteners into the walls to ensure that the brackets support the shelf and its load adequately.

INSTALLING ADJUSTABLE SHELVES

SKILL LEVEL Low
TIME FRAME Under 2 hours
SPECIAL TOOLS Try square, hand saw or power saw, awl, carpenter's level, electric drill, tenon saw, chisel
SEE PAGES 226–227

Adjustable shelves are an arrangement consisting of several individual shelves that can be easily moved to another position to vary the shelf spacing as your needs change over the years. The brackets usually fit into slots or channels in vertical tracks, called standards, which are screwed to the wall.

ALCOVE SHELVING

SKILL LEVEL Low to medium
TIME FRAME ½ day
SPECIAL TOOLS Try square, hand saw, power saw, carpenter's level, awl, sliding t-bevel
SEE PAGES 228–229

Alcoves can accommodate shelves that are as long as the width of the alcoves; they rest on support strips fastened to the walls. The shelf positions are fixed on the walls, giving the appearance of a built-in unit. This type of shelving is the strongest one—the walls take the weight of the load.

STORAGE OPTIONS

PAGES 230–231

Turning unused space in the home into storage for every-day items—from video tapes to linen to pots and pans—is one of the most common home improvements today. The ways of creating storage is limited only by your own creativity. Follow the steps as described in this section or combine techniques to come up with your own design.

MAKING A BUILT-IN CABINET

SKILL LEVEL Medium to high
TIME FRAME 1 to 2 days
SPECIAL TOOLS Try square, carpenter's level, hand saw or jigsaw, electric drill, mallet, tack hammer, profile gauge
SEE PAGES 232–233

Alcoves can be used for more elaborate storage needs than simple shelving. By adding a wood framework to the flanking walls, you can add cabinet doors and create enclosed storage either at low level or extending to the full height of the alcove. By adding glass doors, you can turn it into a display cabinet for a collection.

CREATING A MULTIMEDIA STORAGE UNIT

SKILL LEVEL High
TIME FRAME 2 days or more
SPECIAL TOOLS Try square, hand saw or jigsaw, electric drill plus hole saw bit, drill stand or drill press, tack hammer, profile gauge, carpenter's level, mallet
SEE PAGES 234–235

Many homes now have an array of electrical equipment, from stereos, televisions, and video recorders to computers and video games. They come with space-taking accessories

ROUTER

MASONRY DRILL BITS

HINGE SINKER BIT

PHILLIPS SCREWDRIVERS

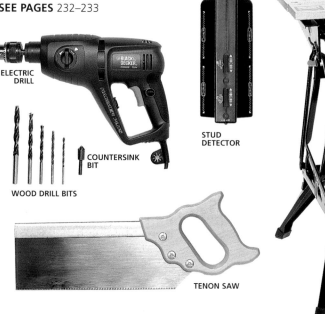

ELECTRIC DRILL

COUNTERSINK BIT

WOOD DRILL BITS

STUD DETECTOR

TENON SAW

such as CDs, albums, video tapes, and manuals.

By starting with the step-by-step instructions for a built-in cabinet (see pp.232–233), you can build a media storage unit customized to your own needs. Take time to decide what should be stored together, and make sure you carefully plan and measure each storage unit before you start the job.

CREATING A WORK CENTER

SKILL LEVEL HIgh
TIME FRAME 2 days or more
SPECIAL TOOLS Carpenter's level, sliding T-evel, tenon saw, panel saw or jigsaw, electric drill, router
SEE PAGES 236–237

Whether you want a home office for your computer, a garden center for potting plants, an organized workshop, or a kitchen island or breakfast bar, you can follow the principles here to create your own work center, with custom-designed storage. This section instructs how to build a freestanding cabinet and attach a countertop to it and the wall. Alter the design to suit your own needs: add legs to one end or extend the countertop from wall to wall and add extra cabinet units below (leave knee room if you want to sit while you work). To add storage units above a countertop, see pp.234–235.

GIVING CABINETS A FACELIFT

SKILL LEVEL Low
TIME FRAME ½ day
SPECIAL TOOLS Paint brush, electric drill
SEE PAGES 238–239

If you want to give a facelift to a room containing built-in cabinets or closets, you may be tempted to strip everything out and start again. However, if there is nothing structurally wrong with the carcases themselves, you can give the units a new lease on life by painting them or treating them to one of the many decorative paint effects, and by attaching new hardware such as handles and hinges. For the neatest results, remove the doors and drawer fronts to paint them.

REPLACING CABINET DOORS AND DRAWER FRONTS

SKILL LEVEL Low to medium
TIME FRAME 1 day
SPECIAL TOOLS Try square, electric drill plus hinge sinker bit, drill stand, awl or nail set
SEE PAGES 240–241

Another way of making a dramatic change to existing built-in units in the kitchen, bedroom, and bathroom is to save the carcases, which should have years of life left in them, and to fit new doors and drawer fronts to them. You'll need to take careful measurements to get replacements that fit exactly.

REPLACING A COUNTERTOP

SKILL LEVEL Medium to high
TIME FRAME 1 to 2 days
SPECIAL TOOLS Jigsaw, electric drill, circular saw, caulking gun, router or laminate trimmer plus miter template
SEE PAGES 242–243

Replacing a worn kitchen countertop is just another part of the process involved in updating your custom kitchen. The job can be easy if it won't involve cut-outs and the countertop is in a straight line. However, the presence of inset sinks and cooktops and the need to make 90° joints between adjacent countertop lengths at corners make the job more complicated. Careful cutting and the use of a router or special jigs can help minimize these problems.

MAKING GOOD USE OF STORAGE SPACE

SKILLS LEVEL Low
TIME FRAME ½ to 1 day
SPECIAL TOOLS Electric drill, tack hammer, hacksaw
SEE PAGES 244–245

There is always a finite limit to the amount of storage space available in any home. Once that has been reached, all that you can do is to make the best use of the space you have. There are numerous clever space-saving devices that you can buy and install to enable even the most inaccessible corner to be reached. In addition, some will allow for better airing of clothes and linen.

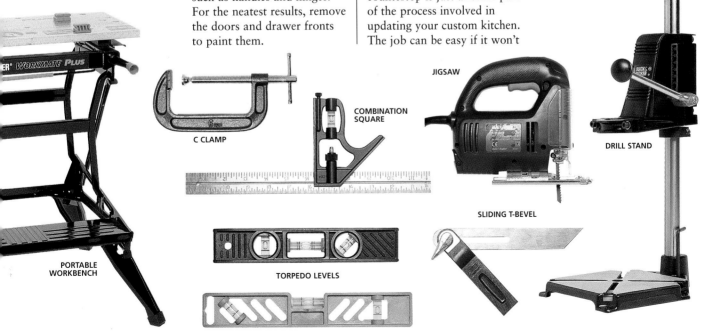

PORTABLE WORKBENCH

C CLAMP

COMBINATION SQUARE

JIGSAW

DRILL STAND

SLIDING T-BEVEL

TORPEDO LEVELS

SHELVING OPTIONS

POSSIBLE MATERIALS

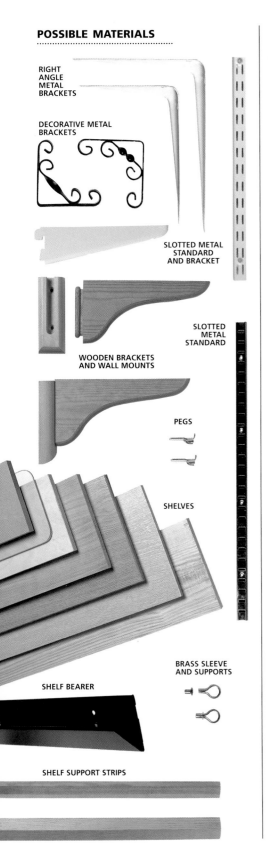

RIGHT ANGLE METAL BRACKETS

DECORATIVE METAL BRACKETS

SLOTTED METAL STANDARD AND BRACKET

SLOTTED METAL STANDARD

WOODEN BRACKETS AND WALL MOUNTS

PEGS

SHELVES

BRASS SLEEVE AND SUPPORTS

SHELF BEARER

SHELF SUPPORT STRIPS

After painting, putting up shelves is the one do-it-yourself activity that everyone tackles. Display and storage space is a necessity in virtually every room in the house, and there are several options you can choose to meet your needs. These range from open wall shelving to alcove shelving to freestanding units. Use different paint finishes and clever lighting to place your individual stamp on the shelves you choose to make, as well as on ready-made ones from stores.

▶ Color is used here to blend in the alcove shelving with their surroundings. The combination of the shelves with the cabinets turns the shelving into a piece of built-in furniture.

◀ Built-in shelving makes efficient use of space and is inexpensive to install. These two units are fitted in the same way as traditional alcove shelving, but the top arches were custom designed. Because it's supported by walls on three sides, you can use this type of shelving to store large, heavy books. Store lighter items on high shelves to avoid removing or lifting up heavy objects above your head.

◀ Deep storage shelves can look dark. However, you can make them seem lighter by having no back on the unit (as long as it won't be supporting heavy items) and by painting bright colors inside the unit.

▶ High display shelves should be narrow enough for you to to see what is on them from below. These are suitable for items that you'll rarely need to take down.

▶ Downlighting your shelves highlights the items on them and casts mood lighting over the whole room. The same effect can be achieved by placing a table lamp on the shelf or a small light behind a large opaque item such as a vase.

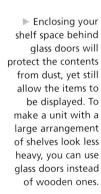

◀ Add a splash of color by painting your shelves in colors that contrast with your wall. The curve of these shelves is not hard to achieve if you use the right material, such as MDF, and cover the edges with a veneer.

◀ Open shelving can be as simple as two brackets and a plank of wood—or as intricate and ornate as these, where the shelves are as interesting as the items on display.

▶ Enclosing your shelf space behind glass doors will protect the contents from dust, yet still allow the items to be displayed. To make a unit with a large arrangement of shelves look less heavy, you can use glass doors instead of wooden ones.

PUTTING UP FIXED SHELVES

YOU WILL NEED

Tape measure and pencil
Try square
Awl
Screwdriver
Hammer (if required)
Torpedo level
Electric drill plus twist **or** masonry drill bits

MATERIALS

Shelf
Shelf brackets
Wood screws
Hollow-wall fasteners (for plasterboard wall) **or** plastic anchors (for masonry wall)

SEE ALSO

Using three brackets on this shelf is the best way to ensure that treasured items are safe from a disastrous fall.

If you want just a single shelf, the simplest way of putting it up is to use individual shelf brackets. These come in a range of decorative styles and finishes and are screwed to the wall and the shelf. A pair of brackets is all that is needed to support a short shelf, but longer shelves will require extra brackets. The spacing between the brackets will depend on what material is used for the shelf, how thick it is, and the weight placed on it.

The maximum bracket spacing for ¾-inch- (20-mm-) thick shelves made from solid wood or most manmade boards is 32 inches (800 mm) for lightweight loads, 28 inches (700 mm) for medium loads, and 24 inches (600 mm) for heavy loads such as stereo equipment and hardback books. For particleboard, reduce the measurements to 30 inches (750 mm), 24 inches (600 mm), and 18 inches (450 mm) respectively.

With a plasterboard wall, you may have to locate the wall studs before you start any drilling (see p.228). If you are not securing the brackets to wall studs, use hollow-wall fasteners that are strong enough to support the shelf and its load (see p.227).

1 For long shelves that require three or more brackets, first determine the length of the shelf and where you want it. Measure the distance of the brackets and use a try square to mark their positions on the bottom of the shelf.

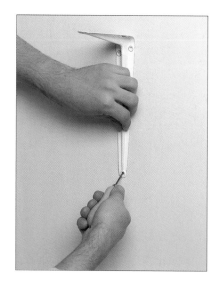

2 Place one of the outer brackets in position on the wall. The longest section should always be against the wall, with the shortest one supporting the shelf. Using an awl, mark the lowest screw position on the wall.

3 Drill a hole for the screw; use a twist drill for plasterboard or a masonry bit for a masonry wall. If the wall is masonry (see p.227), insert a plastic anchor into the hole and use a hammer to gently tap it flush with the wall. With the bracket in place, drive the screw into the hole (or anchor), but leave it slightly loose.

4 Set a level on the bracket; when the bubble in the liquid is centered, the bracket will be level. Mark the other screw holes, swing the bracket away, and drill holes at the marks (if needed, insert anchors). With the bracket realigned, drive in the remaining screws partway. Once all the screws are in place, tighten them.

5 With the first bracket on the wall, rest the edge of the shelf on it, with the level above the shelf, to align the top of the brackets. At the guideline on the shelf, mark the position of the other end bracket and fasten it in place as you did the first one. Use the same procedure to add any intermediary brackets.

6 Place the shelf on the brackets, using the guidelines previously marked on the bottom of the shelf. Drive the screws from the bottom of the bracket up into the shelf. The screws should be long enough to go two-thirds of the way through the shelf, but not any longer.

TWO-BRACKET SHELF

A short shelf that requires only two brackets is easier to install by first securing the brackets to the shelf with screws. You can use a straightedge or a strip of wood in a workbench to help align the back of the brackets to the back edge of the shelf.

With the brackets in place, hold the shelf the right way up against the wall, align it horizontally with a level (as in step 5), and mark the positions for the screws. Drill the holes for the screws (see step 3), and screw the brackets to the walls.

Helpful hints

If you are putting up a shelf with just two brackets, position them one-quarter of the shelf length in from the ends to help prevent sagging. For more than two brackets, set the outer ones in from the ends by the shelf depth and set any additional brackets at equal spacings between them.

You can drill pilot holes into the shelves to make driving in the screws easier. To ensure that you don't drill all the way through the shelf, use a depth guide—if you don't have one, wrap masking tape around the drill bit.

INSTALLING ADJUSTABLE SHELVES

YOU WILL NEED

Tape measure and pencil
Try square
Hand saw **or** power saw
Awl
Screwdriver
Carpenter's level
Electric drill plus twist drill
bit **or** masonry drill bit
Tenon saw (if required)
Chisel (if required)

MATERIALS

Shelves
Tracks
Brackets
Wood screws
Wall anchors

SEE ALSO

Putting up fixed shelves
pp.224–225
Alcove shelving
pp.228–229

Adjustable shelving is perfect for storing children's toys—the shelves can be moved up and down to accommodate new toys and other belongings as the children grow up.

Atrack shelving system is easy to install. It consists of two or more lengths of vertical metal track and a series of matching shelf brackets that fit into slots or channels in the tracks. They are available in white, bright primary colors, and metallic effects.

The system can support shelves made of a variety of materials, including wood and MDF. You can use ready-made ones or cut and finish your own. Even with the shelves attached, the brackets are easy to reposition. Three or more tracks give greater flexibility in the lengths of the shelves and how you stagger them, allowing you to make the most of the space available.

The spacing of the tracks must be set as brackets on fixed shelves are: by the shelf type, thickness, and load (see pp.224–225). The easiest way of putting up the shelves means that the tracks hold the rear edges of the shelves away from the wall. If you want them to fit flush with the wall, notch the rear edges of the shelves.

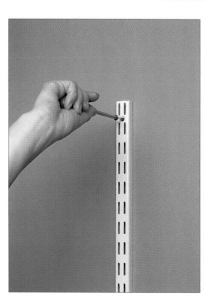

1 After you decide on the positioning and spacing of the tracks, hold the first end track against the wall and mark the position of its topmost screw with an awl. Drill the hole, and install an anchor if you have a masonry wall (see *Helpfuls Hints*, facing page). Drive in the screw partway.

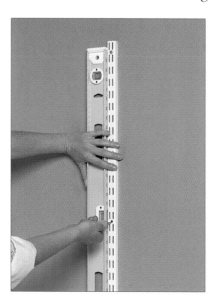

2 To position the track vertically, hold a level against it and adjust it until the bubble is centered in the appropriate tube of fluid. Then mark the positions for the other screws, swing the track aside so you can drill the holes (and install anchors, if necessary), then reposition the track and insert the remaining screws.

3 To position the other end track, slip a bracket into the same slot in both tracks. Standing a shelf on end on the bracket on the first track, with a level on top to keep it horizontal, set the other end track in place and mark the topmost screw. Then repeat steps 1 and 2 to secure the track to the wall. Repeat for any intermediary tracks.

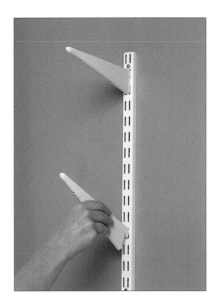

4 Slip the shelf brackets into place in the slots in the track, checking that they are level with each other—count the number of slots above or below the brackets. If necessary, cut the shelves to length (see p.229)—you can add strips of veneer to the ends to hide cut ends.

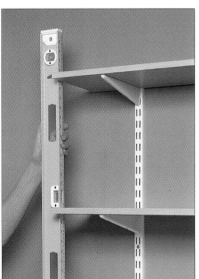

5 Some brackets have a bump on the end to prevent the shelf from slipping forward. If your shelf is wider than the bracket, mark the location of the bump on the bottom of the shelf, and drill a hole partway through so the shelf can rest level on the bracket. Position the shelves on the brackets; use a level or plumb line to align their ends.

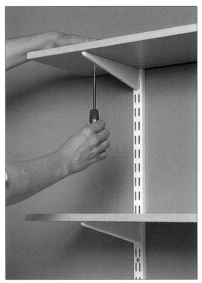

6 Unless the shelves are in an alcove and, therefore, captive, it is best to screw the shelves to the brackets. Drive the screws up from the bottom of the brackets, supporting the top of the shelf with your other hand. Make sure the screws penetrate only about two-thirds of the shelf's thickness (see *Helpful hints*, p.225).

NOTCHING THE SHELF

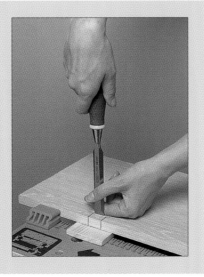

Use a tenon saw to cut down the sides of the marked notch. Clamp the shelf securely, with scrap wood under it. With the chisel perpendicular to the depth line, firmly press the chisel down; then gently tap it with a wood mallet to increase the depth of the cut. Remove a thin layer of the waste by pressing the chisel, bevel side up, against the edge of the shelf. Continue these procedures until you remove all of the waste wood.

Helpful hints

Shelf brackets and tracks exert considerable force on the fasteners securing them to the wall, so you must use the correct type. On solid masonry walls, use screws at least 1½ inches (38 mm) long, and drive them into wall anchors inserted into drilled holes. On wallboard walls, locate the studs (see p.229), which are usually 16 inches (400 mm) apart, then drive 1½-inch- (38-mm-) long screws into the wallboard and studs. You can use hollow-wall fasteners such as toggle bolts to mount shelves to plasterboard alone, but only if the shelves will be lightly loaded.

ALCOVE SHELVING

YOU WILL NEED

Tape measure and pencil
Try square
Fine abrasive paper
Backsaw
Jigsaw (if required)
Torpedo level
Carpenter's level
Awl
Electric drill plus twist bit **or** masonry drill bit
Measuring sticks
Sliding T-bevel
Screwdriver

MATERIALS

Shelves
1 inch x 1½ inches (25 mm x 38 mm) soft wooden strips
Wood screws
Wall anchors

SEE ALSO

Putting up fixed shelving
pp.224–225
Installing adjustable shelving
pp.226–227

Many homes have alcoves, often at either side of a fireplace or a similar structure. They are an ideal site for built-in shelves or other forms of storage because the walls of the alcove can provide the support you need, especially for heavier loads.

The simplest method involves screwing wooden strips to the side walls and resting the shelves on these. In wide alcoves, add a third strip along the rear wall to prevent the shelf from sagging. If you encounter uneven plaster on alcove walls, trim each shelf individually to get a good fit. The shelves can be made from wood, plywood, veneered particleboard, or MDF, which can be stained or painted.

If you are planning to fasten a strip across the rear wall of an alcove, take care if there is a wall light installed there. The electrical cable running to the light will be inside the wall, and a hole drilled in the wrong place could pierce it. Professional electricians

A wooden strip along the front edge of these shelves hide the ends of the side strips attached to the walls.

always run cables vertically or horizontally against wall framing, so knowing where the wall studs are can help you avoid piercing the cable. For ways to locate wall studs, see *Helpful hints*, facing page.

1 Start by deciding where you want the shelf to be (to locate studs, see facing page) and what spacing you require if you plan to install several shelves. Then measure and mark each shelf position on one side wall of the alcove.

2 Using a backsaw, cut as many strips as you will need to support the shelves you are installing; sand the cut ends smooth. If you use a strip at the front of the shelves (see step 7), subtract its width from the width of the shelves to establish the length of the side strips; otherwise, cut the side strips to the width of the shelves.

3 Drill two screw holes through each side strip, about 1 inch (25 mm) from the ends. Hold a strip at a mark and use a torpedo level to find a true horizontal; mark the position for a screw with an awl. Drill the hole and install an anchor, if necessary (see p.227); drive the screw in. Secure the second screw as the first.

4 Once all the strips are in place on one wall, balance a carpenter's level on each strip and mark horizontal lines across the alcove to the facing wall. Use these lines as a guide to install the strips on the opposite wall, following the instructions in step 3. For long shelves, install strips along the back wall.

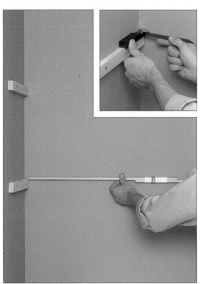

5 Measure for each shelf separately, using measuring sticks—two wood strips held together with rubber bands—to find the width of the back wall (they are more accurate than a retractable tape measure). Use a sliding T-bevel (inset) to find the correct angle of each corner.

6 Transfer the measurements to each shelf and cut them to length. (At this stage, you can finish the shelves by applying stain and/or varnish or painting them, then letting them dry.) Carefully set the shelves on top of the strips; try to avoid marring the walls. To hide the ends of the strips, see the next step.

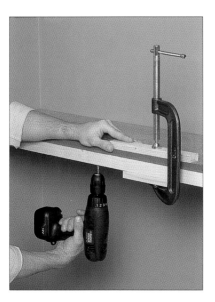

7 Cut a strip to fit under the edge of each shelf. Clamp it in place, using scrap wood to protect the surfaces of the work. Drive screws long · enough to penetrate up through the strip but only two-thirds into the shelf. Use wood filler to fill the cracks between the strips and shelves. Once it has dried, apply a coat of paint.

Helpful hints

One way to find wood studs behind wallboard is to use a battery-power stud detector. Simply hold it against the wall where you want to install the fasteners; follow the manufacturer's directions. A more traditional method is to tap your knuckles along the wall until you hear a solid, instead of hollow, sound. Studs are often spaced 16 inches (400 mm) apart; once you find one stud, the others will be easier to find.

STORAGE OPTIONS

POSSIBLE MATERIALS

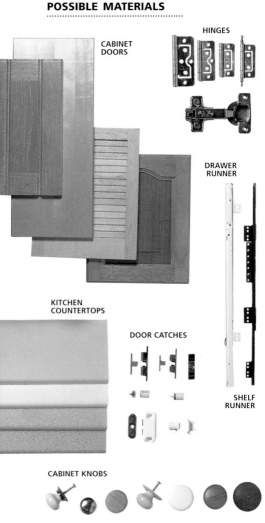

CABINET DOORS

HINGES

DRAWER RUNNER

KITCHEN COUNTERTOPS

DOOR CATCHES

SHELF RUNNER

CABINET KNOBS

CABINET DOOR HANDLES

TIE HANGER

KITCHEN CAROUSEL

SWIVEL CLOTHES HANGER

Successful storage means having a place for everything, and keeping everything in its place. Every home seems to have ever-increasing belongings to fit into it, yet new homes are often less spacious than those built in earlier times. With careful planning, you can make the best possible use of the space available by using any combination of the techniques described on the following pages.

You may be fortunate in having enough storage space, but you may still want a change of style. This is particularly relevant in the kitchen and bedroom, which often contain a lot of built-in furniture. They can be easily updated with little expense and effort.

▶ A custom kitchen is an expensive investment. If your tastes change as time goes by, consider changing the way the units look. Use one of the many paint effects available; change paint for varnish or wood stain; or discard old doors and drawer fronts and fit replacements to the existing cupboards.

◀ Modular units are a hybrid between built-in and freestanding furniture. The open shelves allow you to display crockery, but be aware that the pieces will be exposed to dust.

◄ Louvered doors allow for good ventilation, making them suitable for a clothes or linen closet. These doors were made into a feature by using a strong color and distressed finish.

▲ When pressed for storage, there's no such thing as wasted space—you can create storage in the most unlikely places such as these steps to a platform area.

▲ Clothes that are properly stored will last longer, so make sure there is adequate room and ventilation by using a combination of shelves and hanging space.

▶ When working from home, it is essential to separate living and working spaces. If you cannot convert a whole room to an office, create a work space in the corner of a room.

◄ To work most effectively, your home-office storage space should be organized to allow you easy access to frequently used items. You can keep items rarely used on high, hard-to-reach shelves.

▶ When organizing storage for home entertainment, remember to allow for an ever-expanding collection of compact discs and video tapes, as well as to create room for your treasured albums.

MAKING A BUILT-IN CABINET

YOU WILL NEED

Tape measure
Try square and pencil
Level
Backsaw **or** jigsaw
Electric drill plus twist bits
and masonry drill bits (if
required)
Screwdrivers
Wooden mallet
Tack hammer
Profile gauge (if required)

MATERIALS

Softwood strips for the
framework
Dowels
PVA glue
Finishing nails
Manmade boards for
shelves
MDF (medium density fiber)
board for plinth
Doors
Handles, hinges, and
catches
Woodscrews
Wall anchors (if required)

SEE ALSO

Fitting a bifold wardrobe
door pp.90–91
Alcove shelving pp.228–229
Creating a multimedia
storage unit pp.234–235
Making good use of storage
space pp.244–245

Start by deciding what type of storage you'll need. For example, you can adapt a cabinet to store linen or toys, or you can turn it into high-level storage with hanging space for clothes below. With careful planning, you can even fit a storage cabinet under an open staircase.

You'll have to decide whether to fit the doors flush with the face of the protruding wall, to recess them slightly or, if the alcove is shallow, to build out beyond the face of the wall. Use ready-made doors if possible, adjusting the frame measurements so they'll fit. If you do make the doors, use dowel joints for the frames and glazing beads to enclose and support the panels.

BEFORE YOU START

Check whether the alcove is square and has truly vertical flanking walls (see pp.228–229). Out-of-true walls affect how you make the frame; insert packing between walls and uprights to

This cabinet may provide ample storage space in your living room, but you can increase its capacity by adding shelves or a glass-front display unit above it.

get the latter truly vertical, or scribe the wall profile onto the uprights and cut along the scribed line (see p.166).

1 A top horizontal strip is needed to support the back edge of the top of the cabinet. After measuring the wall (see p.229, step 5), cut the strip to fit, using a tenon saw; then screw it to the rear wall of the alcove (see p.227, *Helpful hints*).

2 To support a flush-fitting or recessed front frame, mark the positions for the vertical strips. (For a protruding cabinet, see p.235.) Use a level to align the top of each vertical strip with the top of the horizontal strip on the back wall. Install the top screw, then align the strip vertically. End the strips above any baseboards.

3 To make a front dowel-joint frame, use a backsaw to cut each of the four lengths of wood to fit (with the vertical lengths sandwiched between horizontal ones). Clamp each length to a work surface; drill holes in the appropriate ends for dowels. Assemble the frame with dowels and glue; tap with a mallet for a snug fit.

4 Attach a mounting strip to each side of the frame so you can screw through this into the wall strip and not have any screws visible on the face of the unit. Add another mounting strip across the bottom to support the front edge of the lower shelf. Screw the frame to the vertical strips on the wall.

5 Cut a plinth made of MDF (you may have to scribe it to fit around the baseboard, see p.169); nail it to the bottom of the frame. Fit the bottom horizontal strip to the wall as you did the top, using the top of the mounting strip on the front of the frame to find its level. Add side and back strips for any middle shelves (see pp.228–229).

6 Cut the shelves to size after measuring the width and depth of alcove for each shelf. Rest the bottom shelf on the wall strip and mounting strip on the frame (then, from the bottom up, any middle shelves on their strips). Glue the top shelf to the frame and mounting strip; or screw corner blocks to the frame (see inset) and shelf.

7 To make your own doors, make a pair of dowel-joint frames (see step 3). Glue and nail thin lengths of wood to the inside edges at the back of the frames. Fit glass, plywood, or MDF panels in place, then fasten them by gluing and nailing glazing beads around the inside edges at the front of the frame.

8 To hang a door, attach hinges to the door with screws. Fasten the hinges to the frame. Drive a screw in one hinge, then the other; add the other screws. Drive them in loosely so you can make adjustments as you go; once all the screws are in place, tighten them. Drill holes for the handles and screw them in place; add a catch.

CREATING A MULTIMEDIA STORAGE UNIT

Most houses contain a range of home entertainment equipment, which can take over a room unless it is kept under control. Work out the best solution to your storage requirements by making a list of the equipment you own and thinking about how you use it. This will dictate whether you house everything in one large unit or create several storage solutions. For example, it makes sense to house the television and VCR in one unit, along with the stereo equipment, tapes, CDs, and albums. If you have a home computer, house it in another room if it is used for homework or business.

After deciding on the configuration, measure each component so you can include it in your design. Remember to provide enough depth for electrical and cable connections at the back of each component, and to allow air to circulate. Make sure outlets are accessible for the equipment; you may need to call in an electrician.

A home entertainment center fits comfortably in this custom-made unit. Inside the cabinet there are shelves for a video recorder and cable or satellite box, and room for VCR and cassette tapes. Wires are hidden behind the CD storage columns.

1 If you don't already have a basic fitted cabinet, start by making one (see pp.232–233), then follow the steps here to adapt it. For wires and cables above the cabinet to reach equipment or outlets below, bore a hole in a back corner of the top of the cabinet, using a hole saw attached to an electric drill.

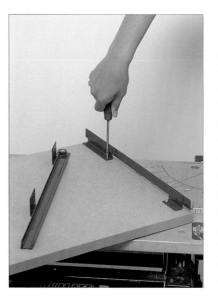

2 Sliding shelves allow you to pull out a VCR or receiver to reach the wire connections, or can hold a computer keyboard. Cut a shelf to fit, allowing room for the sliders (see pp.228–229). Fit one slider at a time; attach one half to the shelf and the other half to the wall. The parts are easy to confuse, so do a test-fit first.

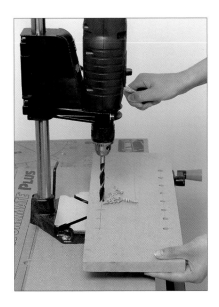

3 Begin to make a storage column for CDs or tapes. Measure and cut the four sides of the box. Mark the positions for two rows of holes (which will take shelf-support pegs) along the front and back of the two vertical sides of the box. Use a drill stand or drill press to make the holes (jigs are available to help drill the holes).

4 Assemble the sides of the box and secure them with screws; use screws long enough for one-third of their length to go into the far piece. Then attach a back to the box, using brads and a hammer—it will prevent items from falling out of the back.

5 Finish the face of the columns by gluing and nailing pine strips to the edges of the box. If you plan to paint the column, this is a suitable time to give it a priming coat.

6 Measure, cut, and fit a shelf (or shelves) in place; follow the instructions on pp.228–229. If electrical equipment will be stored on the shelf, bore a hole in a back corner to correspond with the one in the cabinet below (see step 1). You can use adjustable shelves; however, the finished result will be less sophisticated.

7 Position the storage columns on the top of the cabinet; these two will be staggered to allow wires and cables to run down the shaft created in the corner. Drive a screw down through the front of the column to hold it in place. Fit sleeves for pegs in the holes, then the pegs and shelves. If you want, fit a swivel bracket for a television.

INCREASING A CABINET'S DEPTH

You can increase the depth of a cabinet in a narrow alcove so it can hold large equipment. Cut a piece of MDF to the desired width (scribe it at the baseboard, see p.169). Attach a strip to the wall about 1 inch (25 mm) from the corner. Butt the MDF against the strip; attach a second one over where the two meet.

CREATING A WORK CENTER

YOU WILL NEED

Tape measure and pencil
Level
Sliding T bevel
Tenon saw
Panel saw **or** jigsaw
Electric drill plus twist and masonry drill bits
Screwdrivers
Router
Hex key (if required)

MATERIALS

MDF for cabinet
Woodscrews and wall anchors
Hardboard for cabinet back
Nails
2 inch x 2 inch (50 mm x 50 mm) softwood strips for frame and wall
Wood for base
Premade door
Hinges and hardware for door
Countertop
Table legs (if required)

SEE ALSO

Alcove shelving pp.228–229
Making a built-in cabinet pp.232–233
Creating a multimedia storage unit pp.234–235
Replacing cabinet doors and drawer fronts pp.240–241

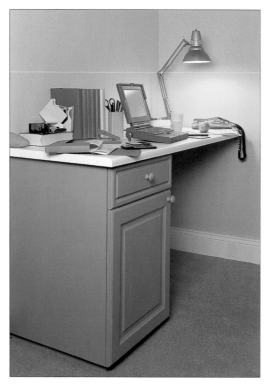

The work center here is for a home office. However, you can adjust the design for other uses such as a sewing center, kitchen island, or a breakfast bar.

A work center can be created anywhere that you have available space. The one shown here is designed to illustrate several techniques, which you can then adapt to create your own customized center. For example, you may choose to attach the work surface to wood strips mounted to two walls, perhaps in a corner. Or you can leave the strips out altogether and use a pair of the drawer/cupboard combination units—which can also be adapted, for example, by increasing the size of the cabinets and dropping the drawers, or by creating a stack of drawers. Yet another option is supporting one end with a strip on a wall and the other end with legs. If you position it high enough, you can store stools below it and use it as a breakfast bar.

It is important to decide exactly how you want to use the center. Whether you'll be standing or sitting, make sure it will be at a comfortable height to work on, and also make sure it will be within easy reach of any necessary outlets. Using premade doors and drawers will make the center much easier to build.

1 For the sides of a base unit, cut two pieces of MDF to the depth of the drawer and the height of the door and drawer. Use a router to cut dadoes for holding a shelf (the shelf also makes the frame more sturdy); make rabbets along the back end of the pieces. Use a strip to guide the router; set it to cut at half the MDF thickness.

2 For the top and bottom, cut two pieces of MDF as deep as the drawer and as wide as the door. Drill three countersunk pilot holes through the edges of the rabbets of the side pieces. Assemble the box, enclosing the ends of the top and bottom pieces in the rabbets on the side pieces. Use an electric screwdriver to drive in the screws.

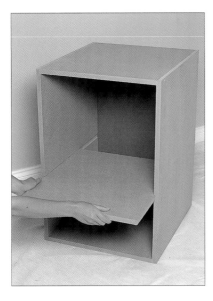

3 A back will help support the cabinet. Cut a sheet of hardboard for the back; nail it in place. To make a shelf, cut a piece of MDF the width and depth of the cabinet and insert it into the dadoes. Drill pilot holes into the dadoes from outside the cabinet; countersink them, then screw the shelf in place.

4 Mark the positions of the drawer runners on the inside of the cabinet. Drill holes for the screws, then fasten the runners in place. Insert the drawer to ensure it opens and closes properly; then take it out and put it to one side until the work center is completed.

5 Make a base so that the door can open: cut four lengths of wood 2 inches (50 mm) shorter than the top's dimensions; butt and screw together. Screw the base to the bottom of cabinet. Screw the hinges onto the door. Position the hinges against the cabinet. Mark and drill screw holes; attach the hinges (see p.241).

6 Cut a wood strip the width of the countertop. Move the cabinet to the wall, set the countertop on it and mark its height on the wall. Draw a horizontal line from the mark for the top of the strip. Drill holes in the strip; mark their positions on the wall. Drill holes at the marks, insert wall anchors, and screw the strip in place.

7 Cut the countertop to the correct length, and place one end on top of the cabinet and the other end on the wall strip. Use white plastic corner brackets to screw the countertop to the strip. To fasten the cabinet to the countertop, drill holes up through the top of the cabinet into the countertop before screwing it in place.

USING LEGS

If you want a freestanding end, turn the countertop over and position a pair of leg brackets on it. Mark and drill the screw holes, then screw on the brackets. Slip the legs onto the brackets and tighten with a hex key. Turn the countertop over and fasten the other end to the cabinet or wall strip.

GIVING BUILT-IN CABINETS A FACELIFT

YOU WILL NEED

Screwdriver
Sanding block plus fine
wet-and-dry sandpaper
Workbench
Paint brushes **or** a spray gun
Electric drill plus twist bit
(if required)

MATERIALS

Paint
Trisodium Phosphate (TSP)
or detergent
Replacement handles **or**
knobs

SEE ALSO

Painting basics pp.114–115
Using paint brushes
pp.116–117
Using a spray gun p.121
Paint effects pp.122–129
Replacing cabinet doors
and drawer fronts
pp.240–241

Sooner or later you will tire of the look of your built-in furniture, whether it is in the kitchen, living room, or bedroom. A coat of paint and new hardware can be all that's needed to create a modern look.

Updating the look of your built-in furniture, especially if it is still in good working order, doesn't mean replacing it. Instead, use the existing finish as the base for a new coat of paint (a primer and paint are available for melamine surfaces), whether it has a plastic or a natural wood finish.

Decide how extensive the paint job will be. You may want to tackle just the doors and drawer fronts—the parts that are visible when the units are closed up. Or you might decide to repaint the cabinet and drawer interiors too, but this is seldom necessary. Apart from all the extra painting involved, you would have to remove everything stored in the units.

Plan the job as a production-line operation. It is easier to paint doors and drawer fronts when they are laid flat on your workbench instead of attached to their units. You can apply the new paint with a brush or a spray gun. Store a small quantity of the paint you use in an airtight container, so you can touch up any chips and knocks to the units in the future.

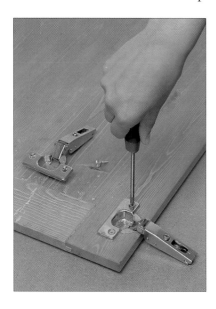

1 Take the doors off their hinges one by one, then unscrew any handles or knobs. In theory, all the door hardware should be interchangeable, but it's always a good idea to keep the parts in separate, labeled piles or plastic bags and return them to their original postions.

2 Wash the surfaces that you plan to paint using trisodium phosphate (TSP) or strong household detergent to remove any dirt, grease, and fingermarks. Rinse them in clean water and let dry.

3 Sand the surfaces with fine wet-and-dry sandpaper to roughen them so they will receive the new paint. Wipe the surface with a cloth moistened in mineral spirits, or use a tack rag, to remove the fine dust that the sandpaper produces.

4 Paint the doors; if they are paneled, start in any recessed areas, move on to the panels, then finish off around the edges. When the base coat has dried, you can add a decorative paint effect if you want. Reattach the hinges and fit the doors in their original positions (see pp.240–241).

5 Remove the drawers from their tracks. After pulling out a drawer to its full extent, tilt it down to release the runner on the drawer from the runner inside the unit. When you replace the drawers, tilt them to the same angle to engage the two runners. Make sure you put the drawers back into their original slots.

6 Remove the handles or knobs by unscrewing them. If the drawers have separate fronts attached to their carcases, unscrew them to release the front. (Screws from the handles or knobs may be holding the fronts in place.) The fronts are easier to paint if not attached to the carcases.

7 If you want to replace two-screw handles with one-screw knobs, or vice versa, fill the original screw holes with a wood or acrylic filler. Center the new hardware on the fronts, mark the screw hole positions, and drill the screw holes.

8 Set the drawer fronts on small pieces of cardboard or hardwood so that you can paint their edges without painting the work surface. (Clamp drawers without a separate front standing on their ends.) Apply the paint (and paint effect if desired); let them dry. Reattach the fronts and handles to the drawers; fit them in the runners.

REPLACING CABINET DOORS AND DRAWER FRONTS

YOU WILL NEED

Screwdrivers
Workbench
Tape measure
Try square
Pencil
Electric drill plus twist drill
bits and 1⅜-inch- (35-mm-)
diameter hinge sinker bit
(if required)
Drill stand (if required)
Awl **or** nail set and hammer

MATERIALS

Replacement doors and
drawer fronts

SEE ALSO

If repainting your existing cabinets does not appeal to you, fit new doors and drawer fronts to the existing carcases. You can achieve a new look or style that you cannot create with paint—and it is less expensive than replacing the complete units.

The carcases, or the boxes, of cabinet units have no movable parts; therefore, they are not exposed to a great deal of wear and tear. There is little point in wasting both time and money replacing a series of perfectly sound carcases. Modern storage units are all modular in size, so buying new doors and drawer fronts to fit them is straightforward—as long as you take exact measurements. There is a wide range of materials, including solid and veneered wood and plastic laminates, and surface finishes include high-gloss coatings and decorative paint effects.

Both doors and drawer fronts are generally supplied as blanks. For European-style hinges (as shown here), you'll need a 1⅜-inch- (35-mm-) diameter hinge sinker bit to drill holes in the doors. Drawer fronts are usually attached to their carcases with screws.

1 Remove an existing door by releasing its hinges from the cabinet. If it has European-style concealed cabinet hinges, release the baseplates by loosening the screw in the center of the cross. Hand-tighten the retaining screws back into the holes in the baseplates so they are not lost before the new door is hung.

2 Release the retaining screws securing the hinges to the door; if they are concealed cabinet hinges, pry the hinges out of their recesses. Put the screws in a safe place. Then use the old door as a template to mark the hinge positions on the inner face of the new door.

3 For concealed cabinet hinges, use a 1⅜ inch (35 mm) hinge sinker bit to drill holes for the hinges at all the marks made in step 2. Use a drill stand to support the drill, and bore a hole to a depth that matches the thickness of the hinge bosses. For other types of hinges, drill pilot holes for their screws.

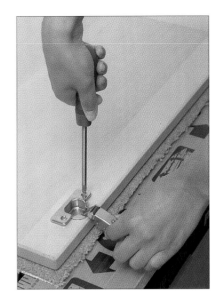

4 Fit the old concealed cabinet hinges in the blind holes. For all types of hinges, secure them with the retaining screws you had previously removed from the old door.

5 Hang a new door on its cabinet by attaching first the top hinge, then the others. For European-style cabinet hinges, use the adjustment screws on their baseplates to get the door to hang squarely. Make additional adjustments to align the doors with each other when you have hung them all.

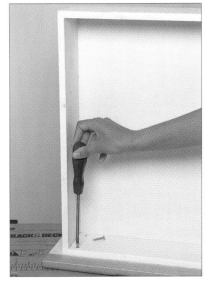

6 To replace a drawer front, undo the screws securing the old front to its carcase and set it aside. Lay the new drawer front face down and position the carcase over it.

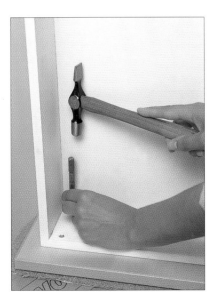

7 Insert an awl or nail set in the screw holes to mark their positions on the inner face of the drawer front. Drill pilot holes, then attach the new drawer front to the carcase by driving in the screws. Check that it is attached squarely, then slide the drawer back into the unit (see p.239).

Helpful hints

For a detailed shopping list, make a sketch of your units and number each door and drawer front. Measure each one and record its size on the sketch. Then count how many items you need in each size to make up your final order.

To change the exposed areas of the carcases, apply a veneer finish—a thin layer of wood. Trim veneer (underside face up) with a veneer saw or utility knife, using a straightedge as a guide. Apply woodworking glue to the back of ordinary veneer. Edging strips have adhesive already applied; use a clothes iron to fasten it in place. (Leave the bottom of the top units a light color to reflect light onto the countertop.)

REPLACING A COUNTERTOP

YOU WILL NEED

Replacing a countertop
Screwdrivers
Tape measure and pencil
Jigsaw
Electric drill plus twist bits
Circular saw
Caulking gun

Turning a corner
Router or laminate trimmer
plus miter template (can
be rented)

MATERIALS

Replacing a countertop
Countertop
Retaining clips and
wood screws
Silicone sealant

Turning a corner
See above

SEE ALSO

Making a built-in cabinet
pp.232–233
Creating a work center
pp.236–237
Giving built-in cabinets a
facelift pp.238–239
Replacing cabinet doors and
drawer fronts pp.240–241

The countertop in a kitchen endures considerable abuse, and one that is in poor condition can make a kitchen that is otherwise in good condition look tired and shabby. The best solution is to replace it with a new countertop, which come in a wide range of designs.

Kitchen countertops have to put up with more wear and tear than any other surface. Hot pans are placed on them, potentially staining sauces are spilled on them, and all manner of food items are chopped and sliced on them.

The easiest type of countertop to install is of a slab of particleboard covered with a durable layer of plastic laminate. The front edge is usually rounded off—a detail known as post-forming, where the laminate is shaped and bonded to the rounded-off board edge. The standard depth for countertops is 25½ inches (650 mm). Most stores stock lengths from 6 to 12 feet (1830 to 3660 mm), but custom lengths are readily available by special order .

The same techniques can be used to fit a top to a vanity in the bathroom or to create a work station.

1 If the countertop has an inset sink or cook top, disconnect their supplies (see *Helpful hints)*; release clips holding them to the countertop to lift them out. Undo the screws holding the countertop to base cabinets. Tape the screws to the inside of the cabinet near their mounting position (use them to attach the new countertop).

2 Lift the old countertop off the base cabinets—it may come off in sections— and set it (or them) aside. Clean away any old strips of sealant from the walls where the countertop was fitted against them.

3 You can use the old countertop section as a template to measure and mark out the new one. Mark any holes needed for inset sinks or cook tops. Rest the countertop, underside face up, on a workbench, with clearance below the inset. Drill a hole at each corner of the inset, making sure you bore the holes in the waste area.

4 Insert the blade of a jigsaw into one of the holes, and start to cut out the inset. Continue until all four sides have been cut.

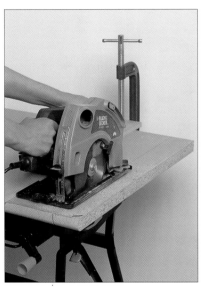

5 With the countertop underside face up, clamp a straightedge as a guide for a circular saw, and trim the end of the section to the correct length, if necessary. If an end will be exposed, finish it off with specially shaped metal trim, similar to that used at corners (see *Turning a corner*, below).

6 Lift the countertop into place, and secure it to the base cabinets with screws and mounting clips. If you're using more then one section, join them with trim as described in *Turning a corner*, below. Seal the gap at the corner between the countertop and the walls, using a silicone sealant (see pp.160–161).

TURNING A CORNER

To finish a joint between adjacent sections at a corner, attach specially shaped metal trim to fill the gap between the rounded front edge of one strip and the straight side edge of the other. A more complex method involves using a router or laminate trimmer with a special bit and template.

Helpful hints

If your countertop has an inset sink, first turn off the water supply and disconnect the taps and trap. If there is an inset cook top, the gas or electricity supply has to be cut off. You can disconnect an electric cook top after turning off the circuit breaker at the service panel. You must call a gas company representative or a qualified appliance technician to disconnect and reconnect a gas cooktop.

If there is more than a ⅜ inch (10 mm) gap between the wall and countertop, scribe it, before attaching it, by holding a pencil against the wall and tracing the wall's shape onto the countertop. Trim along the line with a jigsaw.

MAKING GOOD USE OF STORAGE SPACE

YOU WILL NEED

Fitting a carousel unit
Tape measure and pencil
Electric drill plus twist bits
Screwdrivers
Tack hammer

Fitting a closet pole
Tape measure and pencil
Electric drill plus twist bits
Screwdrivers
Panel saw or hacksaw

Fitting a swivel hanger
Tape measure and pencil
Electric drill plus twist bits
Screwdrivers

Wardrobe system
Tape measure and pencil
Electric drill plus twist bits
Screwdrivers

MATERIALS

Space-saving fittings

SEE ALSO

Making a built-in cabinet
pp.232–233
Creating a multimedia
storage unit pp.234–235
Creating a work center
pp.236–237

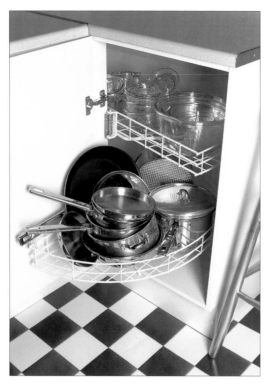

A carousel unit is the perfect storage device for corner units in a kitchen. It swings out or revolves to make items stored on it accessible.

E ven with the most ingenious use of space in the home, there comes a point where you can't fit in any more storage units. When you reach that stage, you'll have to make better use of your existing storage space. The kitchen and the bedroom are the main areas for storage, and there are many space-saving fittings available to make use of even the most inaccessible areas.

In the kitchen, some useful ideas include carousels to increase storage in corner base units, and wire baskets and racks in all shapes and sizes to fit in pull-out storage units and on door backs. In the bedroom, wire baskets come into their own as versatile organizers of storage space. You see at a glance what each basket contains and the clothes are better aired than in closed drawers. Other ideas include fitting split-level closet poles and making use of space under beds.

Take time to research what is available in space-saving fittings. Apart from scouring specialty retailers and home centers, look for advertisements in home interest magazines from mail-order suppliers.

FITTING A CAROUSEL UNIT

1 Start by deciding on the relative positions of the trays—this will depend on the height of the items that you want to store in them. Position the hinge bracket on the cabinet frame, mark the position of the screw holes, and drill pilot holes for the screws.

2 Screw the brackets into the frame, then continue with the other brackets until they have all been mounted.

3 Position the lower carousel tray on the appropriate bracket, making sure that the top flange on the tray goes on the top flange of the bracket. Insert the bracket pin and gently tap it down with a small hammer.

4 Fit a follower bracket to the door—it pulls the tray out when the door is opened. Pull the tray out so it meets the open door, position the follower bracket on the door with its hook over the tray, and mark the screw holes. Remove the bracket, drill the holes, then screw the bracket in place with the tray under the hook.

FITTING A CLOTHES POLE

1 To fit a clothes pole, measure and mark the position of the brackets on each side of the closet. They should be in the center of the side uprights and equidistant from the top of the closet. Mark the screw hole positions, drill the holes, and screw the brackets in place.

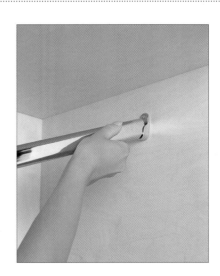

2 Measure from the inside of one bracket to the inside of the other. Cut a solid wood pole or length of metal tubing to this length, using a panel saw or hacksaw. Insert one end of the pole or tubing into one bracket, then bring the other end up and drop it down into the opposite bracket.

FITTING A SWIVEL HANGER

This hanger swivels outside of the closet, so when you decide on its position bear this in mind. Mark the position of the screw holes, drill the holes, then screw the swivel hanger to the side of the closet. You can buy a similar type of hanger designed to hold ties and scarves.

CLOSET SYSTEMS

Ready-to-be assembled storage systems make the best use of the space in your closet, with low rails for hanging short items and shelves above them for other items. To install one, follow the directions from the manufacturer.

GLOSSARY

ACCESS EQUIPMENT Ladders, platforms, scaffolding, and any other equipment used to reach high, inaccessible areas. These made be used in combination, especially when painting or papering walls at a staircase.

AGGREGATE Sand and small stones mixed with cement and water to form concrete.

ANGLED TRIM BRUSH A type of brush with bristles cut at an angle to assist painting neatly at an edge such as at baseboards and crown and casing moldings.

BALUSTER A post (one of a set) used to support a handrail along an open staircase.

BALUSTRADE The complete barrier installed along open staircases and landings. It consists of the balusters, newels, and handrail.

BASEBOARD A wood molding used horizontally along the walls where they meet the floor; they hide any gaps between the two surfaces.

BEVEL A surface that meets another surface at an angle of less than 90°.

BIND When a door or hinged casement rubs against its surrounding frame.

BLIND NAILING A method of securing components together, including as tongue-and-groove floorboards, using fasteners at an angle and driven below the surface of the workpiece.

BLOCKING Short horizonal framing pieces between studs in a partition wall or between floor joists.

BORE To drill a hole that is greater than ½ inch (12 mm) in diameter.

BUTT To fit together two pieces of material side by side or edge to edge.

CARCASE The boxlike, five-sided structure that forms the base of certain types of furniture such as a kitchen cabinet or chest of drawers.

CASING The molding that frames a door or window opening.

CHAIR RAIL A decorative molding, also called a dado or cap rail, installed on walls about waist height, originally to prevent furniture from marring the walls.

CHAMFER A narrow, angled surface, often at 45°, running along the corner of a piece such as a beam or post.

CONCAVE A surface that curves inward.

CONTOUR The outline or shape of an object.

CONVEX A surface that curves outward.

CROWN A decorative molding fastened at the junction between the walls and ceiling, often used to hide cracks.

COUNTERSINK A tapered recess made in the top section of a screw hole to allow the head of the screw to sit flush with the surface of the material.

COVING A concave molding, often used as crown molding.

DOWEL A small cylindrical wooden peg, sometimes with grooves running the length of its surface. It can be used to plug holes or to form a joint by inserting it into holes in two pieces of wood.

ENAMEL PAINT Any paint that dries with a hard, shiny finish. It's used on interior and exterior woods and metals.

END GRAIN The fibers in the end of the wood exposed after cutting across the wood.

FEATHER To dull or taper an edge to make it less noticeable, a technique often used in sanding and painting.

FILLET A small, often wooden, piece of molding with a square cross section.

FURRING STRIP A thin length of wood; a number of them are mounted in parallel lines across a wall or ceiling, forming a framework to which paneling can be attached.

GLAZER'S POINT A small triangular-shape piece of metal for holding a pane of window glass in a rabbet.

GLOSS FINISH The amount of reflectiveness of a painted or other surface. Typical grades .are satin, semi-gloss, gloss, and high-gloss.

GRAIN The direction of the fibers in a piece of wood.

GROUT A water-resistant paste used to seal the gaps between ceramic, terracotta, or other similar tiles attached to walls or floors.

HALF-ROUND MOLDING A type of molding that has a profile that forms half a circle. It's often used for edging and as decoration.

HARDWOOD Wood that comes from broad-leaf—usually deciduous—trees such as ash, beech, and oak. This type of wood is typically hard; however, balsa is classified as a hardwood but is a soft, lightweight material.

HEAD Or head jamb, the highest horizontal member of a window or door frame.

JOIST A horizontal wood beam that is used to support a heavy structure such as a floor or ceiling.

KERF The groove created in a material when cut by any type of saw.

KEY To roughen a surface, often by sanding, to provide a better grip for a material such as paint or adhesive.

LATEX PAINT A water-base paint with a matte or gloss finish. It dries quickly and is easy to clean off equipment.

MASTIC A nonsetting compound that seals a joint between two surfaces such as a tiled wall and a countertop, bathtub, or shower tray.

MATTE Or matt, a flat nonreflective finish on a material, such as paint or quarry tiles. Matte paint is often preferred for interiors.

MITER A joint between two beveled pieces that forms an angle, often a 45° angle.

MORTISE A rectangular-shape recess cut into wood. It may be used to form a joint by combining it with a tenoned end. Alternatively, it is used to hold a strike box in a door frame for a lock or latch.

MOLDING A narrow, usually decorative, strip of wood or other material. It is available shaped in different profiles. Baseboards, casings, and chair and picture rails are all types of molding.

MULLION A vertical dividing component of a window.

MUNTIN A vertical component between panels; they are used to form a paneled door or wall paneling.

NEWEL Part of the balustrade, the wider post at both the top and bottom of a staircase for supporting the handrail.

NOSING The front, often rounded, edge of a stair tread.

PARE To use a chisel, bevel side up, to remove fine

shavings from wood—often done to smooth a surface from which wood was removed.

PARTING STOP The innermost strip of wood in a double-hung window. It separates the channels of the upper and lower sashes.

PATTERN REPEAT The distance of a motif before it begins to be duplicated, or repeated.

PICTURE RAIL A type of decorative molding that is normally attached horizontally to the walls above head height.

PILE The fabric raised from a backing—often used to classify a type of carpet.

PILOT HOLE A hole drilled in a material to guide a screw. It should be smaller in diameter than the shank of the screw without its threads.

PLINTH A four-sided base on which a structure, such as a base cabinet or chest of drawers, is placed.

PRIMER A liquid substance used to seal a material, such as plaster, wallboard, wood, or metal, before applying an undercoat.

PROFILE The contour or outline of an object.

PROUD When an object protrudes from the surface.

RABBET A step-shape recess in the edge of a workpiece, often as part of a joint but also used for exterior door frames to prevent the door from swinging through.

RAIL The horizontal piece of wood that joins vertical pieces in a frame or carcase.

RAISED GRAIN When the wood's surface is roughened by damping, which causes its fibers to swell.

REVEAL The vertical side of a window or door opening.

RISER The vertical component of a step or stair.

SASH The structure of a window that holds the glass. It usually opens, either up and down or sideways, but it is sometimes stationary.

SCARF Or scarph, a joint between two pieces of material cut at matching angles—unlike a miter, the faces of the pieces are flush.

SCRIBE To mark a line with a pointed tool, or to copy the profile of a surface onto a piece of material, which will be trimmed to butt against the surface.

SCORE A line that marks a division or boundary, or the act of making the line.

SETTLING The movement of a house that occurs when normally firm, stable ground has been undermined by excess moisture.

SHIM A thin piece of material, such as cardboard or plywood, used as packing to fill a gap between materials.

SIDE JAMB Or jamb, the vertical side member of the frame that surrounds a door or window.

SILL The lowest horizontal component of a window or door frame or a wooden house frame.

SIZE Or sizing, a thin gelatinous solution used to seal a surface, such as a plaster wall, prior to covering it with wallpaper.

SPANDREL The triangular material that is used to fill the space below an outside stringer on a staircase.

SOFTWOOD Wood that comes from coniferous trees, including cedar and pine. Although softwood is typically soft in nature, yew is one type that is hard.

SOLE PLATE The lowest horizontal member of a wood-frame partition wall.

STAIN A liquid that changes the color of wood but does not protect it. It comes in water-base, oil-base, and solvent-base versions.

STILE A vertical side component of a window sash or door.

STRAIGHTEDGE A length of either metal or wood that has at least one true straight edge. It is often used for marking straight lines or making a surface level.

STRINGER Also known as a string, one of a pair of boards that runs along the staircase, from one floor to another, supporting the treads and risers. If against a wall, it's called an inside stringer; if there is an open side, it's an outside stringer.

STRIP A thin length of wood, typically of 1 inch × 2 inch (25 mm × 50 mm) softwood.

STUD A vertical member of a wood-frame wall.

STUD PARTITION WALL A wall constructed with a wood frame, usually covered with wallboard.

TRISODIUM PHOSPHATE Or TSP, a strong powder detergent for cleaning painted and other types of surfaces.

TEMPLATE Paper, card, metal, or other type of sheet material formed in a specific shape or pattern to be used as a guide for transferring a shape to the workpiece.

TENON A projecting end of a wood component, which fits into a mortise to form a joint.

TONGUE AND GROOVE A joint between two pieces of material—such as floorboards or paneling—in which one piece has a projecting edge that fits into a groove, or slot, on the edge of the adjacent piece.

TOP COAT The last coat of a finish applied to a surface. There may be several coats underneath it.

TOP PLATE The highest horizontal component of a stud partition wall.

TREAD The horizontal part of a step that is walked on.

UNDERCOAT One or more layers of a paint or varnish to cover a primer or hide another color before applying a top coat.

UNDERLAYMENT Or underlay, a layer of material to provide a smooth surface for laying a decorative flooring. Rubber, felt, or paper may be used under carpeting; hardboard or plywood may be used for other floorings.

UTILITY KNIFE Also referred to as a Stanley knife, a handle that holds a replacable blade, which may or may not retract.

VALENCE A decorative wood unit used to hide the top edge of curtains or a structure such as the track of a sliding door.

VAPOR RETARDER An impervious material, usually polyethylene sheeting, laid under a concrete floor or behind wallboard to prevent moisture seeping through it.

VARNISH A liquid applied to wood materials, it hardens to form a protective surface. It may be clear or colored.

WET-AND-DRY ABRASIVE PAPER A paper with silicon-carbide particles attached to it for smoothing surfaces. It may be used wet.

VENEER A thin decorative layer of wood or other material applied to a less attractive, inexpensive base material.

USEFUL ADDRESSES

GENERAL

BROOKSTONE CO.
1655 Bassford Dr.
Mexico, MO 65265
1-800-846-3000
*General merchandise, including
hand tools. Small fee for catalog.*

NORTHERN
P.O. Box 1499
Burnsville, MN 55337
(800) 533-5545
*General merchandise, including
power tools.*

THE TOOL CRIB OF THE NORTH
P.O. Box 14930
Grand Forks, ND 58208
(800) 358-3096
*Hand tools, power tools and
accessories, masonry tools, and
fasteners. Small fee for catalog.*

TOOLS ON SALE
Division of Seven Corners
Ace Hardware, Inc.
216 W. 7th St.
St. Paul, MN 55102
(800) 328-047
*Hand tools, power tools and
accessories.*

CERAMIC TILE, GLASS, AND PLASTICS

PITTSBURGH CORNING CORP.
800 Presque Isle Dr.
Pittsburgh, PA 15239-2799
(724) 327-6100
Glass blocks.

RALPH WILSON PLASTICS CO.
2400 Wilson Place
Temple, TX 76504
(800) 433-3222
Sheet plastic laminates.

CONCRETE, BRICKS AND STONES

BOMANITE CORP.
232 S. Schnoor Ave.
Madera, CA 93637
(800) 854-2094
Concrete stamping tools.

CENTURY IN STONE
1325 6th Ave. N.
Nashville, TN 37208
(615) 256-6697
Stone veneers.

STAMPCRETE
209 Oswego St.
Liverpool, NY 13088
(800) 233-3298
Stamped concrete system.

FLOORING

CHICKASAW
Hardwood Floor Products of
Memphis Hardwood Flooring
1551 Thomas Street
Memphis, TN 38107
(901) 526-7306
Wood planks, strips, and parquets.

MANNINGTON RESILIENT FLOORS
P.O. Box 30
Salem, NJ 08079
(800) 356-6787
Resilient sheet flooring.

HARDWARE

GARRETT WADE COMPANY, INC.
161 Ave of the Americas
New York, NY 10013
(800) 221-2942
*Brass furniture hardware. Small fee
for catalog.*

IMPORTED EUROPEAN HARDWARE
A Division of Woodworker's
Emporium
5461 S. Arville
Las Vegas, NV 89118

(702) 871-0722
*Furniture, cabinet, and door
hardware. Minimum order required.
Small fee for catalog.*

PAXTON HARDWARE LTD.
7818 Bradshaw Rd.
Upper Falls, MD 21156
(410) 592-8505
*Antique reproduction furniture
hardware; lamp fittings.*

WOODWORKER'S HARDWARE
P.O. Box 180
Sauk Rapids, Mr 56379
(800) 383-0130
*Furniture and cabinet hardware,
moldings, and wood turnings.
Minimum order required.*

GLASS

HUDSON GLASS CO. INC.
219 N. Division St.
Peekshill, NY 10566
(800) 431-2964
*Stained glass, tools, and related
supplies.*

S.A. BENDHEIM CO., INC.
61 Willet St.
Passaic, NJ 07055
(800) 221-7379
*Restoration glass. They do not do
millwork.*

METALWORKING

ALLCRAFT TOOL AND SUPPLY CO.
45 W. 46 St.
New York, NY 10036
(800) 645-7124
*Metals, tools, and other supplies for
jewelers and metalsmiths.*

ARE, INC.
636 11th Ave. S.
Hopkins, MN 55343
(800) 736-4273
Metals, tools, and other supplies for

jewelers and metalsmiths. Small fee for catalog.

COUNTRY ACCENTS
P. O. Box 437
Montoursville, PA 17754
(570) 478-4127
Decorative tin panels—both prefinished and in kits. Small fee for catalog.

FREI & BOREL
126 2nd St.
Oakland, CA 94607
(510) 832-0355
Metalworking tools.

GROBET FILE CO. OF AMERICA, INC.
750 Washington Ave. Carlstadt, NJ 07072
(201) 935-0100
Tools, metals, and other supplies for jewelers and metalsmiths. Small fee for catalog.

PAINTS AND FINISHES
GENERAL FINISHES
P.O. Box 857
Davis, CA 95617
New Berlin, WI 53151
(800) 783-6050
Natural wood finishes.

PLASTICS
AIN PLASTICS
249 E. Sanford Blvd., Box 151
Mt. Vernon, NY 10550
(800) 431-2451
Acrylic, fiberglass, and PVC. Minimum order required.

POWER TOOL COMPANIES
CTD MACHINES, INC.
2300 E. 11th St.
Los Angeles, CA 90021
(213) 689-4455

DREMEL
4915 21st St.
Racine, WI 53406-9989
(414) 554-1390

WOODWORKING
NATIONAL MANUFACTURING OF CANADA
600 Fenton's Crescent
Swift Current, SASK
59H 4J8
(800) 667-7466
Furniture fastening systems.

THE BEALL TOOL CO.
541 Swans Rd. NE
Newark, OH 43055
(800) 331-4718
Power tool accessories for making threads in wood.

THE BEREA HARDWOODS CO.
6367 Eastland Rd.
Brookpark, OH 44142
(440) 243-4452
Exotic hardwood lumber and turning blocks. Minimum order required. Small fee for catalog.

BRISTOL VALLEY HARDWOODS
4054 Rt. 64
Canadaigua, NY 14424
(800) 724-0132
Domestic and exotic hardwood lumber, turning blocks, and flooring planks. Small fee for catalog.

CERTAINLY WOOD
13000 Rt. 78
East Aurora, NY 14052-9515
(716) 655-0206
Veneers. Minimum order required.

EAGLE AMERICA CORP.
P.O. Box 1099
Chardon, OH 44024
(800) 872-2511
Router bits and drill bits. Small fee for catalog.

GARRETT WADE COMPANY, INC.
161 Ave. of the Americas
New York, NY 10013
(800) 221-2942
Hand tools, power tools and accessories, inlays, and finishes. Small fee for catalog.

GRIZZLY IMPORTS, INC.
(East of Mississippi River)
2406 Reach Rd.
Williamsport, PA 17701
(800) 523-4777
Hand tools, power tools and accessories.

GRIZZLY IMPORTS, INC.
(West of Mississippi River)
P.O. Box 2069
Bellingham, WA 98225
(800) 541-5537
Hand tools, power tools and accessories.

LEIGH INDUSTRIES LTD.
P.O. Box 357
104-1585 Broadway St.
Port Coquitlam, B.C.
V3C 4K6 Canada
(800) 663-8932
Dovetail jig and router accessories.

VINTAGE WOOD WORKS
P.O. Box R
Hwy. 34 S.
Quinlan, TX 75474
(903) 356-2158
Turnings and architectural details. Small fee for catalog.

WILKE MACHINERY CO.
3230 Susquehanna Trail
York, PA 17402
(717) 764-5000
Power tools and accessories. Can arrange to lease tools.

INDEX

ACKNOWLEDGMENTS

Photographic Credits
All photography by John Freeman, with the exception of the credits listed below.

Page 8 Robert Harding Picture Library/Ben Wright *bottom right*, Peter Willis *bottom left*; 9 Houses & Interiors *top*; 10–11 Houses & Interiors; 12 Peter Willis; 13 Reproduced by permission of Building Research Establishment Ltd; 110 Robert Harding Picture Library/Dominic Blackmore *center* and *bottom left*, Tony Stone Images/Oliver Benn *bottom right*; 111 Robert Harding Picture Library/Homes & Gardens *top* and *bottom left*, Camera Press *top right* and *center*, Robert Harding Picture Library/Bill Reavell *bottom right*; 112 Camera Press *center*, Elizabeth Whiting Assoc *bottom*; 113 Abode *top left* and *center*, Elizabeth Whiting Assoc *top right* and *bottom*; 130 Houses & Interiors *center*, Camera Press *bottom*; 131 Camera Press *top* and *center*, Robert Harding Picture Library/Homes & Ideas *bottom left*, Robert Harding Picture Library/Ideal Home *bottom right*; 150 Camera Press *center*, Robert Harding Picture Library/Christopher Sykes *bottom*; 151 Houses & Interiors *top* and *bottom right*, Robert Harding Picture Library/Nick Carter *center*, Camera Press *bottom left*; 162 Robert Harding Picture Library/Country Homes & Interiors *center*, Houses & Interiors *bottom*; 163 Camera Press *top* and *center left*, Robert Harding Picture Library/Jonathan Pilkington *top right*, Abode *center right*, Robert Harding Picture Library/James Merrell *bottom left*, Robert Harding Picture Library/Dominic Blackmore *bottom right*; 178 Camera Press *center*, Robert Harding Picture Library/Mark Luscombe-Whyte *bottom*; 179 Camera Press *top left* and *center*, Elizabeth Whiting Assoc *top right*, Robert Harding Picture Library/Tom Leighton *bottom left*, International Interiors/Paul Ryan *bottom right*; 196 Robert Harding Picture Library/Simon Upton *center*, Houses & Interiors *bottom*; 197 Robert Harding Picture Library/Dominic Blackmore *top left*, Camera Press *top right*, *center left*, and *bottom*, Robert Harding Picture Library/Tim Beddow *center right*; 208 Camera Press *center*, Robert Harding Picture Library/Flavio Galozzi *bottom*; 209 Robert Harding Picture Library/Dominic Blackmore *top left*, Elizabeth Whiting Assoc *top right* and *bottom left*, Camera Press *center left* and *bottom right*, Robert Harding Picture Library/Brian Harrison *center right*; 222 Robert Harding Picture Library/Trevor Richards *center*, Robert Harding Picture Library/Ken Kirkwood *bottom*; 223 Robert Harding Picture Library/Bill Reavell *top left*, Robert Harding Picture Library/James Merrell *top right*, Robert Harding Picture Library/Christopher Drake *center left*, Robert Harding Picture Library/Polly Wreford *center right*, Robert Harding Picture Library/Ariadne *bottom left*, Robert Harding Picture Library/Jan Baldwin *bottom right*; 230 Camera Press; 231 Robert Harding Picture Library/Dominic Blackmore *top left*, Camera Press *top*, *center*, and *bottom*.

Illustration Credit
All illustrations by Amzie Viladot Lorente

Acknowledgments
The publishers are grateful to the following individuals and companies for their assistance in compiling this book: Abru Henderson Ltd, for ladders; Black & Decker Ltd, for power tools; Colefax and Fowler, for wallpaper borders; Cottage Flooring, for carpet and flooring demonstration; Daniel Platt Ltd, for quarry tiles; Farrow & Ball, for paint samples; Fired Earth, for flooring and wall tiles; Forbo Nairn Ltd, for vinyl floor coverings; GET plc (Rapitest), for stud detector; HSS Hire, for hired equipment; Ideal Standard Ltd, for bathroom suite and faucet; Junckers Ltd, for wood flooring; LASSCo London Architectural Salvage & Supply Co Ltd, for cast iron fireplace surround; LASSCo Flooring, for floorboards and flooring; Sheen Interiors, for wallcoverings; Stanley Tools, for hand tools; The Tool Shop, for hand tools; Vitrex Ltd, for tiling tools and accessories and safety equipment; John Wilman Ltd (Coloroll), for wallcoverings and borders; Woodfit Ltd, for storage and sliding door equipment; Bob Cleveland, Barry Edwards, and Martyn Judd, for studio assistance; and Simon Garrett, John McKeever, and Jill Streeten for the loan of their homes.